Management Science, Operations Research and Project Management

Management Science, Operations Research and Project Management

JOSÉ RAMÓN SAN CRISTÓBAL MATEO
University of Cantabria, Spain

Routledge
Taylor & Francis Group
LONDON AND NEW YORK

First published 2015 by Gower Publishing

Published 2016 by Routledge
2 Park Square, Milton Park, Abingdon, Oxon OX14 4RN
711 Third Avenue, New York, NY 10017, USA

Routledge is an imprint of the Taylor & Francis Group, an informa business

Gower Applied Business Research
Our programme provides leaders, practitioners, scholars and researchers with thought provoking, cutting edge books that combine conceptual insights, interdisciplinary rigour and practical relevance in key areas of business and management.

British Library Cataloguing in Publication Data
A catalogue record for this book is available from the British Library

Library of Congress Cataloging-in-Publication Data
San Cristóbal Mateo, José Ramón
Management science, operations research and project management : modelling, evaluation, scheduling, monitoring / by José Ramón San Cristóbal Mateo.
pages cm
Includes bibliographical references and index.
ISBN 978-1-4724-2643-7 (hardback) -- ISBN 978-1-4724-2644-4 (ebook) -- ISBN (invalid) 978-1-4724-2645-1 (epub) 1. Project management. 2. Management. 3. Operations research. I. Title.
HD69.P75S3242 2015
658.4'04--dc23

2014029453

ISBN 13: 978-1-4724-2643-7 (hbk)

Contents

List of Figures

List of Tables

Introduction

Owing to its societal and economic relevance, Project Management has become an important and relevant discipline and a key concept in modern-world private and public organizations. Project Management is an academic discipline discussed both in Management Science and in Operations Research. Management Science tends to focus on quantitative tools and the soft skills necessary to manage projects successfully. Operations Research gives the essential scientific contribution to the success of Project Management through the development of models and algorithms. The aim of this book is to fill the gap between scientific research and practical application of that research. The chapters explore the use of the existing Management Science models providing valuable tools for the project modelling, evaluation, scheduling, and monitoring.

This book will provide project managers with the tools and methods necessary to make sound decisions in the complex environments that they face today in order to manage projects successfully. With this aim, the book will include numerous examples of these tools for problem-solving applied to Project Management.

What is a Project?

Generally speaking, a project consists of a number of tasks that must be done for the project to be completed. These tasks have durations, they typically cost money, and they often require non-financial limited resources such as people and facilities. They also have precedence relationships which put constraints on what can be done and when.

Following the definition in BS 6079-1 'Guide to Project Management', a project is: 'a unique set of coordinated activities, with definite starting and finishing points, undertaken by an individual or organization to meet specific objectives within defined schedule, cost and performance parameters'. This concept of project implies:

1. The identification of the system to be transformed.

2. The description of the initial state and the final state that should represent the targets of the project.

3. An organizational framework. Projects need the skills and talents from multiple professions and organizations which usually have something at stake, because failure would jeopardize the organization or its goal.

4. A set of resources.

5. A methodological support.

Projects were traditionally the prerogative of the engineering disciplines, but with the dynamics of business, Project Management has moved into business' main street. A project could be the building of a house, a ship, or the development of a software program, and many others actions such as military campaigns or recovery programmes from natural disasters also meet the criteria of projects.

Dimensions of a Project

Typically, projects have three primary objectives: to finish the project quickly, to consume as few resources as possible (especially, to minimize costs), and to produce a high-quality project. In addition, in certain industries like airlines, railways, etc., some people add a fourth dimension – safety – which is considered to be equally important. In today's highly competitive business environment, Project Management's ability to schedule activities and monitor progress within time, cost, and performance guidelines is becoming increasingly important to obtain competitive priorities. This implies that there are trade-offs that must typically be made when scheduling a project.

The usual decision of Project Management focuses primarily on the time dimension. The typical questions in the mind on any project manager that need to be answered are: how long will the project take to complete if everything goes according to schedule? Which tasks form bottlenecks that prevent the project from being completed earlier? And which tasks have some slack in the sense that they can be delayed to some extent without delaying the project?

The second dimension refers to resources. The project must be accomplished within the budgeted cost. The tasks in a project almost always compete for resources, whether dollar or non-financial resources, and no real Project Management application can afford to ignore these resources. How to spend money optimally in order to speed up the completion of the project is a typical problem in Project Management that requires problem-solving techniques, such as optimization problems, and decision-making, as well as management skills.

The third dimension, scope, is the most difficult to quantify. The project must meet the performance requirements, and scope must include not only quality but also safety or any other performance measurements. The project manager must know what it is intended to do and what features the project should include.

Who is a Project Manager?

A project manager may be defined as that person who has the responsibility, authority, and the necessary management skills to achieve the project objectives within agreed time, cost, and performance criteria. The project manager must be an effective leader that makes all major decisions based on their individual insights and experience. The issues of interest to a project manager may be grouped under four general headings (Elmaghraby, 1995):

1. Representation and modelling for visualization analysis.
2. Scheduling activities subject to resource constraints.
3. Financial issues, either related to project 'compression' or to cash flows.
4. Uncertainty in activity durations as well as in resource availabilities and/or cash flows, and how to cope with it.

What is Project Management?

The definition of Project Management given by the PM book guide (PMI, 2004) can be used as a starting point: 'Project management is the application of knowledge, skills, tools, and techniques to project activities in order to meet or exceed stakeholder needs and expectations from a project.' However, scholars, practitioners, and academic and professional societies have different definitions and interpretations of the subject of Project Management (Kwak and Anbari, 2009). Behavioural scientists may think of the matrix organization or emotional intelligence; operational researchers may think of network analysis, queuing theory, or optimal plant design; strategic scholars may think of strategic alliances among different organizations during project evaluation.

Project Management is the process of conceiving, designing, preparing, evaluating, scheduling, organizing, monitoring, and controlling the transformation of a system from an initial state, to a specific state, and the motivation of all those involved in it in order to achieve the project objectives within defined schedule, cost, and performance parameters. It is usually admitted that modern Project Management appeared during WWII and was initially dedicated to big military and construction projects. Today, projects seem to have become increasingly common in all kinds of organizations (Mawby and Stupples, 2002). They are increasingly large, complex and constrained, and may involve large numbers of interested parties and professional and technical disciplines. As projects became more and more apparent in organizations, and as they had much larger amounts at stake, it became impossible to sustain them without specific and rigorous methodology. Project Management has then grown up and spread around the world to become what it is today, that is to say, a set of theories, principles, methodologies and practices, sometimes included in standard body of knowledge as Project Management Institute (PMI, 2004) and Association for Project Management (PMA, 2006).

There has been a long debate in the management education community as to whether Project Management is a practice or an academic discipline. In several disciplines such as the Construction, Engineering, and Management disciplines people learn planning, managing, and controlling engineering construction projects to meet the time, budget, and specifications. However, when it comes to the Business and Management discipline, scholars often appear puzzled and unconvinced of the notion of Project Management. Project Management is more applied and interdisciplinary than other management discipline so it is more difficult to justify the field as a distinguishable academic discipline within the academic management community. Kwak and Anbari (2009) identified eight categories that represent the disciplines where one can find Project Management research:

1. Operations Research/Decision Sciences/Operations Management/ Supply Chain Management. This refers to the discipline associated with quantitative decision analysis and management principles including

various optimization tools and techniques, network analysis, resource levelling, simulation, etc.

2. Organizational Behaviour/Human Resources Management. This refers to the discipline associated with organizational structure, organizational dynamics, motivations, leadership, conflict management, etc.

3. Information Technology/Information Systems. This refers to the discipline associated with the use of computers and computer systems to process, transmit, store, and retrieve information for better management decisions.

4. Technology applications/Innovation/New product development/ Research and Development. This refers to the discipline associated with the concepts of making innovative and technological improvements and the research and development of entirely new products, services, and processes.

5. Engineering and Construction/Contracts/Legal aspects/Expert witness. This refers to the discipline associated with the use and application of a broad range of professional expertise to resolve issues related to engineering and construction, contracts, expert witness, and their legal implications.

6. Strategy/Integration/Portfolio Management/Value of Project Management/ Marketing. This refers to the concepts of organizing and managing resources to maximize profit, minimize cost, and support the overall strategy of the organization.

7. Performance Management/Earned Value Management/Project Finance and Accounting. This refers to the concepts and techniques that measure project progress objectively by combining measurements of technical performance, schedule performance, and cost performance.

8. Quality Management/Process Improvement. This refers to the concepts of improving processes, minimizing defects, and reducing costs by implementing continual improvement principles and specific measures and metrics.

In recent years, the range of Project Management applications has greatly expanded. Today project managers have gained recognition and employment opportunities beyond construction, aerospace, and defence, in pharmaceuticals, information systems, and manufacturing. Project managers are interested in finding out to what extent the Project Management profession would accommodate the needs of any industry. Business organizations are interested in finding out to what extent is the Project Management profession fragmented into industry-specific areas, or to what extent would an academic degree in Project Management accommodate industry-specific needs. Universities and other training institutions are interested in accommodating the needs of both individuals and organizations involved in Project Management.

Following Popper (1972), we reduce the complexity of the world into experiments which may be validated in that they are repeatable and, we build knowledge through regulation of our theories. Management Science, the application of scientific method to management, is far from being a robust body of scientific knowledge in the way say that physics or chemistry is, in the sense that there can be reducible, repeatable, and refutable laws of management (Morris, 2004). Significant parts of Project Management can be developed along 'theory' lines with reasonable scientific rigour. There are examples of Project Management benefiting from scientific knowledge such as network scheduling, linear programming, dynamic programming, or Goldratt's theory of constraints. Project Management is a discipline in the sense that there is a substantial and, in places, significant literature on it. There are defined 'Bodies of Knowledge' on it and there are many people who believe that they practise it and professional societies who promote it and who examine and qualify people in it.

Project Management has become a key concept in modern world of private or public organizations which are considered open and complex systems interacting with the environment and pursuing objectives according to their specific mission and nature (Drucker, 1974; Ackoff, 1970; Simon, 1977). The achievement of such objectives implies structuring the activities of the organizations through projects with specific targets that should be consistent with the adopted organizational objectives (Tavares, 2002).

The current vision of Project Management tends to rely upon the notions of planning and control, to propose models and prescriptions as ways to increase the ability of humans to control complex worlds (Stacey, 2001; Wood, 2002). It emphasizes the role of project actors regarding the issues of time, cost, and scope (Cicmil and Hodgson, 2006). The increasing use of computers has given rise to a new generation of operations researchers devoted to computer applications and expert systems for project planning, control, and risk analysis.

Project Modelling

A project can be modelled by a discrete and finite set of entities usually called jobs or activities; a set of precedence conditions; a discrete and finite set of attributes defined for each activity and describing its properties such as time, cost, quality, safety, etc.; and a discrete and finite set of criteria, such as total duration, net present value, etc., that express the values and the preferences of the project manager to compare alternative decisions concerning the management of the project. According to Tavares (2002), the improvement of the network models to describe each of these components has been pursued along seven different lines:

1. Construction of 'generalized networks' (Kaufman and Desbazeille, 1964), where some activities just occur with specific probabilities or in terms of the outcomes of previous activities.

2. Construction of 'logical networks' (Battersby, 1967), where the occurrence of each activity is conditioned by logical relationships between precedent activities.

3. Modelling of 'overlapping activities', in terms of the time domain or in terms of the consumed resources expressed by progress lag constraints for activities carried out at each time (Leashman and Kun, 1993).

4. Introduction of 'hammock activities' (Harhalakis, 1990) which are associated to the time span occurred between events concerning other activities. The duration of these activities is equal to the difference of times between two specified events.

5. Morphologic modelling of project networks (Tavares, Ferreira, and Coelho, 1997; Tavares, 1998) which is based on two concepts, the progressive and the regressive levels and it is important to classify or to simulate networks.

6. Construction of hierarchical networks where each project can be viewed as a set of interconnected sub-projects (macro-activities) and each of these macro-activities can be modelled by another network constructed in terms of more detailed activities. This process of modelling has been studied using multiple hierarchical levels (Speranza and Vercellis, 1993) or partitioning methods (Rafael, 1990).

7. Aggregation of project networks to be transformed into simpler and more synthetic networks. Two approaches have been proposed: the method of modular decomposition, based on the identification of modules that can be synthetized by equivalent macro-activities (Muller and Spinrad, 1989) and the method of network reduction (Bein, Kamburovski, and Stallman, 1992) based on three different types of reduction: series, parallel, and node reduction.

Project Evaluation

Evaluation can be regarded as a joint learning process for all the agents involved in the project, generating useful and relevant information and knowledge to assess the relevance, efficiency, and effectiveness of projects. The evaluation of projects has been traditionally studied using monetary criteria such as net present value (NPV), payback period, return on investment, etc. Indicators such as NPV or the risk of delay strongly depend on the schedule as early (late) starting times tend to be responsible for lower (higher) NPV and risk of delay (Tavares, 2002). In addition, this type of index does not consider other important non-monetary criteria such as quality, safety, etc. The evaluation process must include appropriate focus on safety, quality, cost, schedule, etc., attributes that need not be mutually exclusive. The development of multi-criteria decision-making theory can enrich this domain with new contributions as a decision-aid to support the process of multi-criteria evaluation of a project (Tavares, 1998).

The purpose of project evaluation is to calculate the benefits and/or costs of projects in such a way as to provide credible and useful information as to whether the project should be undertaken, its design, effectiveness of implementation, short-term and long-term effects on the scope. Evaluation should lead to a decision to continue, rectify or stop a project, look for cost reduction opportunities, along with opportunities to reduce planning budgets, working hours, etc., at every stage of the project. One of the most important problems in project evaluation concerns the treatment of uncertainty. The problem is that the stream of future benefits and costs is not known with certainty.

Project Scheduling

Initially, the study of project scheduling has been done considering just the duration and precedence conditions of the activities and ignoring the resource requirements. Two basic methods were proposed to schedule a project assuming deterministic duration: the Critical Path Method and the Method of Potentials. Since most activity durations have a random nature, PERT was proposed to determine the distribution of the project completion.

Next, the problem of project scheduling under resource constraints was considered and formulated as an optimization problem (Tavares, 2002) where the decision variables are the scheduled starting times of the activities; the constraints include the precedence conditions and the maximal (and/or minimal) bounds concerning the available resources; the objective function describes the main criteria such as minimization of the total duration, maximization of the net present value, or other cost-benefit indicators. The process of decision-making concerning the scheduling of activities and the allocation of resources to the implementation of activities can be considered static or dynamic: static if the decision should be made before starting the project without the acceptance of any latter correction or change, dynamic if the decision can be changed along the process of implementing the project.

The deterministic static single-mode problem is based on a model defined in terms of $x_i(t) = 0$ (1) if the activity i is (or is not) carried out at time unit t. This problem has been structured by binary optimization methods that belong to two major groups (Pritsker, Watters, and Wolfe, 1969; Davies, 1972; Patterson, 1984; Demeulemeester and Herroelen, 1997): Exact methods and Heuristic methods. Whereas the Exact methods explore the full space of the scheduling activities, the Heuristic methods do not guarantee the obtention of the optimum but tend to be faster. In the case of the deterministic continuous-mode problem, the decision concerning the implementation of each activity includes its starting time and also its intensity in terms of time. Several approaches have been used to solve this problem. Weglarz (1981) used Optimal Control Theory assuming that the processing speed of each activity at time t is a continuous, non-decreasing function of the amount of resource allocated to the activity at that instant of time. Tavares (1987, 1989) presented a model based on the decomposition of the project into a sequence of stages using dynamic programming.

Project Monitoring and Control

Projects are highly unlikely to proceed according to plan. In order to be able to identify and measure the differences between the plan and the actual work performance, progress on the project is required to be controlled and monitored. The monitoring and control of projects involves the following stages:

1. Measuring the state of the project.

2. Compare actual and planned parameters.

3. Report the variations between these parameters

4. Take corrective actions.

Monitoring project performance involves making measurements as the project proceeds and comparing these measurements with the desired or expected values. Small deviations between plan and actual performance may be seen as being within the limits of uncertainty of the model building process. Larger differences may require control action to try to bring the actual performance on course within the desired state of the plan (Al-Jibouri, 2003). Some of the most commonly used instruments for the monitoring and control of projects are:

1. Development of information systems under several labels such as Management Information Systems or Executive Information Systems to produce updated pictures of how the project is progressing in terms of completion of activities, consumption of resources, delays, quality and safety control, etc., (Drigani, 1989).

2. Multivariate data analysis of completed activities or of previous projects to learn how to improve and to correct initial estimates adopted for Project Management (Kelley, 1982).

3. Decision Support systems to assess the progress of the project and to update the adopted models for Project Management (Mitra, 1986).

4. Leading parameters. Under this technique one or more of the major types of work is chosen as measures of the performance of the project. The actual cost per leading parameter as well as the total cost of the project is compared with the planned during the same period of time. One disadvantage of this technique is that projects often involve many important types of work and the goodness of the single parameter selected for assessing the project performance may vary with time. To overcome this problem, different parameters can be used at different stages of the project (Al-Jibouri, 2003).

5. Activity duration. This financial technique (Mawdesley, Askew, and O'Reilly, 1997; Al-Jibouri and Mawdesley, 2001) employs ratios between the earnings and expenditures of the project activities as measures of performance.

6. Variances (Staffurth, 1975; Lockyer and Gordon, 1996; Harrison, 1992). In project monitoring and control, variances are the differences between the planned and actual expenditures, incomes or between any other values. Two main types of variances can be determined by plotting different expenditures curves: the budget revision variance and the total cost review variance. These variances indicate an increase in the unit cost of the project with its budgeted expenditure. In order to help to recognize the reasons for the changes in cost, these variances can be broken down into more detailed subdivisions.

7. An extension of the method of variances is the Earned Value analysis (Fleming and Koppelman, 2006). Under this technique, the original tender prices are used, together with the schedule, to establish what should have been spent (or earned) at any time. As the project progresses, the actual work performed is evaluated using the original tender figures and the budgeted value of work performed is calculated. The use of the planned and actual values of work performed enables comparisons of the future and current states of the project.

Chapter 1
Network Models

The theory of networks plays an important role in the planning and scheduling of projects primarily because of the ease with which these projects can be modelled in network form. Networks are easily understood by all levels of personnel in the organizational hierarchy, facilitate the identification of pertinent data, present a mechanism for data collection and can be used for both communication and analysis purposes (Drezner and Pritsker, 1965). In this chapter we begin by introducing the different types of network representations. Next, the characteristics that define both the structure and the parameters of a network are shown. Finally, according to the types and parameters of the network's elements and based on the combinations of different logical operations, the following network modes are considered: generalized network models (GNM), decision box, decision-CPM model; graphical evaluation and review technique (GERT), venture evaluation and review technique (VERT), generalized alternative activity network (GAAN), and controlled alternative activity network (CAAN).

Types of Network Representations

Networks of flow have been extensively studied in the literature (Ford and Fulkerson, 1962; Charnes and Cooper, 1962; Elmaghraby, 1964). The US Navy's successful application of PERT to the development of the Polaris Fleet Ballistic Missile System in 1958 generated a very large body of network analysis methodology (Moeller and Digman, 1981). Pritsker and Happ (1966) attributed the increasing use of network analysis to (i) the ability to model complex systems by compounding simple systems, (ii) the need for a communications mechanism to discuss the operational system in terms of its significant features, (iii) a means for specifying the data requirements for analysis of the system, and (iv) a starting point for analysis and scheduling of the operational system.

Call a network model a set of nodes and arrows, which connect certain events, together with a variety of links between the project's activities, the pre-given project's time parameters and various resources assigned to activities. Both nodes and arrows may be evident and dummy, both of them may be either of deterministic or of stochastic nature (Voropajev et al., 2000).

Normally, the representation of a project in terms of a discrete and finite set of entities called activities and a set of precedence relations among them can be done by adopting two ways of representation. The activity-on-arc (*AoA*) representation (Figure 1.1), where each arc describes an activity and each node represents the completion of the activities concerning on it, and the alternative hypothesis, the activity-on-node (*AoN*) representation (Figure 1.2), where each node represents and activity and each arc between two nodes describes a precedence relationships between the activities associated to such nodes.

The *AoN* representation is the most straightforward and natural representation, and is unique. On the other hand, the *AoA* representation is not unique and is clustered with dummy activities and dummy events for three reasons: (i) to comply with the requirement of each activity is uniquely identified by its terminal nodes; (ii) to respect the specified precedence relation; and (iii) to comply with the requirement that the resulting network is 'two-terminal'.

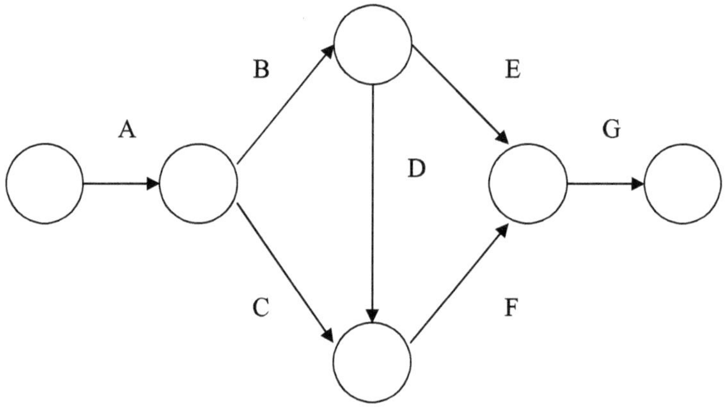

Figure 1.1 Notation *AoA*

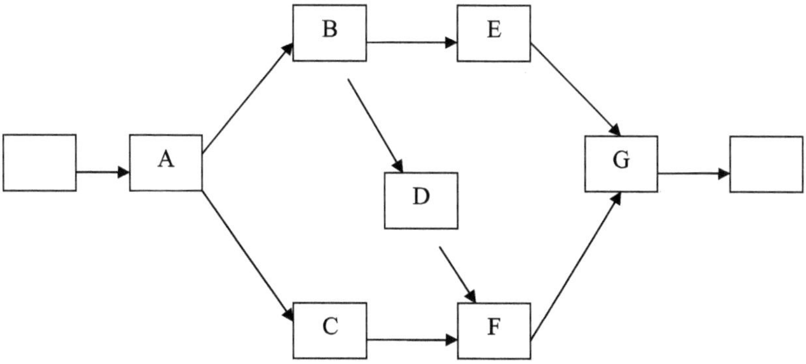

Figure 1.2 Notation *AoN*

The adoption of the *AoA* assumption is more common in the operations research literature as it was used by the popular methods of PERT/CPM, but an alternative method proposed by Roy (1964) has adopted the *AoN* assumption. From a purely representation point of view, the *AoA* mode of representation is preferred when:

1. Payment is related to the realization of certain events, in which case the *AoA* representation is convenient to highlight these key events.

2. It is desired to visually identify all completed activities at a particular event, or the activities leading to the event's realization.

3. It is desired to give a visual representation of the duration of the activities; then the arc length is made proportional to the duration of the activity.

From an analytical point of view, the *AoA* mode of representation is preferred when:

1. There are more complex relations among the activities of the project, such as in the presence of generalized precedence relations.

2. It is desired to represent the activity floats.

3. We wish to construct mathematical models that depend on the definition of nodes, such as the linear programming models for the optimal time-cost trade-off, or any of the various models for the determination of the probability distribution functions of time of realization of events.

Characteristics of Network Models

Based on the *AoA* representation, Voropajev et al. (2000), suggest three main groups of characteristics which define both the structure and the parameters of network models: (i) types of network's elements; (ii) parameters of network's elements; and (iii) degree of alternativity:

1. Types of network's elements

We consider two types of network's elements, events and links, defined by the following characteristics:

a) Events. An event's realization means that (i) all activities entering that event are already accomplished and, (ii) all activities leaving the event may start.

b) Links. Links may be used to define:

   - 'Finish-start' links. To define order of realizing the project's activities.
   - 'Finish-finish', 'start-finish', 'start-start' links. To define a variety of possible logical restrictions in order to realize two different activities.
   - Generalized links. To define more complicated logical situations (i.e., when a certain part of a certain activity may start to be operated only after completing a certain part of another activity).
   - Reverse links. To define a logical restriction for a fragment's duration not to exceed a pre-given time value. In this case the fragment's output and input are connected by a reverse arrow (acyclic networks).
   - Implicit algorithmic links. To define technological links as well as resource restrictions, various organization activities, etc. These links have a non-evident influence upon the network model.

2. Parameters assigned to a network's elements. Two types of parameters, deterministic and stochastic parameters are considered:

a) Deterministic parameters:

   - Number. It usually defines the activity duration, the delay interval, etc.

- Numerical interval. An interval denotes a continuous set of values with pre-given upper and lower bounds. For example, an activity duration is restricted by a given interval and has to be set within these bounds.
- Function. It determines a certain parameter as a function of a certain value (e.g., an activity duration can be often determined by dividing the activity volume by the team's speed). The attribute function can be classified as follows:
  - Non time-dependent function. Linear continuous function; step-wise linear continuous function (e.g., when the number of workers changes in the course of activity's realization); step-wise non-continuous function (e.g. when realizing an activity is stopped for a certain period).
  - Time-dependent function. It can be subdivided into relative time (e.g. time interval depending on the moment of the event's realization); and calendar time (e.g. when activity duration depends on seasonal changes).
  - Function as a set of variants. It defines one possible choice from a set of different values (e.g., an activity duration is defined by choosing a device to operate the activity).

b) Stochastic parameters:

- Discrete random value. It defines a random choice from a full group of events with given probabilities. For example, a random choice of an activity duration from several possible values, $t_1, t_2, \ldots, t_n$, with the corresponding probabilities, $p_1, p_2, \ldots, p_n$, $\sum_{i=1}^{n} p_i = 1$.
- Continuous random value. It determines the probability density function of various random parameters, e.g., random activity durations.
- Parametric random value. It determines the probability density function of a certain random attribute which depends parametrically on another attribute (e.g., random activity duration depending parametrically on the budget assigned to that activity).

3. Degree of alternativity by classifying alternative logical operations at the receiver and at the emitter of the project's events. This classification is as follows:

- 'AND'. It has a 'must follow' emitter for all activities leaving a certain node and the 'AND' receiver for all operations entering the node. Thus, all activities entering the node or leaving the node are realized. The node will be realized only if all the branches leading into the node are realized. The time of realization is the largest of the completion times of the activities into the node.
- 'Exclusive Or'. It enables only one activity to be realized from a set of activities entering a node or leaving a node. The realization of any branch leading into the node causes the node to be realized. This operation is subdivided into two classes:
  - 'Stochastic Exclusive Or', denoted by 'Or*'. Each alternative activity entering a set corresponds to a certain probability value while a set of activities is a full group of events. The choice of an alternative activity at the node's receiver or emitter is carried out by a random trial in accordance with the activities' probability values. Each set comprises no fewer than two alternative activities.
  - 'Deterministic Exclusive Or', denoted by 'Or**'. The choice of an alternative activity from a set of activities at the receiver or at the emitter is carried out by the project manager.
- 'AND + Or*'. Two different sets of activities are either entering a certain node or leaving a node. All activities entering the first set have to be realized while only one activity has to be chosen from the second set on the basis of a random trial.
- 'AND + Or**'. The difference between this operation and the previous one is that the choice of an activity from the second set is carried out by the project manager.
- 'Or* + Or**'. Two alternative sets of activities are either entering a node or leaving a node. The choice of an alternative activity from the first set is of random nature and is uncontrolled, while for the second set, choosing an alternative activity is a control action.
- 'AND + Or*+ Or**'. Three sets of activities are entering or leaving a certain node. All activities entering the first set have to be realized while the choice of an alternative activity from the second and third sets is carried out by means of random trials and control actions, correspondingly.

Types of Networks

According to the types and parameters of the network's elements and based on the combinations of different logical operations at the nodes' receivers and emitters, the network models shown in Table 1.1 can be considered.

Table 1.1 Network models

Model	Types and parameters of network's elements
List of events	It is the simplest network. It comprises only events and there are no number parameters.
GANT	A diagram that comprises both events and activities. The parameters are only positive numbers which denote the activities' durations.
CPM-PERT	Finite, oriented, connected, acyclic networks that comprise both events and activities with the logical 'must follow' emitter and the 'AND' receiver, as well as the 'finish-start' links. The parameters assigned to activities are deterministic in CPM and of random duration in PERT networks.
Decision-CPM	All the events have an 'AND' receiver while certain events have controlled deterministic alternative outcomes. The choice of an alternative network is supervised by the project manager.
Generalized network model (GNM)	A generalized time-oriented network model which includes both events and activities together with various terms' restrictions, all kinds of connecting links, reverse links and generalized links between activities. The parameters which are usually links' durations, are both positive and non-positive as well. A generalized resource constrained network model is a GNM network with an additional implementation of implicit algorithmic links.
Graphical evaluation and review technique (GERT)	Besides the logical 'AND' receiver and 'must follow' emitter, comprises certain events with 'Stochastic Exclusive Or*' either at the emitter or at the receiver. The choice of an alternative activity is realized by a random trial of a full group of events with fixed probabilities.
Venture evaluation and review technique (VERT)	It is a computerized mathematically oriented network based simulation model made of arcs and nodes There are two types of nodes, split-logic nodes and single-unit logic nodes.
Controlled alternative activity network (CAAN)	It comprises, besides events with the logical 'must follow' emitter and the logical 'AND' receiver, certain events with 'Exclusive Or*' of stochastic nature at the receiver or at the emitter. Certain other events entering the model have an 'Exclusive Or**' receiver or emitter but these are not events which comprise simultaneously two types of alternative sets of activities of 'Exclusive Or*' and 'Exclusive Or**' entering or leaving one and the same node.
General alternative activity network model (GAAN)	A finite, oriented, acyclic network with one source node and no less than two sink nodes. Three different types of activities may leave one and the same node of activities: PERT, ASA (alternative stochastic activity), and ADA (alternative deterministic activity). Unlike the CAAN model, the GAAN model is not a fully divisible network.
Stochastic alternative time-oriented network (SATM)	It is a further extension of the generalized network model GNM and GAAN. SATM differs from GNM by implementing various types of alternative relations (stochastic or deterministic alternatives) and a broad spectrum of stochastic values.

Decision-CPM Model

The increased complexity of major projects through the 1940s led many groups to research methods of better control. This culminated in the late 1950s in CPM and PERT. CPM and PERT are finite, connected, oriented, acyclic networks, with one source node and one sink node. They are limited in terms of the types of logical elements permitted. Both networks comprise events and activities with the logical 'must follow' emitter and the 'AND' receiver, as well as the 'finish-start' links. Thus, all activities entering and leaving a node must be realized. The parameters assigned to activities are deterministic in CPM and of random duration in PERT networks.

CPM was developed independently at the same time as PERT for a construction project at DuPont. The method was instituted by Kelley and Walker (1959a,b), and further developed by Fulkerson (1961) and Kelley (1961). It was refined by Moder and Philips (1964) and has been extended to CPM/Time by Gessford (1966).

PERT has also been used quite extensively (Malcolm et al., 1959; Murray, 1963; MacCrimmon and Ryavec, 1962, 1964; Clark, 1961; Grubbs, 1962; Hartley and Wotham, 1966). Some extensions of PERT include PERT/Cost (Office of the Secretary of Defence, 1962) which added resource cost to the PERT/Time schedule and PERT/Reliability (Malcolm, 1963) which is an extension similar to PERT/Cost. A comprehensive review for both methods can be found in Davis (1966) and Levine (1986).

There are many situations in which the logical structure of PERT and CPM models are highly inadequate and too limited in its applicability. Industrial and economic systems are replete with different logical classes of events, uncertain activities, multiple-source and multiple-terminal projects, etc., which cannot be handled by these models (Eisner, 1962). Examples abound in the areas of computer programming systems, bidding and contracting situations, missile countdown procedures, investment selections, etc.

In many cases it is desirable to represent probabilistic flows from one activity to another or flows in the opposite direction. For example, it is necessary that there to be two output branches from a maintenance activity where, depending on whether the item passed or failed a test, it would continue normal flow or be routed to appropriate maintenance activities, or if the item failed the test one possible decision would be to retest in order to ensure proper test results. This requires a flow in the opposite direction (Drezner and Pritsker, 1965).

Despite CPM is considered to be a technique for planning and scheduling of projects, there is no interaction between these two phases of the CPM analysis unless the technique of the job crashing is used (Crowston and Thompson, 1967). The planning phase is usually identified with the construction of the project graph, during which time specific decisions are made on the method of performing the jobs as well as their technological ordering. At the completion of the planning stage it is possible to schedule the starting time of each task in the project using the conventional CPM calculations.

A much greater degree of interaction between the planning and scheduling phases is essential in order to obtain an overall optimum. Thus, if there are a number of competing methods of performing some of the tasks, each method having a different cost, a different time duration and different technological dependencies, the effects of alternative methods of performing a task can be considered, and decisions previously optimal may be changed during the execution of the project. Crowston and Thompson (1967) call this problem, the decision-CPM problem.

Crowston and Thompson (1967, 1970), Crowston (1971) and later on Hastings and Mello (1979) introduced the concept of multiple choices at such alternative nodes, when decision-making is of a deterministic nature. In a decision project graph, for each job set a decision must be made as to which job of the set is to be done. If we decide to do one of the jobs in a job set, then all immediate predecessor relations that the job satisfies must hold in the final graph. If we decide not to do that job, then none of its immediate predecessor relations hold and we must remove that job together with all edges that impinge on it from the decision project graph. Once such decision is made for each job set, the result is an ordinary CPM project.

Let $J = \left\{S_1, S_2, S_3, \ldots\right\}$ be a set of job sets that must be done to complete the project. Some of the job sets are unit sets, $S = \left\{S_{i1}\right\}$, and other sets have several members, $S_{ij} = \left\{S_{i1}, S_{i2}, S_{i3}, \ldots\right\}$. If all job sets are unit sets, then all of the jobs in the project are independent and the project reduces to the ordinary project of the usual CPM variety. If one or more of the job sets have more than one member, then for each such set a decision must be made as to which job of the set is to be done. Once such decision is made for each job set, the result is an ordinary CPM project.

Consider a job set $S_{ij} = \left\{S_{i1}, S_{i2}, \ldots, S_{ik(i)}\right\}$ and its associated $k(i)$ variables $d_{i1}, d_{i2}, \ldots, d_{ik(i)}$ with constraints given by

$$d_{ij} = \begin{cases} 1 & \text{if job } j \text{ is to be performed} \\ 0 & \text{otherwise} \end{cases} \tag{1.1}$$

If exactly one of the jobs must be performed then, the mutually exclusive interdependence condition is expressed by

$$\sum_{j=1}^{k(i)} d_{ij} = 1 \tag{1.2}$$

However, the design problem may not always be the simple choice of one job from each job set. For instance

$$\sum_{j=1}^{k(i)} d_{ij} = 3 \quad (1.3) \qquad \sum_{j=1}^{k(i)} d_{ij} \le 4 \quad (1.4) \qquad \sum_{j=1}^{k(i)} d_{ij} + \sum_{j=1}^{k(l)} d_{lj} = 3 \quad (1.5)$$

Note that Equation (1.3) says that we must choose exactly three alternatives; Equation (1.4) says that we may choose at most four alternatives; and Equation (1.5) says that at two decision nodes i and l we must choose exactly three alternatives.

In addition to the relations described above there will be precedence relations between the jobs of a decision project. Let $S_{ij} \le S_{mn}$ denote a relation between two pairs of jobs, S_{ij} and S_{mn}, and is read S_{ij} is an immediate predecessor of S_{mn}, indicating that all immediate predecessors of a job must be completed before that job can be started. If we decide to do one of the jobs in a job set, then all immediate predecessor relations that the job satisfies must hold in the final graph. If we decide not to do that job, then none of its immediate predecessor relations hold and we must remove that job together with all edges that impinge on it from the decision project graph to obtain the final project graph. If on any path, two jobs are separated by a job which could be eliminated, and if it is desired to maintain a technological ordering of the two jobs, a dummy immediate predecessor relation must be established between them.

We associate with each job, S_{ij}, a time t_{ij}, and a cost c_{ij}. Also we assume a reward payment or 'r' dollars per day for each day the project is under the required due date D, and a penalty payment 'p', for each day beyond D. We can now formulate the integer programming problem of selecting the best project graph and finding its critical path.

$$\text{Min} \quad C = \sum_{i=1}^{h}\sum_{j=1}^{k} d_{ij}c_{ij} - rw_F^- + pw_F^+ \tag{1.6}$$

$$\text{subject to} \quad w_F - w_F^+ + w_F^- - D = 0 \tag{1.7}$$

$$w_i + t_i \leq w_m \tag{1.8}$$

$$-M\left(1 - d_{ij}\right) + w_{ij} + t_{ij} \leq w_m \tag{1.9}$$

$$\sum_{j=1}^{k(i)} d_{ij} = 1 \tag{1.10}$$

$$0 \leq d_{ij} \leq 1, \text{ integer} \tag{1.11}$$

where w_F is the early start time of finish the last job in the project; w_i is the early start time of job S_i. The first term in Equation (1.6), $\sum_{i=1}^{h}\sum_{j=1}^{k} d_{ij}c_{ij}$, calculates the costs of all the decision jobs that are to be performed and the second term, $-rw_F^- + pw_F^+$, is explained by constraint (1.7). If $w_F > D$, then the project is not completed until after the due date so that $w_F^+ = w_F - D$, and a penalty of pw_F^+ is included in the objective function. If $w_F < D$, then the project is completed before the due date so that $w_F^- = D - w_F$, and a reward of $-rw_F^-$ is included in the objective function. Constraint (1.8) indicates that if job sets S_i and S_m are unit sets, then S_i is to be performed before S_m. If S_m is a unit-job set and S_{ij} is from a multi-job set, constraint (1.9) says that job S_{ij} is to be performed before S_m. Since M is a large enough number the inequality is restrictive only if $d_{ij} = 1$. If S_{ij} is not performed (i.e., $d_{ij} = 0$), the inequality does not constrain the variables. Thus all paths though the jobs which are not performed will be broken.

Next, the multi-objective linear programming problem is applied to the project shown in Table 1.2. A graphical representation of the combined planning and scheduling problem is shown in the decision project graph of Figure 1.3, where the circular 'AND' nodes represent jobs that must be performed and the triangular 'OR' nodes introduce the mutually exclusive job alternatives of a job set. In Figure 1.3, the additional interdependence of a contingent relationship between jobs S_{41} and S_{22} ($S_{41} \geq S_{22}$) is included. We may include job S_{22} if and only if we perform job S_{41}. Therefore, the possible sets of decisions are $\left\{S_{21}, S_{42}\right\}$, $\left\{S_{21}, S_{41}\right\}$, and $\left\{S_{22}, S_{41}\right\}$. The project graphs resulting from each of these sets of decisions are shown in Figures 1.4, 1.5, and 1.6 respectively.

Table 1.2 Data of the project

Task	S_{ij}	Time (days)	Cost (€*10⁶)
A	S_1	27	4.06
B	S_{21}	36	3.74
	S_{22}	31	4.20
C	S_3	25	0.35
D	S_{41}	29	5.67
	S_{42}	26	7.09
E	S_5	39	4.79
F	S_6	20	0.35
G	S_7	3	0.13

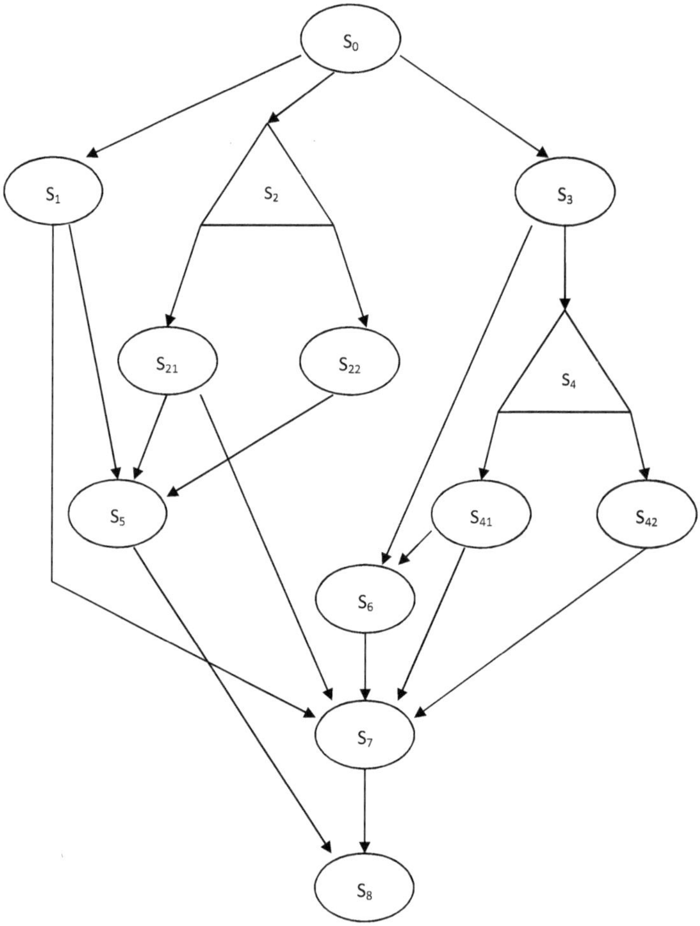

Figure 1.3 Decision-CPM network

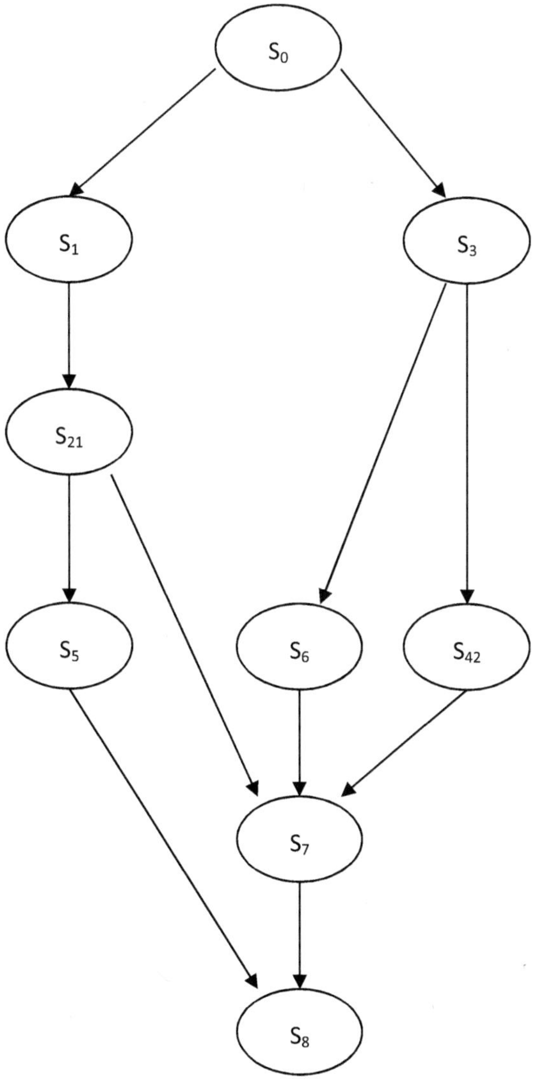

Figure 1.4 Decision set {S_{21},S_{42}}

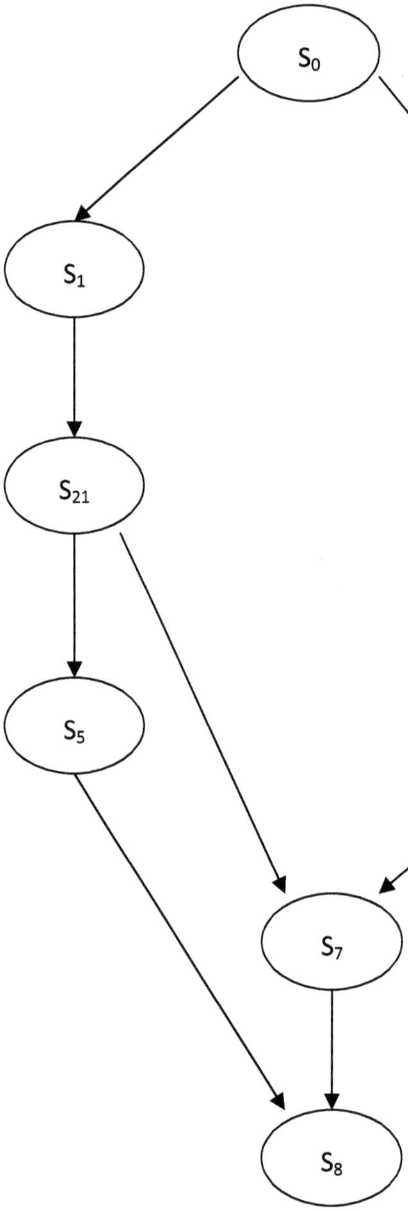

Figure 1.5 **Decision set** $\{S_{21}, S_{41}\}$

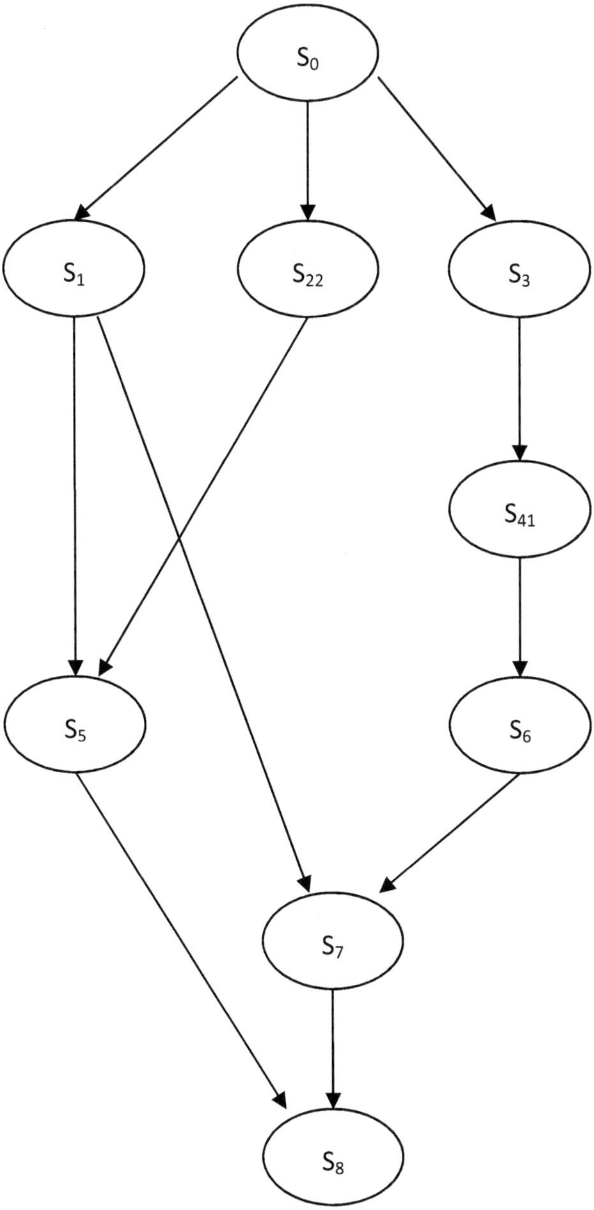

Figure 1.6 Decision set $\{S_{22}, S_{41}\}$

We assume a reward payment of €10,000 dollars per day for each day the project is under the required due date D = 105 days, and a penalty payment of €15,000, for each day beyond D. The multi-objective linear programming problem of selecting the best project graph and finding its critical path minimizing total costs can be expressed as follows:

Min $\quad C = 5.67d_{41} + 7.09d_{42} + 3.74d_{21} + 4.20d_{22} - 0,01w_F^- + 0,015w_F^+ + 9.68$

Subject to

$t_1 + t_7 \le w_8 \quad w_8 - w_F^+ + w_F^- = 105$

$t_1 + t_5 \le w_8 \quad d_{22} \le d_{41}$

$t_3 + t_6 + t_7 \le w_8 \qquad d_{21} + d_{22} = 1$

$t_1 - M\left(1 - d_{21}\right) + t_5 \le w_8 \qquad d_{41} + d_{42} = 1$

$t_1 - M\left(1 - d_{22}\right) + t_7 \le w_8 \qquad t_1 = 27; t_3 = 25; t_6 = 20; t_7 = 3$

$-M\left(1 - d_{22}\right) + t_5 \le w_8 \qquad w_8 = 78;\ 103;\ 105$

$t_3 - M\left(1 - d_{42}\right) + t_7 \le w_8 \qquad 0 \le d_{ij} \le 1$, integer

$t_3 - M\left(1 - d_{41}\right) + t_7 \le w_8$

$t_3 - M\left(1 - d_{41}\right) + t_6 + t_7 \le w_8$

Given a daily penalty and premium of €15,000 and €10,000 respectively, the project can be completed in 105 days selecting jobs S_{21} and S_{42} at a minimum cost of €19.07 million. As can be seen in Table 1.3, the total project cost will change with the due date established given any sets of decisions because of overtime penalties and early finish premiums. For example, if jobs $\left\{S_{21}, S_{41}\right\}$ are selected the project can be completed in 103 days at a cost of €19.09 million.

Table 1.3 Total cost of the project with given decision sets and due date

	Decision set		
Due date	$\{S_{21}, S_{41}\}$	$\{S_{22}, S_{41}\}$	$\{S_{21}, S_{42}\}$
105	19.07	19.28	20.51
103	19.09	19.30	20.54
90	19.28	19.43	20.73

Generalized Network Model

A generalized network model (GNM) is a generalized time-oriented network that includes both events and activities, together with various terms' restrictions, all kinds of connecting links, reverse links and generalized links between activities. The parameters which are usually the link's durations, are both positive and non-positive as well. Various logical restrictions that can be implemented in the model are the following (Voropajev et al., 2000):

1. Consider the two activities, (i_1, j_1) and (i_2, j_2) shown in Figure 1.7, and their durations $t(i_1, j_1)$ and $t(i_2, j_2)$.

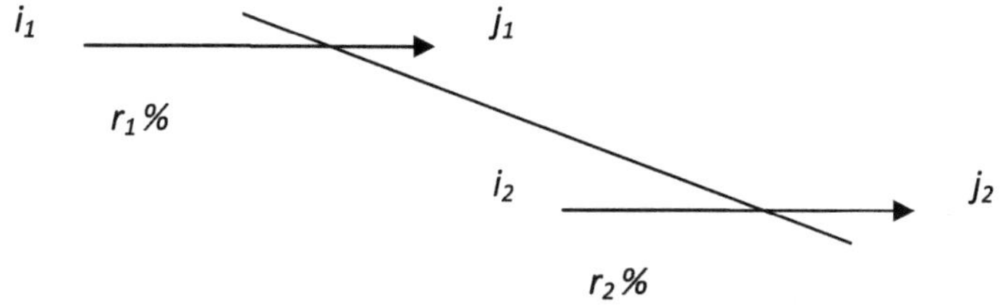

Figure 1.7 A generalized network model

Call $(i,j)_r$ a sub-activity which, being the first part of activity (i,j), contributes r per cent of the total volume of that activity, and call $F(i,j)_r$ the actual moment the sub-activity $(i,j)_r$ is finished. A restriction is introduced such that the difference between $F(i_1, j_1)_{r_1}$ and $F(i_2, j_2)_{r_2}$ has to be no less than a deterministic time $d(r_1, r_2)$, i.e.,

$$F(i_2, j_2)_{r_2} \geq F(i_1, j_1)_{r_1} + d(r_1, r_2) \tag{1.12}$$

where (i_1, j_1), (i_2, j_2), r_1, r_2, and $d(r_1, r_2)$ are pre-given values. Restriction (1.12) can be used in real examples, e.g., software integration testing can only start when software coding has produced at least two components.

2. For a certain set of activities $A(i,j)$ and $B(i,j)$, their starting and finishing times, $S(i,j)$ and $F(i,j)$, may be restricted from above or from below, as shown in Figure 1.8.

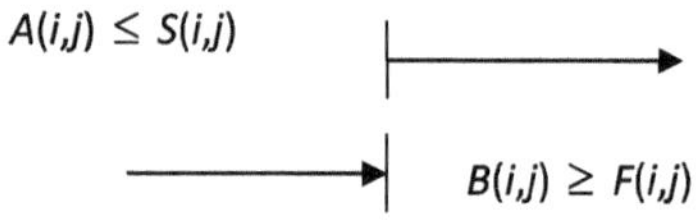

Figure 1.8 Starting and finishing times in a generalized network model

3. For a certain pair of consecutive activities (i_1, i_2), (i_2, i_3), the starting times of activity (i_2, i_3) must not exceed the finishing time of (i_1, i_2) by more than $f(i_1, i_2, i_3)$ where f is a pre-given deterministic value. Thus,

$$S(i_2, i_3) \leq F(i_1, i_2) + f(i_1, i_2, i_3) \tag{1.13}$$

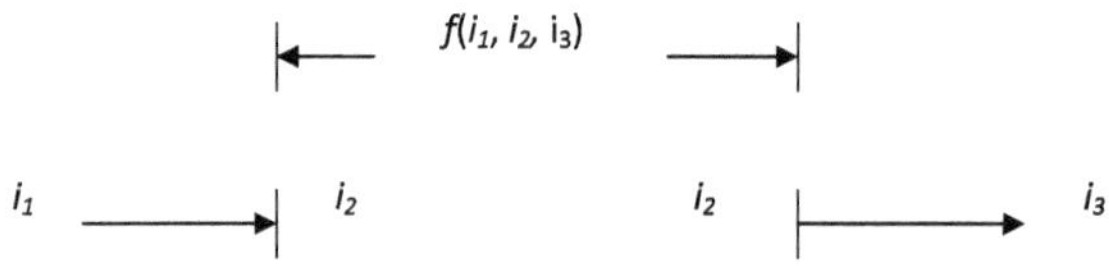

Figure 1.9 Finishing time in a generalized network model

Decision Box Network

The first significant development in the area of alternative networks to incorporate more stochastic flexibility was the pioneering work of Eisner (1962) in which a 'decision box' with both random and alternative outcomes was introduced. Since CPM and PERT networks are severely restricted from a logical point of view, Eisner (1962) suggested the use of logical elements in the PERT-type network and Elmaghraby (1964, 1967) introduced additional logic and algebra developing a notation for a multi-parameter type network. Elmaghraby coined the phrase 'Generalized Activity Networks' to describe such networks. His algebra was limited to branches that had constant times associated with them. Hespos and Strassman (1965) introduced the concept of the stochastic decision tree which is particularly applicable to projects characterized by high uncertainty and requiring a sequence of related decisions to be made over a period of time. The method makes it possible to evaluate all or nearly all feasible combinations of decisions in the decision tree, using subjective probability estimates or empirical frequency distributions for some or all factors affecting the decision.

Decision box networks are made of events and paths. Events that lead to alternatives are called decision boxes. Two paths that branch from a decision box are called 'conjunctive' if they are both to be performed, and if one or the other is to be performed, they are called 'disjunctive'. Since the decision box network allows the presentation of alternatives, not all the events shown on the network will be performed. Similarly, not all the end events or objectives of the various paths will be achieved.

An example of a decision box network is shown in Figure 1.10. Decision boxes 2 and 2_1 represent the case of a conjunctive path dependency. Decision box 4 represents a conjunctive merger point, that is, a point at which two or more conjunctive paths merge together after each has incorporated a decision box. As we can see, it is required that both decision boxes 2 and 3 be answered affirmatively in order for decision box 4 to be reached. Events *A* through *H* represent all the objectives or end events and dummy variables *X* and *Y* are introduced as the merge point activities leading to decision box 4.

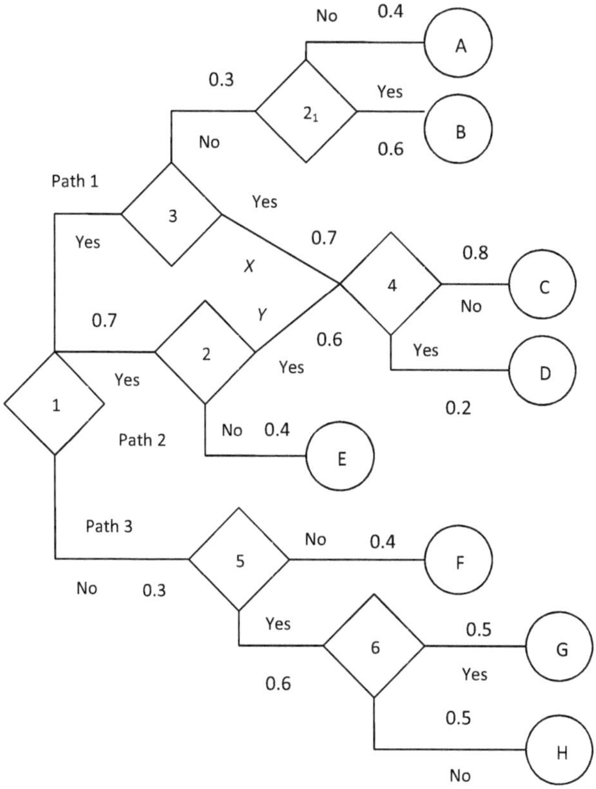

Figure 1.10 A decision box network

Source: Eisner 1962.

The following expression indicates, in the logical form, a tentative set of outcomes of the network:

$$\{[(A \cup B) \cup X] \cap (Y \cup E)\} \cup \{(G \cup H) \cup F\} \tag{1.14}$$

where $X \cap Y = C \cup D$

In Equation (1.14) the symbol $\cup$ represents a disjunctive path operation and the symbol $\cap$ represents a conjunctive path operation. Expansion of Equation (1.14) yields the outcomes: (*A* and *Y*) or (*A* and *E*), or (*B* and *Y*), or (*B* and *E*), or (*X* and *Y*) = (*C* or *D*) or (*X* and *E*), or *G*, or *H*, or *F*.

The conjunctive path dependency represented by decision boxes 2 and 2_1 further restricts the outcomes by making some of them impossible. For example, the outcomes (*A* and *Y*) and (*B* and *E*) are impossible since they call for contradictory answers to the same decision box, namely, decision box 2. Since (*X* and *Y*) is equal to (*C* or *D*), the final list of outcomes is:

(*A* and *E*); (*B* and *Y*), *C*; *D*; (*X* and *E*); *F*; *G*; *H*.

Now, the question is to know what combinations of objective events are possible, i.e., what are the possible outcomes of the project? or which of the possible outcomes are most likely to occur? The probabilities of each of the possible outcomes can now be calculated on the basis of the individual decision box a priori probabilities assigned to each of the alternatives of each decision box. These calculations are shown in Table 1.4.

In the example given, outcome *C* has the highest probability of occurrence associated with it (0.235). The latter outcome in terms of achieving the objectives events is outcome *D* (0.059).

Table 1.4 Probabilities of each outcome

Outcomes	Probability components	Substitution	Final outcome probabilities
A and *E*	$p(A)p(E/A)$	(0.4)(0.3)(0.7)	0.084
B and *Y*	$p(B)p(Y/B)$	(0.6)(0.3)(0.7)	0.126
C	$p(C)p(X)p(Y)$	(0.8)(0.7)(0.6)(0.7)	0.235
D	$p(D)p(X)p(Y)$	(0.2)(0.7)(0.6)(0.7)	0.059
X and *E*	$p(X)p(E/X)$	(0.7)(0.7)(0.4)	0.196
F	$p(F)$	(0.4)(0.3)	0.120
G	$p(G)$	(0.5)(0.6)(0.3)	0.090
H	$p(H)$	(0.5)(0.6)(0.3)	0.090
			1.000

Graphical Evaluation and Review Technique (GERT)

Pritsker and Happ (1966) and Pritsker and Whitehouse (1966) developed a new graphical technique, called GERT, for the study of alternative stochastic networks composed of 'Exclusive Or', 'Inclusive Or', 'AND' nodes and multi-parameter branches. Whitehouse (1973) describes GERT as an analytical procedure which combines the disciplines of flow graph theory, moment generating functions and PERT to obtain solutions to stochastic problems. GERT derives both the probability that a node will be realized and the conditional moment generating function (MGF) of the elapsed time required to traverse between any two nodes (Moeller and Digman, 1981). The steps in applying GERT are (Pritsker, 1966):

1. convert a qualitative description of a system or problem to a model in network form;

2. collect the necessary data to describe the branches of the network;

3. obtain an equivalent one-branch function between two nodes of the network;

4. convert the equivalent function into the following two performance measures of the network:

   - the probability that a specific node is realized; and
   - the MGF of the time associated with an equivalent network;

5. make inferences concerning the system under study from the information obtained in 4 above.

The components of GERT networks are directed branches (arcs, edges, transmittances) and logical nodes (vertices). A directed branch has associated with it one node from which it emanates and one node at which it terminates. Two parameters are associated with a branch:

1. The probability that a branch is taken, *p*, given that the node from which it emanated is realized; and

2. A time, *t*, required, if the branch is taken to accomplish the activity which the branch represents.

A node in a stochastic network consists of an input (receiving) side and an output (emitting) side. Table 1.5 shows the three logical relations on the input side and the two types of relations on the input side which will be considered.

Table 1.5 Logical relations of stochastic networks

Name	Symbol	Characteristic
	INPUT SIDE	
Exclusive Or	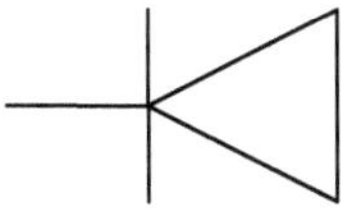	The realization of any branch leading into the node causes the node to be realized. One and only one of the branches leading into this node can be realized at a given time.
Inclusive Or	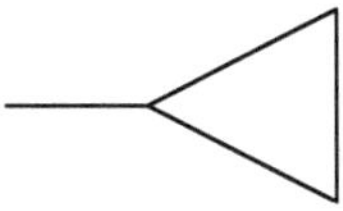	The realization of any branch leading into the node causes the node to be realized. The time of realization is the smallest of the completion times of the activities leading into this node.
AND		The node will be realized only if all branches leading into the node are realized. The time of realization is the largest of the completion times of the activities into the AND node.
	OUTPUT SIDE	
Deterministic	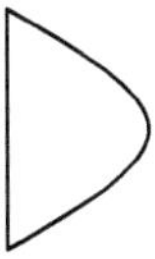	All branches emanating from the node are taken if the node is realized, i.e., all branches emanating from this node have a probability equal to 1.
Probabilistic	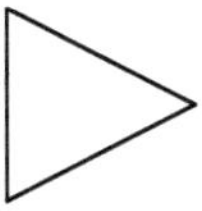	Exactly one branch emanating from the node is taken is the node is realized.

The input and output symbols are combined in Figure 1.11 in order to show six possible types of nodes:

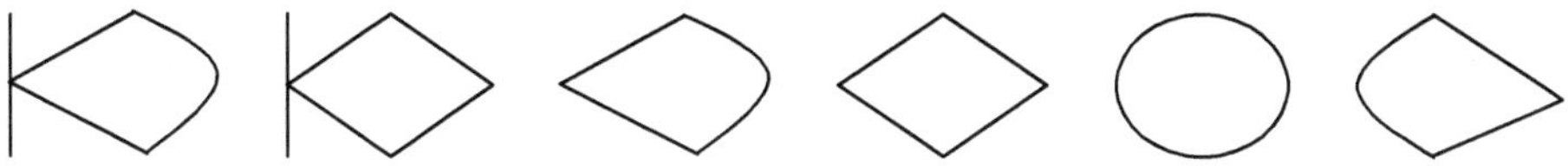

Figure 1.11 Types of nodes in a GERT network

Let us discuss the method for analysing stochastic networks. For two branches in series, the probabilities (p) associated to each branch are multiplied to obtain the equivalent probability for the two branches and the time parameter (t) is added. For parallel branches, the probabilities add and the time parameter is a weighted average. Following Pritsker (1966), these observations suggest the transformation of p and t into a single function known as the trasmittance function (w-function):

$$w_E(s) = p_i e^{st_i} \tag{1.15}$$

where p_i is the probability that activity i will be realized, s is the parameter of trasmittance, and t_i is the time activity i will take.

Then, for two branches in series (Figure 1.12), the w-functions of the branches will be multiplied:

$$w_E(s) = w_a(s)\, w_b(s) = \left(p_a e^{st_a}\right)\left(p_b e^{st_b}\right) \tag{1.16}$$

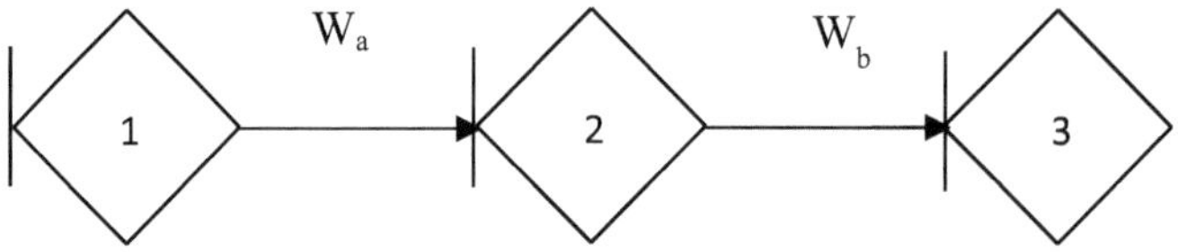

Figure 1.12 Branches in series

and for two branches in parallel (Figure 1.13), the w-functions of the branches will be added:

$$w_E(s) = w_a(s) + w_b(s) = \left(p_a e^{st_a}\right) + \left(p_b e^{st_b}\right) \tag{1.17}$$

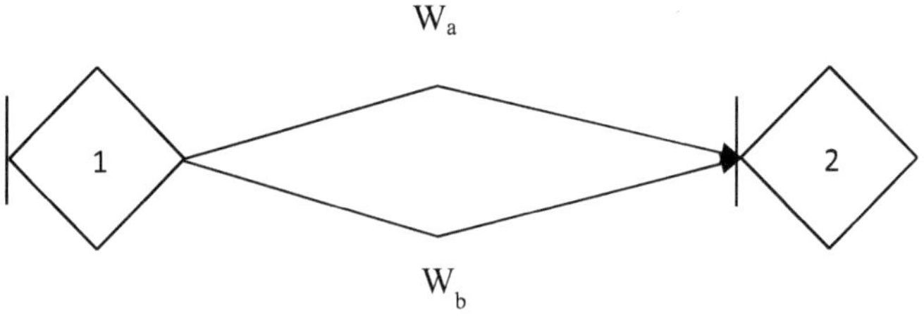

Figure 1.13 Branches in parallel

The equivalent probability that a system will be realized, p_E, is obtained by setting the dummy variable, s, equal to zero. Thus, for two branches in series:

$$p_E = w_E(0) = p_a p_b \tag{1.18}$$

and for two branches in parallel

$$p_E = w_E(0) = p_a + p_b \tag{1.19}$$

For the equivalent time, it is seen that by differentiation of $w_E(s)$ with respect to s and then setting $s = 0$, and expression proportional to the expected time results:

for two branches in series,

$$\left.\frac{\partial w_E(s)}{\partial(s)}\right|_{s=0} = p_a p_b (t_a + t_b) \tag{1.20}$$

and for two branches in parallel

$$\left.\frac{\partial w_E(s)}{\partial(s)}\right|_{s=0} = p_a t_a + p_b t_b \tag{1.21}$$

For both of these expressions the division by p_E will yield the desired results for the equivalent expected time:

for two branches in series

$$\frac{p_a p_b (t_a + t_b)}{p_a p_b} = (t_a + t_b) \tag{1.22}$$

and for two branches in parallel

$$\frac{(p_a t_a + p_b t_b)}{(p_a + p_b)} \tag{1.23}$$

Consider the self-loop in Figure 1.14. The path from node 1 to node 2 is $w_a(s) = p_a e^{st_a}$ and the function for the closed portion of the graph is $1 - w_b(s) = 1 - p_b e^{st_b}$, then

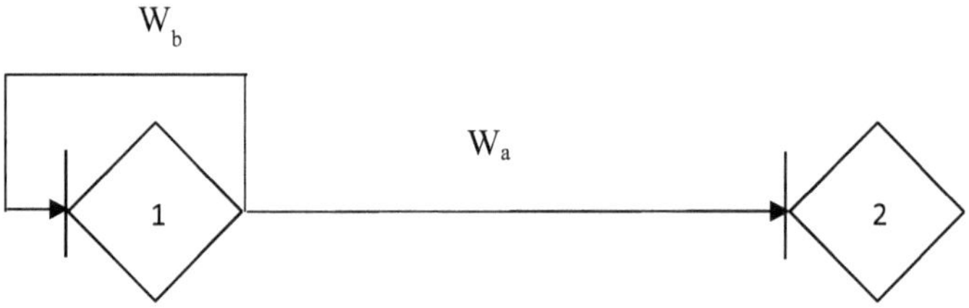

Figure 1.14 Self-loop

$$w_E(s) = \frac{w_a(s)}{1 - w_b(s)} = \frac{p_a e^{st_a}}{1 - p_b e^{st_b}} \tag{1.24}$$

The equivalent probability, p_E, is:

$$p_E = w_E(0) = \frac{p_a}{(1 - p_b)} \tag{1.25}$$

and the equivalent time is obtained by differentiation of $w_E(s)$ with respect to s and then setting $s = 0$:

$$\left.\frac{\partial w_E(s)}{\partial(s)}\right|_{s=0} = t_a + t_b\left(\frac{p_b}{1 - p_b}\right) \tag{1.26}$$

Due to the fact that the equivalent time is a variable conditioned on the branch being realized, the division by $p_E = W_E(0)$ will yield the desired results for the equivalent expected time.

From the above, it is seen that

$$\mu_{1E} = \frac{\partial}{\partial s}\left[\frac{W_E(s)}{W_E(0)}\right]_{s=0} \tag{1.27}$$

where μ_{nE} is defined as the nth moment about zero of the equivalent branch, and

$$\frac{W_E(s)}{W_E(0)} = M_E(s) \tag{1.28}$$

is the moment generating function of the equivalent time, t_E. Table 1.6 shows the equivalent function and the equivalent MGF for a series, parallel and self-loop network.

Table 1.6 Network reduction employing the topological equation

Network type	**Equivalent function ($w_E(s)$)**	**Equivalent MGF ($M_E(s)$)**
Series	$(p_a e^{st_a})(p_b e^{st_b})$	$e^{s(t_a+t_b)}$
Parallel	$(p_a e^{st_a}) + (p_b e^{st_b})$	$\frac{1}{p_a + p_b}\left[p_a e^{st_a} + p_b e^{st_b}\right]$
Self-loop	$\frac{(p_a e^{st_a})}{1-(p_b e^{st_b})}$	$(1 - p_b)e^{st_a}\left[1 - p_b e^{st_b}\right]^{-1}$

Consider the GERT network shown in Figure 1.15. For each branch of the network, the probability that the branch is realized, given that the preceding node is realized, and the time and cost associated with the activity represented by the branch, if the activity is performed, are shown in Table 1.7 by an ordered triple of probability, time (days), and cost in €10³ (p, t, c).

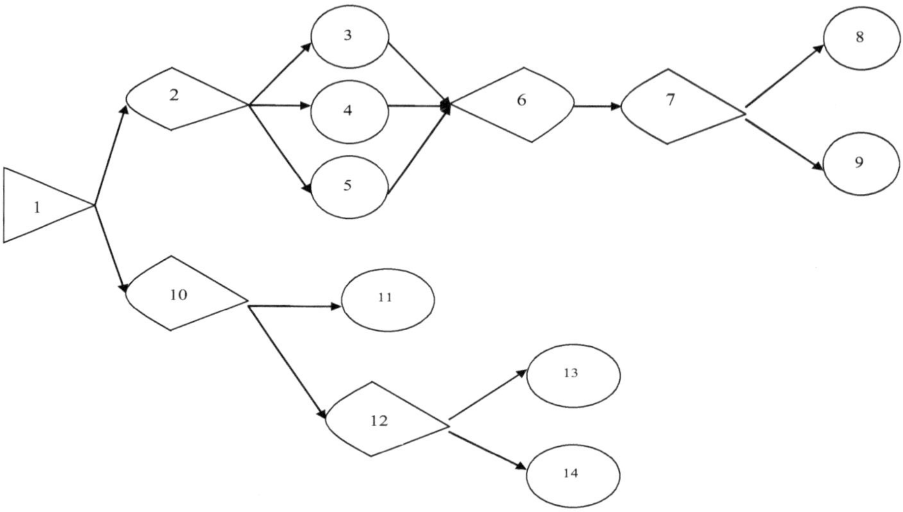

Figure 1.15 A GERT network

Table 1.7 Ordered triple of probability, time, and cost

Task	(p, t, c)	Task	(p, t, c)
1–2	(0.6; 7; 30)	6–7	(1; 4; 20)
2–3	(0.24; 1; 2.5)	7–8	(0.3; 1; 1.5)
2–4	(0.32; 1; 2.5)	7–9	(0.7; 1; 1.5)
2–5	(0.44; 0; 0)	1-10	(0.4; 6; 35)
3–6	(1; 1;10)	10–11	(0.7; 1; 1.5)
4–6	(1; 1; 10)	10–12	(0.3; 4; 35)
5–6	(1; 2; 20)	12–13	(0.5; 1; 1.5)
		12–14	(0.5; 1; 1.5)

The performance measures associated with, say, event 8 are computed by:

$$w_{1-8}\left(S_1S_2\right) = \left(.6e^{7S_1+30S_2}\right)\left[\left(.24e^{2S_1+12.5S_2}\right)+\left(.32e^{2S_1+12.5S_2}\right)+\left(.44e^{2S_1+20S_2}\right)\right]\left[\left(e^{4S_1+20S_2}\right)\left(.3e^{S_1+1.5S_2}\right)\right]$$

$$p_{1-8} = w_{1-8}\left(0,0\right) = \left(.6\right)\left(1\right)\left(.3\right) = 0.18 \quad \left(18\%\right)$$

$$E\left\{t_{1-8}\right\} = \frac{\partial}{\partial S_1}\left[\frac{1}{p_{1-8}} w_{1-8}\left(S_1, 0\right)\right]_{s_1=0} = 14 \text{ weeks}$$

$$E\{c_{1-8}\} = \frac{\partial}{\partial S_2}\left[\frac{1}{p_{1-8}} w_{1-8}(0, S_2)\right]_{s_2=0} = 67.3 \text{ (in thousands)}$$

An extension of GERT network is the Q-GERT network model developed by Pritsker (1979) which derives its name from special queue nodes which it has available for modelling situations in which queues build up prior to service activities. Q-GERT contains most of the capabilities and features of GERT plus numerous other features which make it particularly applicable to scheduling multiple projects, especially to R&D planning schemes. A limiting factor in GERT is that as the number of teams and projects increase the GERT network becomes extremely complex. As an alternative, Q-GERT offers even greater potential in planning and scheduling complex projects when several projects and teams exist (Moore and Taylor, 1977). The most important of the features for handling specific and complex network situations is the ability to assign unique network 'attributes' (i.e., activity times, nodal branching probabilities) to each individual project and then process each project through a single generalized network. Q-GERT requires only that the projects under analysis be diagrammed in network form, converted to computer program input data describing the network, and simulated using the prewritten Q-GERT simulation package. The Q-GERT simulation program provides statistical output for individual simulation runs, histograms, and simulation traces.

GERT network modelling, with its capability to include probabilistic branching (stochastic models), network looping (feedback loops), multiple sink nodes (multiple outcomes), multiple node realizations (repeat events), and multiple probability distributions (assigned to activity times), has been explored as a feasible modelling alternative for analysis of industrial engineering and management, R&D projects, etc., which include these complexities (Moore and Taylor, 1977). GERT applications in planning single R&D projects can be found in (Samli and Bellas, 1971; Bellas and Samli, 1973; Whitehouse, 1973). Moore and Taylor (1977) report on a simulation study of multiple R&D projects that are worked on concurrently and sequentially by more than one research team. Moore and Clayton (1976) show the GERT technique being used in planning the drilling of an oil well. Taylor and Moore (1980) describe a simulation study of two cases of R&D development planning. The reader is referred to several excellent sources on GERT and Q-GERT (Moore and Clayton, 1976; Whitehouse, 1973; Pritsker and Happ, 1966; Pritsker and Whitehouse, 1966; Whitehouse and Pritsker, 1969; Whitehouse, 1973; Pritsker, 1979).

Venture Evaluation and Review Technique (VERT)

The venture evaluation and review technique (VERT) is a computerized mathematically oriented network based simulation technique designed to assess the risks involved in projects that enables the project manager to simulate various decisions with alternative technology choices within the stochastic decision tree network (Moeller, 1972; Moeller and Digman 1981; Kidd, 1991). VERT is designed to analyse risks existing in three parameters of most common to managers in projects, time, cost and performance. As such, the technique is more powerful that techniques such as GERT, which are basically time and cost oriented. By allowing each activity to carry these three forms of uncertainty, VERT incorporates a 'realistic' degree of uncertainty into project analysis (Kidd, 1991).

Numerical values for each activity's time, cost and performance parameters may be assigned in terms of (i) one of the standard statistical distributions embedded in the VERT model or (ii) a histogram or (iii) a mathematical relationship if the time and/or cost and/or performance of this activity is dependent upon other nodes and/or arcs which are to be completed prior to this arc (Moeller and Digman, 1981).

A VERT model is made of arcs and nodes. Arcs and nodes are similar in that both have time, cost and performance attributes. Arcs have a primary and cumulative set of time, cost and performance values associated with them while nodes have only the cumulative set. The primary set represents the time expanded, the cost incurred and the performance generated to complete the specific activity this arc represents. The cumulative set represents the total time expanded, cost incurred, and composite performance generated to process all the arcs encountered along the path the network flow came through in order to complete the processing of the arc or node in question.

VERT has two types of nodes. The most commonly used type is the split-node logic which has separate input and output logic operations. The second, more specialized and less frequently used type of node has a single-unit logic which covers both input and output operations simultaneously. There are four basic input logics available for the split-logic nodes: (i) Initial; (ii) AND; (iii) Partial AND; and (iv) OR. And there are six basic split-node output logics available to distribute the network flow to the appropriate output arcs. They are described in Table 1.8 (Moeller and Digman, 1981):

Table 1.8 Split-logic nodes

INPUT LOGICS (ARCS)	
Initial	It serves as a starting point for the network flow. Multiple initial nodes may be used. All initial nodes are assigned the same time, cost and performance values by the project manager.
AND	It requires all the input arcs to be successfully completed before and combined input network flow is transferred over to the output logic for the appropriate distribution among the output arcs.
Partial AND	It is nearly the same as AND input logic except that it requires a minimum of one input arc to be successfully completed before allowing flow to continue on through this node. This input logic will wait for all the input arcs to come in or be eliminated from the network before processing.
OR	It is quite similar to the Partial AND logic. It also requires just a minimum of one input arc to be successfully completed before allowing the flow to continue on through this node. However, this logic will not wait for all the input arcs to come in or be eliminated from the network before the flow is processed.
OUTPUT LOGICS (ARCS)	
Terminal	It serves as an end point of the network. It is a sink for network flow.
ALL	All output logic simultaneously initiates the processing of all the output arcs.
Monte Carlo	It initiates the processing of one and only one output arc per simulation iteration by the use of the Monte Carlo method. This means that the output arcs are initiated randomly by user-developed probability weights that are placed on these output arcs.
Filter 1	It initiates one or a multiple number of output arcs depending on the joint or singular satisfaction of the time and/or cost and/or performance constraints placed on these node's output arcs. These constraints consist of upper and lower time and/or cost and/or performance boundaries.
Filter 2	It is the same as Filter 1 except that only one constraint rather than one to three constraints can be placed on the constraint-bearing output arcs (this constraint consists of an upper and a lower bound on the number of inputs arcs successfully processed), and only Partial AND input logic may be used with Filter 2 output logic.
Filter 3	It employs constraints which are not boundary values but, rather, consist of the name(s) of previously processed arcs. Thus the specified arc(s) must have been successfully completed before the outputs that are being constrained can be initiated.

In addition to the split-logic nodes described above, there are also single-unit logic nodes. This type of nodes enable direct transmission of the network flow from a given input arc to a given output arc. In the event there are more successfully processed input arcs than there are output arcs processing requests, the following logic embedded in each node will be used to select the optimal set of output arcs. The single-unit logic nodes are described in Table 1.9 (Moeller and Digman 1981).

Table 1.9 Single-unit logic nodes

Name	Description
Compare	It selects the optimal output arc set for processing by weights entered for time, cost and performance.
Preferred	It gives preference to the first input-output arc combination over the second and the second is given preference over the third, etc.
Queue	It has the function of transferring network flows in a queuing manner from an input arc to its mating output arc. As the network flows in the line input arcs arrive, they are queued-up and sequently processed by the server(s).
Sort	It has the purpose of transferring flows from input arcs to output arcs by sorting using time and/or cost and/or performance sort weights.

The most significant innovation of VERT is the introduction of its mathematical relationships, giving VERT the capability of establishing a mathematical relationship between any given arc's time and/or cost and/or performance and any other arc and/or node's time and/or cost and/or performance. VERT model has been applied to the evaluation of electric power generating methods and to weapon system developments, including tanks, helicopters, and air defence systems (Moeller and Digman, 1981).

Generalized Alternative Activity Network Model (GAAN)

Based on the idea of discrete optimization Golenko-Ginzburg and Block (1997) developed a more universal activity network model called the Generalized alternative activity network model (GAAN). A GAAN model is a finite, oriented, acyclic activity-on-arrow network, $G(N, A)$, with the following properties:

1. $G(N, A)$ has one source node and no less than two sink nodes.

2. Each activity $(i, j) \in A$ refers to one of the three different types as follows:

a) Activity (i, j) is a PERT activity (*PA*) with the logical 'must follow' emitter at node *i* and the 'AND' receiver at node *j*.

b) Activity (i, j) is an alternative stochastic activity (*ASA*) with the logical 'Exclusive Or' emitter at node *i*. Each $(i, j) \in A$ of *ASA* type corresponds to probability $0 < p_{ij} < 1$, while node *i* comprises at set of no less than two probabilities, p_{ij}, $\sum_j p_{ij} = 1$.

c) Activity (i, j) is an alternative deterministic activity (*ADA*) with the logical 'Exclusive Or' emitter at node *i*. Node *i* is a decision-making node and the corresponding transfer probabilities are assumed to equal one.

3. Activities of all types may leave one and the same node *i*. Thus, unlike the CAAN model, the GAAN model is not a fully divisible network.

4. Activities of all types may enter one and the same node.

An example of a GAAN type graph is shown in Figure 1.16 and Table 1.10.

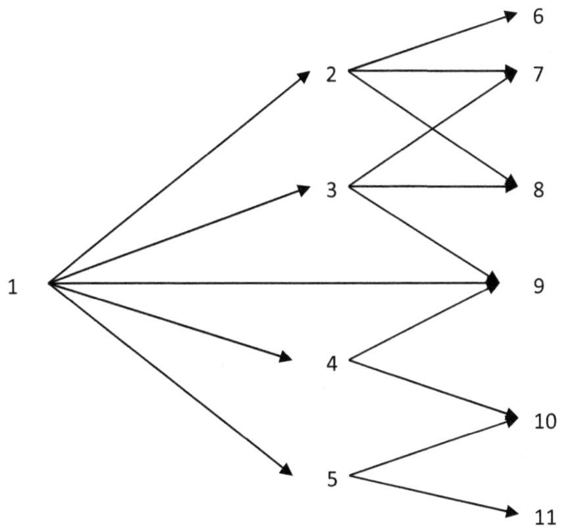

Figure 1.16 A GAAN network
Source: Golenko-Ginzburg and Block 1997.

Table 1.10 Types of activities

Task	Type	p_{ij}	Task	Type	p_{ij}	Task	Type	p_{ij}
(1,2)	ADA	1	(2,6)	PA	1	(3,9)	PA	1
(1,3)	ADA	1	(2,7)	ADA	1	(4,9)	ADA	1
(1,4)	ASA	0.3	(2,8)	ADA	1	(4,10)	ADA	1
(1,5)	ASA	0.7	(3,7)	ASA	0.6	(5,10)	PA	-
(1,9)	PA	1	(3,8)	ASA	0.4	(5,11)	PA	-

In order to solve a GAAN model, the concept of joint variant is introduced. Call a joint variant a sub-network $G^*\left(N^*, A^*\right)$ satisfying the following conditions:

1. $G^*\left(N^*, A^*\right)$ has one source node;
2. If $G^*\left(N^*, A^*\right)$ comprises a certain node *i*, namely $i \in N^*$, then $G^*\left(N^*, A^*\right)$ comprises all activities (i, j) of type *PA* and *ASA* leaving node *i*;
3. If $G^*\left(N^*, A^*\right)$ comprises a certain node i which in the GAAN model $G(N, A)$ has alternative outcomes of *ADA* type, then $G^*\left(N^*, A^*\right)$ comprises only one activity of that type leaving that node;
4. $G^*\left(N^*, A^*\right)$ is the maximal sub-network satisfying conditions 1–3.

The project manager has to determine an optimal decision policy, namely to choose an optimal joint variant together with determining optimal alternative outcomes of *ADA* type from every decision-making node that is reached in the course of the project's realization.

In the GAAN model the problem is to determine the joint variant optimizing the mean value of the objective function, subject to restricted mean values of several other criteria. The exact solution of this problem may be obtained by looking through all the joint variants on the basis of their proper enumeration. To enumerate the joint variants Golenko-Ginzburg and Block (1997) used the lexicographical method in combination with some techniques of discrete optimization and developed an algorithm to single out all the joint variants. If the number of joint variants becomes very high, obtaining a precise solution requires much computation time, especially for networks with many alternatives. For such cases, future research may be undertaken to develop an approximate solution, namely to determine a quasi-optimal joint variant that approximates the optimal solution with a pre-given relative error.

A particular case of GAAN models is the controlled alternative activity network (CAAN) model developed by Golenko-Ginzburg (1988, 1993) for projects with both random and deterministic alternative outcomes in key nodes. CAAN models comprise two types of alternative nodes. The first one reflects stochastic (uncontrolled) branching of the project's development. The second one (which is very common in R&D projects) is a decision node, i.e., the management chooses upon reaching that point the outcome direction. CAAN networks include additional types of nodes with 'Exclusive Or' receiver and 'Must follow' emitter, 'Exclusive Or' receiver and 'Exclusive Or' emitter. A CAAN model has one source and no fewer than two sink nodes. At each routine decision-making node, the developed algorithm singles out all the sub-networks (the so-called joint variants) that corresponds to all possible outcomes from that node. Decision-making results in determining the optimal joint variant and following the optimal direction up to the next decision-making node. A CAAN network covers a broad spectrum of stochastic networks. The CAAN model can only be applied to fully divisible networks that can be subdivided into non-intersecting fragments, thus, this type of model is not relevant to Eisner's model that is usually structured from non-divisible sub-networks. The CAAN model has been used in planning and controlling various R&D projects in the USSR Ministry of Aviation (Golenko-Ginzburg, 1972; Golenko-Ginzburg et al., 1997), in designing Israeli chemical plants and creating optical systems (Golenko-Ginzburg et al., 1997).

GAAN models are applicable to a wide range of managerial and engineering problems, in particular, to the representation and analysis of systems with probabilistic alternatives and events. For example, bidding situations in which the contractor bids on more than one project, projects involving R&D activities in which problems are attached on a wide front, in processing new software or in projects with multiple technologies and with stochastic evolution of technology leading to obsolesce effects (Rajagopalan, 1994), etc. The GAAN model is especially effective for this type of projects with multiple alternative technology choices, where there are several possible alternative ways for reaching intermediate and ultimate goals and where decision-making has to be introduced with incomplete or inadequate information about the alternatives.

Besides applying the GAAN model to a variety of industrial projects, the model was used in designing an artificial blood circulation system for an artificial heart (Lerner, 1990). Kidd (1990) provides an example of how a generalized activity network can be used in managing a software development project. This highlights a growth area in which generalized activity networks have proved useful in the past. The development of software requires a flexible management approach, as various outcomes within these projects are difficult to determine particularly at the preliminary stages (Dawson and Dawson, 1995).

Chapter 2

Multi-Objective Decision-Making Models

Traditional research on project schedule and management focuses on one objective: either the shortest possible project duration or the minimum possible cost. However, in most situations, the optimization problems are multi-objective where two or more independent objectives must be optimized simultaneously, such as the utilization of resources available and balance of workload. In these cases, multi-objective methods are helpful tools for project managers. In this chapter, different types of multi-objective decision-making methods are presented, namely, the traditional time-cost trade-off problem, fuzzy linear programming, goal programming and an integer programming problem.

Linear Programming Formulation of the Time-Cost Trade-off Problem

Linear programming is a powerful tool used by managers to obtain optimal solutions to problems that involve restrictions or limitations, such as available resources, budgets, and time. There are a number of different linear programming techniques, some of these techniques are used to find solutions for specific types of problems, and other are more general.

The literature contains linear, non-linear, and discrete formulations of the time-cost trade-off problem (Liberatore and Pollack-Johnson, 2006). The linear formulation assumes that each activity's time can range over a closed interval, and that the cost of completing the activity is linear and decreasing over the interval. This problem can be formulated as a linear programming problem and there are exact solution algorithms that take advantage of the project network's structure (Fulkerson, 1961; Kelley, 1961). Moore et al., (1978) reported a multi-criteria project crashing problem with linear time-cost trade-off, and proposed a goal programming formulation. The non-linear problem in its simplest form has been modelled using a piecewise linear representation of the time-cost trade-off for each activity (Moder et al., 1983) to represent the common situation in which it becomes proportionately more expensive to reduce duration by each successive time unit. For concave-type relationships, a mixed integer programming problem has to be attempted, but a convex-type relationship appears to be a more practicable assumption in the context of project crashing. If the convex-type relationship is approximated by piecewise linear segments, then the project crashing problem can be converted into equivalent linear programming formulations. Vrat and Kriengkrairut (1986) presented a goal programming model for the project crashing problem with a non-linear convex-type relationship. The discrete version of the time-cost problem requires specifying a set of discrete processing times and associated costs for each activity which is a different way to model non-linearity. The budget version of the discrete problem has been shown to be strongly NP-hard (De et al., 1997).

The linear programming formulation for the traditional deadline makespan problem can be expressed by (Liberatore and Pollack-Johnson, 2006):

$$\text{Min } C = \sum_{i=1}^{n} c_i x_i \tag{2.1}$$

subject to $$t_j \geq t_i + d_i - x_i \quad \forall \ (i, j) \ i \in P(j) \tag{2.2}$$

$$t_1 = 0 \tag{2.3}$$

$$t_n \leq T \tag{2.4}$$

$$0 \leq x_i \leq u_i \tag{2.5}$$

$$t_i \geq 0 \quad \forall \ i \tag{2.6}$$

where

C: total incremental cost for reducing project makespan;

x_i: number of time units to crash (reduce duration of) task *i*;

t_i: time task *i* is scheduled to start (in time units from the beginning of the project);

T: the desired makespan (deadline for total project completion time);

d_i: duration in time units of task *i*;

c_i: cost per time unit to crash task *i*;

u_i: maximum number of time units that task *i* can be reduced (crashed);

n: number of tasks (1 if is the start task, and *n* if is the finish task);

$P(j)$: The set of tasks that are immediate predecessors of task *j*;

The objective is to minimize the total crashing costs such that the earliest start times of each activity must be greater than or equal to the earliest finish times of that activity's immediate predecessors. We assume that the start task (task 1) is the only task with no predecessors, that the finish task (task *n*) is the only task that is not a predecessor of any other task, and that there are no cycles in the network.

Next, the above linear programming problem is applied to the project shown in Figure 2.1. Table 2.1 shows the tasks to undertake, their normal cost, crashing cost, normal duration and crashing time.

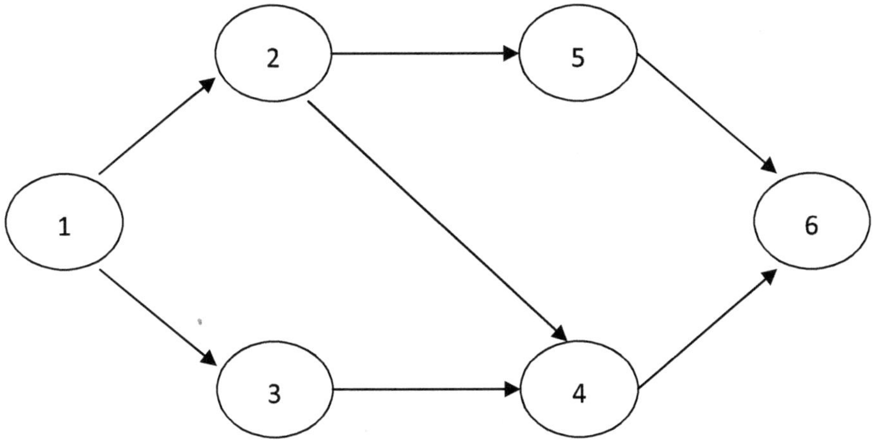

Figure 2.1 Network associated to the time-cost trade-off problem

Table 2.1 Data of the project

Task	Arc (i,j)	Normal cost (€*10³)	Crashing cost (€*10³)	Normal time (days)	Crashing time (days)	x_i	Slope
A	(1,2)	8	14	10	7	3	2
B	(1,3)	7	16	9	6	3	3
C	(2,5)	8	9	6	5	1	1
D	(2,4)	10	18	8	6	2	4
E	(3,4)	6	14	8	4	4	2
F	(5,6)	4	4	5	5	0	0
G	(4,6)	9	24	6	3	3	5

The formulation for this linear programming problem can be expressed as:

Min C: $2x_A + 3x_B + 1x_C + 4x_D + 2x_E + 5x_G$

subject to $t_1 = 0$

$t_2 \geq t_1 + 10 - x_A$

$t_3 \geq t_1 + 9 - x_B$

$t_4 \geq t_2 + 8 - x_D$

$t_4 \geq t_3 + 8 - x_E$

$t_5 \geq t_2 + 6 - x_C$

$t_6 \geq t_5 + 5 - x_F$

$t_6 \geq t_4 + 6 - x_G$

$t_6 \leq 24, \ldots, 17$

$x_A \leq 3$; $x_B \leq 3$; $x_C \leq 1$; $x_D \leq 2$;

$x_E \leq 4$; $x_F = 0$; $x_G \leq 3$

$x_i \geq 0_i$; $t_i \geq 0$; $\forall\ i$

The problem can be solved using Lingo (Lindo Systems, 2002) and different solutions to this problem are given in Table 2.2. As can be appreciated, the reduction in time implies an increase in the crashing cost.

Table 2.2 Different solutions to the linear programming problem

Time (days)	Crashing cost (€*10³)	Task reduced
24	0	
22	6	$x_A = 2$; $x_E = 1$
21	10	$x_A = 3$; $x_E = 1$
20	15	$x_A = 3$; $x_E = 2$; $x_G = 1$
19	20	$x_A = 3$; $x_E = 2$; $x_G = 2$
18	25	$x_A = 3$; $x_E = 2$; $x_G = 3$
17	32	$x_A = 3$; $x_C = 1$; $x_D = 1$ $x_E = 3$; $x_G = 3$

Liberatore and Pollack-Johnson (2006) extend the linear formulation of the deadline time-cost problem and propose a quadratic mixed integer programming approach for reducing project completion time that considers crashing as well as the removal and modification of precedence relationships. Deckro et al. (1995) develop the following quadrating programming model for the traditional time-cost trade-off scenario:

$$\text{Min } z \quad \sum_{(i,j)\in A}\left[b_{ij} + a_{ij}\left(n_{ij} - y_{ij}\right)^2\right] \tag{2.7}$$

$$\text{subject to} \quad -x_i + x_j - y_{ij} \geq 0 \text{ for all } (i,j) \in A \tag{2.8}$$

$$\tau_{ij} \leq y_{ij} \leq \mu_{ij} \text{ for all } (i,j) \in A \tag{2.9}$$

$$X_T \leq D \tag{2.10}$$

$$x_i \geq 0 \text{ for all } i \tag{2.11}$$

where

b_{ij} : normal cost of activity (i, j);

a_{ij} : marginal cost increase for varying the normal time;

n_{ij} : normal time to complete activity (i, j);

y_{ij} : actual duration of activity (i, j);

x_i : realization time of event i;

A: set of all activities in the project;

T: index of the terminal node of the project;

D: target completion date for the project;

The actual duration of activity (i, j), y_{ij}, would be limited to be within a range from τ_{ij} to μ_{ij}, where τ_{ij} and μ_{ij} represent the lower and upper bounds on y_{ij} respectively. Constraint (2.8) ensures that node *j* cannot be realized until after node *i* has been realized, and at least the duration of activity (i, j) has elapsed. Constraint (2.9) creates the upper and lower bounds on the duration of each activity. Constraint (2.10) requires that the terminal node, *T*, be realized on or before the project due date, *D*. Constraint (2.11) requires that each node be realized at some non-negative time.

A Linear Time-Cost Trade-off Model to Find the Critical Path

An alternative way to find the critical path is by using linear programming (Hillier and Lieberman, 2001; Taha, 2003). The idea is based on the concept that a critical path method problem can be thought of as the opposite of the shortest path problem. In order to determine the critical path in the project network it is sufficient to find the longest path from start to finish. Then, the length of this path is the total duration time of the project network. The linear programming formulation assumes that a unit flow enters the project network at the start node and leaves at the finish node.

Let x_{ij} be the decision variable denoting the amount of flow in activity $(i, j) \in A$. Since only one unit of flow could be in any arc at any time, the variable x_{ij} must assume binary variables only. The critical path method problem with *n* nodes is formulated as:

Max D $$\sum_{i=1}^{n}\sum_{j=1}^{n} t_{ij} x_{ij} \tag{2.12}$$

subject to $$\sum_{j=1}^{n} x_{ij} = 1 \tag{2.13}$$

$$\sum_{j=1}^{n} x_{ij} = \sum_{k=1}^{n} x_{ki}\ ,\ i = 2,\ldots,n-1 \tag{2.14}$$

$$\sum_{k=1}^{n} x_{kn} = 1 \tag{2.15}$$

$$x_{ij} = 0 \text{ or } 1\ \ \forall\ i,j \tag{2.16}$$

The objective is to maximize the total duration time of the project network form node 1 to node n. The critical path of this project network consists of a set of activities $(i,j) \in A$ from the start to the finish in which each activity in the path corresponds to the optimal decision variable $x_{ij} = 1$ in the optimal solution to the linear programming model.

The following example is used to illustrate the proposed model. The problem is to find the critical path between node 1 and node 6 in Figure 2.1. The formulation for this particular linear programming problem can be expressed as:

Max D $$10x_{1,2} + 9x_{1,3} + 6x_{2,5} + 8x_{2,4} + 8x_{3,4} + 6x_{4,6} + 5x_{5,6}$$

subject to $$x_{1,2} + x_{1,3} = 1$$

$$x_{1,2} - x_{2,4} - x_{2,5} = 0$$

$$x_{1,3} - x_{3,4} = 0$$

$$x_{2,4} + x_{3,4} - x_{4,6} = 0$$

$$x_{2,5} - x_{5,6} = 0$$

$$x_{4,6} + x_{5,6} = 1$$

$$x_{ij} = 0 \text{ or } 1\ \ \forall\ i,j$$

and the solution is $D = 24$ (days), with $x_{1,2} = 1$; $x_{2,4} = 1$; and $x_{4,6} = 1$.

Fuzzy Linear Programming

When the activity times in the project are deterministic and known, the critical path method has been demonstrated to be a useful tool in managing projects in an efficient manner and a useful tool in the planning and control of complicated projects in a wide range of engineering and management applications (Chen and Hsueh, 2008). However, there are many cases where the activity times may not be presented in a precise manner and have to be estimated subjectively. To deal quantitatively with imprecise data, the Program Evaluation and Review Technique (PERT) was employed. However, in PERT, durations are considered independent and identically distributed. The use of the beta distribution or its variants may not be able to provide an appropriate distribution when the activity time is highly skewed. To construct the probability distribution of activity times requires a prior predictable regularity or a posterior frequency distribution. Variability is neglected in the definition of the critical path, which is determined considering only the average duration of the tasks, etc. (Chen, 2007; Zammori et al., 2007).

An alternative way to deal with imprecise data in determining activity times is to employ the concept of fuzziness (Zadeh, 1978). In recent years many researchers have combined fuzzy set theory with PERT to handle time estimates in project planning and control problems. The result is an approach called Fuzzy PERT, whereby the vague activity times can be represented by fuzzy sets. The main advantages of methodologies based on fuzzy theory are that they do not require prior predictable regularities or posterior frequency distributions, and they can deal with imprecise input information containing feelings and emotions quantified based on decision-maker's subjective judgment (Chen, 2007).

Several studies have investigated the case where activity durations times in a project are approximately known and are more suitable represented by fuzzy sets rather than crisp numbers (Rommelfanger, 1994; Mons et al., 1995; Kutcha, 2001; Chanas and Zielinski, 2003; Chanas et al., 2002; Dubois et al., 2003; Slyeptsov and Tsyhchuk, 2003; Zielinski, 2005). They employed the concept of fuzziness (Kaufmann, 1975; Zimmermann, 2001) to these cases, and developed analysis approaches. Most of them are straightforward extensions of deterministic CPM mainly based on the formulas for the forward and the backward recursions, in which the deterministic activity times are replaced with the fuzzy activity times (Chen and Hsueh, 2008). These studies focus on the identification of the critical path and on the relatively degrees of criticality of activities and paths in project networks. In this section the traditional deadline makespan problem is formulated as a fuzzy decision model.

A fuzzy objective function is characterized by its membership functions and so are the constraints. A decision in a fuzzy environment is defined in analogy to non-fuzzy environments as the selection of activities which simultaneously satisfy (optimize) objective function(s) and constraints. In fuzzy set theory the intersection of sets normally corresponds to the logical 'and'. The decision in a fuzzy environment can therefore be viewed as the intersection of fuzzy constraints and fuzzy objective function(s). The relationship between constraints and objective functions in a fuzzy environment is therefore fully symmetric, i.e., there is no longer a difference between the former and the latter. Applied to linear programming the fuzzy decision can therefore be defined as the intersection of the fuzzy sets describing the constraints and the objective functions. If one defines the solution with the highest degree of membership to the fuzzy 'decision set' as the maximizing decision, then the following approach can be used (Zimmermann, 1984). Starting from the problem:

$$\begin{aligned} \text{Min} \quad & z = cx \\ \text{Subject to} \quad & Ax \le b \\ & x \ge 0 \end{aligned} \tag{2.17}$$

the adopted fuzzy version is

$$\begin{aligned} & cx \le z_0 \\ & Ax \approx b \\ & x \approx 0 \end{aligned} \tag{2.18}$$

where z_0 means an aspiration level of the decision-maker. We now define membership function α_i such that

$$\begin{cases} \propto_i\left(\left(Ax\right),cx\right)=1 & if \quad \left(Bx\right)_i \le b_i^{'} \\ 0 < \propto_i\left(\left(Ax\right),cx\right)<1 & if \quad b_i^{'} < \left(Bx\right)_i \le b_i^{'}+d_i \\ \propto_i\left(\left(Ax\right),cx\right)=0 & if \quad \left(Bx\right)_i > b_i^{'}+d_i \end{cases} \tag{2.19}$$

where i indicates de i_{th} row of B or b', B is the matrix A augmented by the rows of the objective function, b' the right-hand side augmented by the upper bounds for the values of the objective functions and d, the subjectively chosen constant of admissible violations. The membership function of the solution is then

$$\propto\left(Bx\right) = \min_i \propto_i\left(Bx\right) \ge 0 \tag{2.20}$$

and the maximizing decision

$$\max_{x\ge0} \min \propto_i\left(Bx\right) \tag{2.21}$$

Using the simplest kind of membership function, i.e., linear function of the type

$$\propto_i\left(Bx\right) = \begin{cases} 1 & if \quad \left(Bx\right)_i \le b_i^{'} \\ 1-\dfrac{\left(Bx\right)_i - b_i^{'}}{d_i} & if \quad b_i^{'} < \left(Bx\right)_i \le b_i^{'}+d_i \\ 0 & if \quad \left(Bx\right)_i > b_i^{'}+d_i \end{cases} \tag{2.22}$$

and substituting $b_i^{''} = {b_i^{'}}/{d_i}$ and $B_i^{'} = {B_i}/{d_i}$ componentwise, we arrive at the following problem:

$$\max_{x\ge0} \min\left(b_i^{''} - \left(B^{'}x\right)_i\right) \tag{2.23}$$

or

$$\max_{x\ge0} \propto_D\left(x\right) \tag{2.24}$$

where $\propto_D\left(x\right)$ is the membership function of the decision solution set. The problem (2.24) is equivalent to solving the following linear programming problem

$$\begin{array}{ll} \text{Max} & \lambda \\ \text{subject to} & \lambda \leq b_i^{"} - \left(B^{'}x\right)_i, i = 0\left(1\right)m \\ & x \geq 0 \end{array} \tag{2.25}$$

To explain the proposed approach, an application is presented as a numerical example which deals with the realization of the project shown in Figure 2.2. Table 2.3 shows the data of the project.

Table 2.3 Durations (weeks) and costs (€*10⁶) of the project

Arc (i,j)	Task	Normal cost	Crashing cost	Normal time	Crashing time	Slope
(1,2)	A	4.060	6.200	27	20	0.306
(1,5)	B	3.740	4.205	36	31	0.093
(2,4)	C	5.670	7.090	29	26	0.473
(2,3)	D	0.350	0.379	20	16	0.007
(5,6)	E	0.350	0.435	25	21	0.021
(4,7)	F	4.790	6.400	39	33	0.268
(7,8)	G	0.130	0.130	3	3	-
(7,9)	H	0.010	0.025	4.5	3.5	0.015
(5,9)	I	0.590	0.590	29	29	-

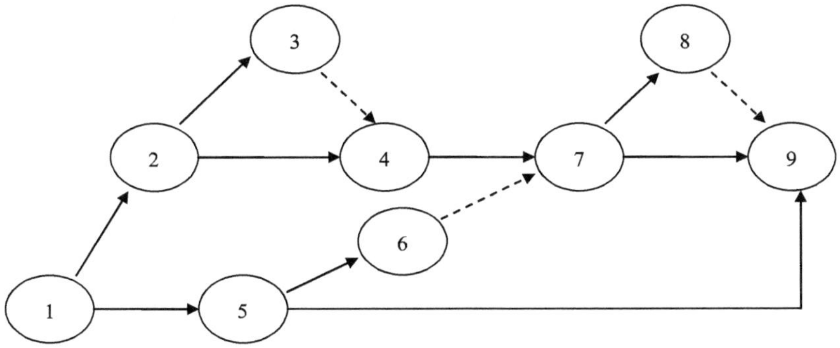

Figure 2.2 Network associated to the fuzzy linear programming problem

The linear programming formulation for the traditional deadline makespan problem which sets up the appropriate execution option for each activity so that the project is completed by a desired deadline T with the minimum cost C can be expressed as follows:

Min
$$C = 0.306X_A + 0.093X_B + 0.473X_C + 0.007X_D$$
$$+0.021X_E + 0.268X_F + 0.015X_H$$

subject to $t_1 = 0$;

$$t_2 \geq t_1 + 27 - X_A$$

$$t_2 \geq t_1 + 27 - X_A$$

$$t_4 \geq t_3 + 0 - X_{f_1}$$

$$t_4 \geq t_2 + 29 - X_C$$

$$t_5 \geq t_1 + 36 - X_B$$

$$t_6 \geq t_5 + 25 - X_E$$

$$t_7 \geq t_4 + 39 - X_F$$

$$t_7 \geq t_6 + 0 - X_{f_2}$$

$$t_8 \geq t_7 + 3 - X_G$$

$$t_9 \geq t_8 + 0 - X_{f_3}$$

$$t_9 \geq t_7 + 4.5 - X_H$$

$$t_9 \geq t_5 + 29 - X_I$$

$$x \geq 0;\ t_9 \leq T$$

$$X_A \leq 7; X_B \leq 5; X_C \leq 3; X_D \leq 4; X_E \leq 4; X_F \leq 6; X_H \leq 1;$$

where X_i is the number of time units to crash (reduce duration of) task i and t_i the time (in time units from the beginning of the project) task i is scheduled to start. Next, we shall apply the fuzzy approach and make the following assumption: the membership function $\propto_i(x)$ of the fuzzy sets characterizing the objective function rises linearly from 0 to 1 at the higher achievable values corresponding to the minimum time to carry out any task. This means that the level of satisfaction with respect to the improvement in the time to undertake, say task *A*, rises from 0 if is undertaken in 27 weeks or more (normal time), to 1 if it is undertaken in 20 weeks or less (crashing time). Thus, we have for task *A*

$$\propto_A(Bx) = \begin{cases} 1 & if \quad (Bx)_A \le 20 \\ 1 - \dfrac{(Bx)_A - 20}{7} & if \quad 20 < (Bx)_A \le 27 \\ 0 & if \quad (Bx)_A > 27 \end{cases}$$

and for the rest of the tasks:

$$\propto_B(Bx) = \begin{cases} 1 & if \quad (Bx)_B \le 31 \\ 1 - \dfrac{(Bx)_B - 31}{5} & if \quad 31 < (Bx)_A \le 36 \\ 0 & if \quad (Bx)_A > 36 \end{cases}$$

$$\propto_C(Bx) = \begin{cases} 1 & if \quad (Bx)_C \le 26 \\ 1 - \dfrac{(Bx)_C - 26}{3} & if \quad 26 < (Bx)_C \le 29 \\ 0 & if \quad (Bx)_C > 29 \end{cases}$$

$$\propto_D(Bx) = \begin{cases} 1 & if \quad (Bx)_D \le 16 \\ 1 - \dfrac{(Bx)_D - 16}{4} & if \quad 16 < (Bx)_D \le 20 \\ 0 & if \quad (Bx)_D > 20 \end{cases}$$

$$\propto_E(Bx) = \begin{cases} 1 & if \quad (Bx)_E \le 21 \\ 1 - \dfrac{(Bx)_E - 21}{4} & if \quad 21 < (Bx)_E \le 25 \\ 0 & if \quad (Bx)_E > 25 \end{cases}$$

$$\propto_F(Bx) = \begin{cases} 1 & if \quad (Bx)_F \le 33 \\ 1 - \dfrac{(Bx)_F - 33}{6} & if \quad 33 < (Bx)_F \le 39 \\ 0 & if \quad (Bx)_F > 39 \end{cases}$$

$$\propto_H(Bx) = \begin{cases} 1 & if \quad (Bx)_H \le 3.5 \\ 1 - (Bx)_H - 3.5 & if \quad 3.5 < (Bx)_H \le 4.5 \\ 0 & if \quad (Bx)_H > 4.5 \end{cases}$$

Including the unfuzzy constraints, we arrive at the following formulation

Max λ

Subject to

$\lambda \le \frac{20}{7} - \frac{0.306}{7} X_A \qquad t_4 \ge t_2 + 29 - X_C$

$\lambda \le \frac{31}{5} - \frac{0.093}{5} X_B \qquad t_5 \ge t_1 + 36 - X_B$

$\lambda \le \frac{26}{3} - \frac{0.473}{3} X_C \qquad t_6 \ge t_5 + 25 - X_E$

$\lambda \le \frac{16}{4} - \frac{0.007}{4} X_D \qquad t_7 \ge t_4 + 39 - X_F$

$\lambda \le \frac{21}{4} - \frac{0.021}{4} X_E \qquad t_7 \ge t_6 + 0 - X_{f_2}$

$\lambda \le \frac{33}{6} - \frac{0.268}{6} X_F \qquad t_8 \ge t_7 + 3 - X_G$

$\lambda \le 3.5 - 0.015 X_H \qquad t_9 \ge t_8 + 0 - X_{f_3}$

$t_1 = 0 \qquad t_9 \ge t_7 + 4.5 - X_H$

$t_2 \ge t_1 + 27 - X_A \qquad t_9 \ge t_5 + 29 - X_I$

$t_2 \geq t_1 + 27 - X_A \qquad x \geq 0;\ t_9 \leq T$

$t_4 \geq t_3 + 0 - X_{f_1} \qquad X_A \leq 7; X_B \leq 5; X_C \leq 3; X_D \leq 4; X_E \leq 4; X_F \leq 6; X_H \leq 1;$

The solution to the above problem corresponding to three different deadlines is shown in Table 2.4. For a deadline equal to 90 weeks, the maximum degree of 'overall satisfaction', $\lambda = 2.860$, is achieved for the solution $X_A = 0$, $X_B = 0$, $X_C = 3$, $X_D = 4$, $X_E = 4$, $X_F = 6$, and $X_H = 1$. This is the 'maximizing solution', which means that the maximum level of satisfaction with respect to the improvement in the time to undertake the project, is obtained by reducing tasks *C*, *D*, *E*, *F*, and *H* in 3, 4, 4, 6, and 1 week respectively. If the deadline to undertake the project is reduced to 88 or 86 weeks, the maximum degree of 'overall satisfaction' is $\lambda = 2.791$ and $\lambda = 2.704$ respectively. For these deadlines, in addition to the above reductions, to obtain the maximum level of satisfaction with respect to the improvement in the time to undertake the project, task *A* must be reduced in 1.50 and 3.50 weeks.

Table 2.4 Solution

Time	λ	X_A	X_B	X_C	X_D	X_E	X_F	X_H
90	2.860	0	0	3	4	4	6	1
88	2.791	1.50	0	3	4	4	6	1
86	2.704	3.50	0	3	4	4	6	1

Goal Programming

Although goal programming is itself a development of the 1950s, it has only been since the mid 1970s that goal programming received truly substantial attention. Much of the reason for such interest is due to goal programming's demonstrated ability to serve as an efficient and effective tool for the modelling, solution and analysis of mathematical models that involve conflicting goals and objectives.

In linear programming only one objective is permitted. Thus, even though multiple goals may confront the project manager, all progress toward these goals must be measured on a common scale, often profit or cost. Linear programming requires unidimensionality in the objective function, i.e., all goals must be expressed in common units and combined to give an overall single measure of effectiveness. This is the largest drawback of linear programming. Decision-makers need a methodology to attack problems in which a multitude of conflicting goals and subgoals exist. Goal programming can be used to help satisfying project managers. The requirements are that the project manager must be able to establish the goals and then to express the relationship between the decision variables and goals with linear functions. Once the project manager has provided an ordinal ranking of his/her goals, the goal programming model minimizes the deviation from the goals that have been set subject to the constraint set such that higher order goals are satisfied to the fullest extent before lower order goals are considered (Hannan, 1978).

In the area of Project Management, goal programming models have been used by quite a few authors. In particular, in the project crashing environment, Hannan (1978) incorporates considerations other than the project completion time and project cost into the typical critical path method. Factors such as share of the market, completion time of individual jobs, contractual agreements, and scarcity of resources such as men, materials, and machines are taken into consideration. Vrat and Kriengkrairut (1986) set four types of project goals: (i) to meet a new specified project completion period, (ii) to ensure that certain activities are not crashed for quality reasons, (iii) to maintain a specific budget target, and (iv) to minimize the total direct cost of crashing.

The general form of a goal programming problem may be expressed as:

$$\text{Minimize} \quad \sum_{i=1}^{m}\left(P_{oi}d_i^{+} + P_{ui}d_i^{-}\right) \tag{2.26}$$

$$\text{subject to} \quad \sum_{j=1}^{n}\left(a_{ij}x_j\right) + d_i^{-} - d_i^{+} = b_i \tag{2.27}$$

$$x_j, d_i^{-}, d_i^{+} \geq 0 \tag{2.28}$$

where d_i^{-} is the amount by which goal i is underachieved and d_i^{+} is the amount by which goal i is overachieved; P_{oi} is the priority associated with d_i^{+}; P_{ui} is the priority associated with d_i^{-}; $x_j\left(j = 1, 2, \ldots, n\right)$ are the variables in the goal equations; $b_i\left(i = 1, 2, \ldots, m\right)$ are the targets or goals; and a_{ij} are the coefficients of the variables.

Next, the above goal programming problem is applied to the project shown in Figure 2.3. Table 2.5 shows the normal time, crashing time, normal cost, crashing cost, and the slope.

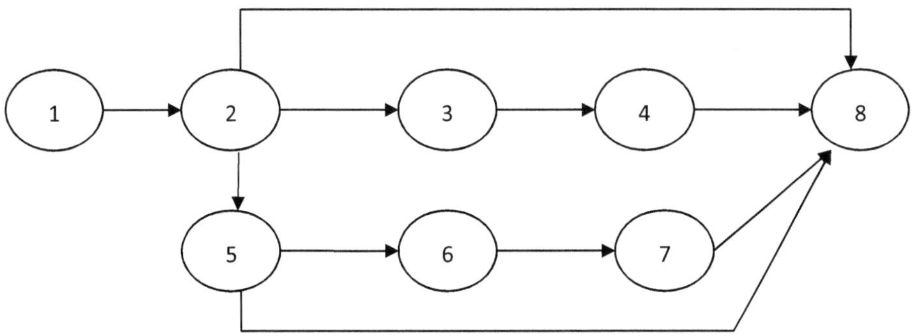

Figure 2.3 Network associated to the goal programming problem

Table 2.5 Normal time, crash time, normal cost, crash cost and cost of crashing per day

Task	Arc (i,j)	$t_{i,j}$		Normal cost (€)	Cost of crashing (€)
		Normal time	Crash time		
A	(1,2)	0.50	0.50	3,200	–
B	(2,8)	3.20	2.30	56,726	7,000
C	(2,3)	0.25	0.25	2,104	–
D	(3,4)	0.20	0.20	1,803	–
E	(4,8)	0.30	0.30	2,705	–
F	(2,5)	0.50	0.25	2,404	500
G	(5,6)	0.75	0.50	5,409	2,500
H	(6,7)	8.50	6.25	42,404	7,700
I	(7,8)	5.25	3.75	28,269	5,500
J	(5,8)	0.15	0.15	2,104	–

Solving the network through the critical path method algorithm (Kelley and Walker, 1999; Kelley, 1961), the normal time to undertake the project is 15.5 days, being the activities *A*, *F*, *G*, *H*, and *I* critical activities. The normal cost undertaking the project in 15.5 days is €147,128.

Five activities (*B*, *F*, *G*, *H*, *I*) can be reduced which will permit reducing the time to complete the project. However, this reduction in time implies an increase in cost. As can be shown in Table 2.5 (last column), e.g., activity *B* may be reduced form 3.20 days to 2.30 days at a cost of $7,000 per unit time. The project manager must set up his/her goals in function of its interests in order to achieve a balance between time and cost.

Suppose that the project manager sets the following goals: (i) to reduce the time to undertake the project to no more than 12 days (goal 1); (ii) as this reduction in time will imply an increase in cost the project manager wants to limit the crashing costs to €100,000 (goal 2). To achieve these goals the project manager must manage the project in such a way that the goals may be achieved. The formulation for this particular goal programming problem can be expressed as follows:

Minimize $P_{o1}d_1^+ + P_{o2}d_2^+$ (2.29)

subject to

Goal 1 $t_8 + d_1^- - d_1^+ = 12$ (2.30)

Goal 2
$$\begin{aligned}&7,000(3.2 - t_{2,8}) + 500(0.5 - t_{2,5}) + 2,500(0.75 - t_{5,6}) + 7,700(8.5 - t_{6,7})\\&+5,500(5.25 - t_{7,8}) + d_2^- - d_2^+ = 100,000\end{aligned} \tag{2.31}$$

$$t_i, d_i^-, d_i^+ \geq 0 \tag{2.32}$$

Also

Crash Time $\leq t_{i,j} \leq$ Normal Time	$t_j - t_i \geq t_{i,j}$
$0.50 \leq t_{1,2} \leq 0.50$	$t_2 - t_1 \geq t_{1,2}$
$2.30 \leq t_{2,8} \leq 3.20$	$t_3 - t_2 \geq t_{2,3}$
$0.25 \leq t_{2,3} \leq 0.25$	$t_4 - t_3 \geq t_{3,4}$
$0.20 \leq t_{3,4} \leq 0.20$	$t_8 - t_4 \geq t_{4,8}$
$0.30 \leq t_{4,8} \leq 0.30$ (2.33)	$t_8 - t_2 \geq t_{2,8}$ (2.34)
$0.25 \leq t_{2,5} \leq 0.50$	$t_5 - t_2 \geq t_{2,5}$
$0.50 \leq t_{5,6} \leq 0.75$	$t_6 - t_5 \geq t_{5,6}$
$6.25 \leq t_{6,7} \leq 8.5$	$t_7 - t_6 \geq t_{6,7}$

$$3.75 \le t_{7,8} \le 5.25 \qquad t_8 - t_7 \ge t_{7,8}$$

$$0.15 \le t_{5,8} \le 0.15 \qquad t_8 - t_5 \ge t_{5,8}$$

where d_1^+ and d_2^+ are the amounts by which goals 1 and 2, are overachieved and P_{01} and P_{02} are the priorities associated with these goals respectively. The t_i and t_j are the times corresponding to nodes i and j, and t_{ij} is the time to complete the activity (i,j). Equations (2.30) and (2.31) show how the goals have been converted into equations through the addition of deviation variables (d_i^- and d_i^+). The amount by which each one of the goals is overachieved (d_i^+) is the variable to be minimized in this particular case. Equation (2.32) is the non-negativity constraint. The set of Equations in (2.33) indicates that the time to complete the activity (i,j) is between the normal time and the crash time and Equations in (2.34) are introduced to comply with the temporal sequence between the arcs. This problem was solved using Lingo (Lindo systems, 2002), and the solution is given in Table 2.6.

Table 2.6 Deviation variables

$d_1^+ = 0$	$d_1^- = 0.75$
$d_2^+ = 0$	$d_2^- = 73,675$

As can be appreciated in Table 2.6, goals 1 and 2 are achieved. The project is carried out in 11.25 (12 - 0.75) days and the total costs do not exceed €100,000.

An Integer Programming Problem

Integer programming models are these optimization models in which some or all of the variables must be integer. The main difference between linear programming and integer programming models is that linear programming models allow fractional values for the decision variables, whereas integer programming models allow only integer values for integer-constrained decision variables. Many complex problems can be modelled using 0–1 variables and other variables that are forced to assume integer values. A 0–1 variable (often called a binary variable) is a decision variable that must be equal to 0 or 1, i.e., an activity that either is or is not undertaken. If the variable is 1, the activity is undertaken; if it is equal 0, the activity is not undertaken. In this section, an integer programming model which enables us to minimize the time to undertake a project meeting quality output standards and the corresponding costs is developed.

To form the model for this problem let T_i^j the duration of activity i $\{i = 1, 2, \ldots, l\}$ in the critical path, and C_i^j the cost of activity i using resource allocation n, with $j = 1, 2, \ldots, n$. To estimate the overall quality performance at the project level the quality function suggested by El-Rayes and Kandil (2005) has been selected, which enables the aggregation of the estimated quality for all considered activities to provide an overall quality at the project level using simple weighted approach.

$$\sum_{i=1}^{l} Wt_i \sum_{k=1}^{k} Wt_{i,k} * Q_{i,k}^n \tag{2.35}$$

where $Q_{i,k}^n$ is the performance of quality indicator k in activity i using resource utilization n; $Wt_{i,k}$ is the weight of quality indicator k compared to other indicators in activity i indicating the relative importance of this indicator to others being used to measure the quality of the activity; and Wt_i is the weight of activity i compared to other activities in the project representing the importance and contribution of the quality of this activity to the overall quality of the project.

Therefore, we may rewrite the final model as:

$$\text{Minimize} \quad \sum_{i=1}^{l} \sum_{j=1}^{n} T_i^j x_i^j \tag{2.36}$$

$$\text{subject to} \quad \sum_{i=1}^{l} \sum_{j=1}^{n} C_i^j x_i^j \leq C \tag{2.37}$$

$$\sum_{i=1}^{l} Wt_i \sum_{k=1}^{k} \sum_{j=1}^{n} Wt_{i,k} Q_{i,k}^n x_i^j \geq Q \tag{2.38}$$

$$x_i^j = \begin{cases} 1 & \text{if activity } i \text{ is undertaken} \\ 0 & \text{otherwise} \end{cases} \tag{2.39}$$

$$\sum_{j=1}^{n} x_i^j = 1 \tag{2.40}$$

where x_i^j is the 0–1 variable and *C* and *Q* are the Cost and Quality target values respectively. Equation (2.39) implies that decision variables are integer and Equation (2.40) implies that each activity is undertaken once. The rest of the variables as above.

Two additional versions of the model can be proposed (San Cristóbal, 2009). The first one enables the project manager to minimize cost meeting quality and time objectives, while the second one enables to maximize quality meeting time and costs objectives respectively.

A) TO MINIMIZE COST MEETING QUALITY AND TIME

$$\text{Minimize} \quad \sum_{i=1}^{l}\sum_{j=1}^{n} C_i^j x_i^j \tag{2.41}$$

$$\text{subject to} \quad \sum_{i=1}^{l}\sum_{j=1}^{n} T_i^j x_i^j \leq T \tag{2.42}$$

$$\sum_{i=1}^{l} Wt_i \sum_{k=1}^{k} Wt_{i,k} Q_{i,k}^n x_i^j \geq Q \tag{2.43}$$

$$x_i^j = \begin{cases} 1 \text{ if activity } i \text{ is undertaken} \\ 0 \text{ otherwise} \end{cases} \tag{2.44}$$

$$\sum_{j=1}^{n} x_i^j = 1 \tag{2.45}$$

where *T* and *Q* are the Time and Quality target values respectively and the rest of variables as above.

B) TO MAXIMIZE QUALITY MEETING COST AND TIME OBJECTIVES

$$\text{Minimize} \quad \sum_{i=1}^{l} Wt_i \sum_{k=1}^{k} Wt_{i,k} Q_{i,k}^n x_i^j \tag{2.46}$$

$$\text{subject to} \quad \sum_{i=1}^{l}\sum_{j=1}^{n} T_i^j x_i^j \leq T \tag{2.47}$$

$$\sum_{i=1}^{l}\sum_{j=1}^{n} C_i^j x_i^j \leq C \tag{2.48}$$

$$x_i^j = \begin{cases} 1 \text{ if activity } i \text{ is undertaken} \\ 0 \text{ otherwise} \end{cases} \tag{2.49}$$

$$\sum_{j=1}^{n} x_i^j = 1 \tag{2.50}$$

where T and C are the Time and Cost target values respectively and the rest of variables as above.

Next the integer programming problem is applied to the project shown in Table 2.7. Solving the network through the critical path method algorithm, the time to undertake the project is 22 weeks, being the activities *A*, *D*, and *G* critical activities.

Table 2.7 Tasks to undertake, predecessors, normal and crash duration

Tasks	Predecessors	Normal time (weeks)	Crash time (weeks)
A	–	9	6
B	–	8	4
C	–	5	1
D	A	8	2
E	B	7	4
F	C	5	3
G	D	5	4

Now suppose that the project manager, in the execution of the project, wants to meet the following objectives: to minimize time so that total costs do not exceed €8,000. In addition, two quality output objectives are established: that the overall quality achieved in the overall project exceeds an output, *Q*, of 98, and the quality achieved by the tasks *D* and *E* must be equal to or to exceed a quality output, *Q*, of 99. The formulation for this particular problem can be expressed as follows:

Minimize $\sum_{i=A,B,C,D,E,F,G} \sum_{j=1,2} T_i^j x_i^j$

subject to $\sum_{i=1}^{l} \sum_{j=1}^{n} C_i^j x_i^j \leq 8,000$

$$\sum_{i=1}^{l} Wt_i \sum_{k=1}^{k}\sum_{j=1}^{n} Wt_{i,k} Q_{i,k}^{n} x_i^j \geq 98$$

$$\sum_{i=D} Wt_i \sum_{k=1}^{k}\sum_{j=1}^{n} Wt_{i,k} Q_{i,k}^{n} x_i^j \geq 99$$

$$\sum_{i=E} Wt_i \sum_{k=1}^{k}\sum_{j=1}^{n} Wt_{i,k} Q_{i,k}^{n} x_i^j \geq 99$$

$$x_i^j = \begin{cases} 1 \text{ if activity } i \text{ is undertaken} \\ 0 \text{ otherwise} \end{cases}$$

$$\sum_{i=1}^{l} \sum_{j=1}^{n} x_i^j = 1$$

Table 2.8 shows the time and cost with two resources utilizations ($n = 1$ and $n = 2$) and the quality indicators (on a 0–100 scale) and the weights considered.

Table 2.8 Time, cost, quality indicators and weights considered

Task	Time (Weeks)		Cost (€)		Wt_i	$Wt_{i,k}$	$Q^n_{i,k}$		$Wt_{i,k}$	$Q^n_{i,k}$	
	n = 1	n = 2	n = 1	n = 2		k = 1	n = 1	n = 2	k = 2	n = 1	n = 2
A*	9	6	1,000	1,600	0.10	0.8	100	98	0,2	98	96
B	8	4	900	1,800	0.10	0.7	100	96	0,3	98	97
C	5	1	700	800	0.15	0.6	100	98	0,4	98	96
D*	8	2	900	1,900	0.10	0.7	100	98	0,3	98	96
E	7	4	700	1,500	0.15	0.5	100	98	0,5	98	96
F	5	3	500	500	0.20	0.7	100	98	0,3	98	96
G*	5	4	800	2,300	0.20	0.8	100	98	0,2	98	96

* Critical activity.

This problem was solved using Solver de Microsoft (Microsoft, 2007), and the optimal solution is given in Table 2.9. The minimum time to undertake the project is 18 weeks with a total cost of €7,600, an amount lower than the objective of €8,000. As regard as quality, the two objectives established are achieved. The quality for the overall project is 98.77 (upper than 98) and the corresponding to the activities *D* and *E*, 99.4 and 99 respectively.

Table 2.9 Optimal solution

Time (*T*) (Weeks)	18
Cost (*C*) (€)	7,600
Quality (*Q*) (Overall Project)	98,77
Quality (*Q*) (Activity *D*)	99,4
Quality (*Q*) (Activity *E*)	99

Table 2.10 shows the activities that must be undertaken with resources utilization n = 1 and n = 2. Activities *B, C, D, E,* and *F,* are undertaken with resources utilization n = 1, while activities *A,* and *G* are undertaken with resources utilization n = 2.

Table 2.10 Activities to undertake with resources $n = 1$ and $n = 2$

Activity	A	B	C	D	E	F	G
n =1	0	1	1	1	1	1	0
n =2	1	0	0	0	0	0	1

Chapter 3

Multi-Criteria Decision-Making Models

Project managers are faced with decision environments where there are a number of conflicting criteria such as project cost, time, safety, quality levels, etc. Multi-criteria decision-making (MCDM) or Multi-criteria decision aid (MCDA) methods belong to a class of Operations Research models which deal with the process of making decision in the presence of multiple objectives. These methods, which can handle both quantitative and qualitative criteria, share the common characteristics of conflict among criteria, incommensurable units, and difficulties in design/selection of alternatives (Pohekar and Ramachandran, 2004). The aim of this chapter is to describe four different multi-criteria decision aid methods, namely, Multi-attribute utility theory, the VIKOR and TOPSIS methods, and the Fuzzy PROMETHEE method, that will be used to determine the critical path of a network.

Multi-Attribute Utility Theory

Multi-attribute utility theory is an extension of utility theory developed to help decision-makers assign utility values, taking into consideration the decision-maker's preferences, to outcomes by evaluating these in terms of multiple attributes and combining these individual assignments to obtain overall utility measures (Keeney and Raiffa, 1976). Multi-attribute utility theory generally combines the main advantages of simple scoring techniques and optimization models. Further, in situations in which satisfaction is uncertain, utility functions have the property that expected utility can be used as a guide to rational decision-making.

Utility theory has generally been used to develop a relationship between utility and costs incurred as a consequence of a particular decision. There are situations where, rational decision-makers who subscribe the Von Neuman-Morgenstern axioms, are sometimes willing to violate the Expected Monetary

Value minimization criterion (when dealing with benefits to maximize the Expected Monetary Value) and to sacrifice it to reduce risk, choosing the alternative that maximizes his or her expected utility.

A utility function is a device which quantifies the preferences of a decision-maker by assigning a numerical index to varying levels of satisfaction of a particular criterion. For a single criterion, the utility of satisfaction of a consequence x' is denoted by $u(x')$. Utility functions are constructed such that $u(x')$ is less preferred to $u(x'')$, i.e. $u(x') < u(x'')$ if and only if x' is less preferred to x'', i.e. $x' < x''$. In other words, a utility function is a transformation of some level of project performance, x', measured in its natural units into an equivalent level of decision-maker's satisfaction.

When choosing one from several alternatives, typically each alternative is assessed for desirability on a number of scored criteria. What connects the criteria scores with desirability is the utility function. The most common formulation of a utility function is the additive model:

$$U_i = w_j u_{ij} \text{ for all } i \tag{3.1}$$

where U_i is the overall utility value of alternative i; u_{ij} is the utility value of the j_{th} criterion for the i_{th} alternative; and u_{ij} equals $u(X_i)$, for $1 \geq i \geq n$ and $1 \geq j \geq m$. X_i designates a specific value of x_{ij}; n is the total number of criteria, m is the total number of alternatives, and w_j is the relative weight of the j_{th} criterion.

Utility functions contain information about the decision-maker's attitude toward risk being reflected in the shape of the utility curve, which combines the decision-maker's preference attitudes, i.e. increasing or decreasing utility with increasing x'. Depending on the decision-maker's attitudes toward risk, utility functions can be concave, convex or linear as shown in Figure 3.1. Concave utility functions describe risk-averse situations whereas convex utility functions describe risk-seeking situations. A linear utility functions describes a risk-neutral situation.

Next, the critical path of a network shown in Figure 3.2 will be determined by using multi-attribute utility theory. Four criteria will be considered, time in days, cost in €*10^6, and quality and safety on a 1–10 scale. The data corresponding to the project are shown in Table 3.1, and the duration of each path with its time, cost, quality and safety are shown in Table 3.2.

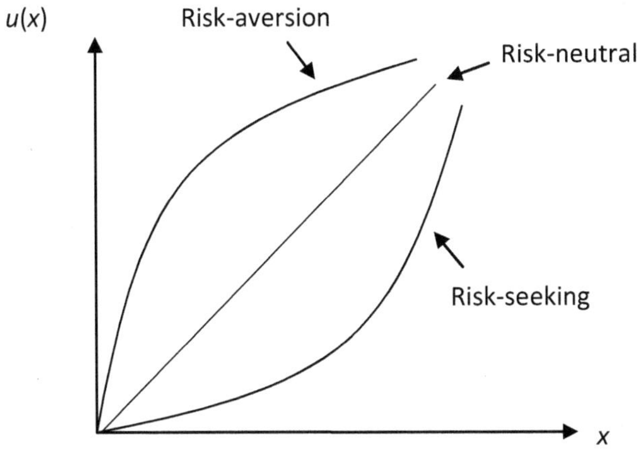

Figure 3.1 Utility curves

Table 3.1 Data of the project

Task	Arc (i,j)	Time (days)	Cost (€*10⁶)	Quality	Safety
A	(1,2)	32	17,750	5	4
B	(2,3)	20	12,667	3	6
C	(3,14)	29	14,400	2	7
D	(3,4)	21	14,117	7	2
E	(3,5)	10	7,300	8	9
F	(5,6)	4	3,000	4	2
G	(6,14)	20	16,300	3	4
H	(2,7)	19	11,550	10	8
I	(7,14)	39	24,413	8	2
J	(2,14)	45	34,883	4	7
K	(1,8)	21	17,250	6	7
L	(8,9)	17	14,375	7	1
M	(9,10)	18	15,125	9	8
N	(10,11)	19	15,125	2	9
O	(11,14)	17	15,000	6	4
P	(1,12)	32	34,142	10	10
Q	(12,13)	18	17,850	4	8
R	(13,14)	20	19,550	9	3

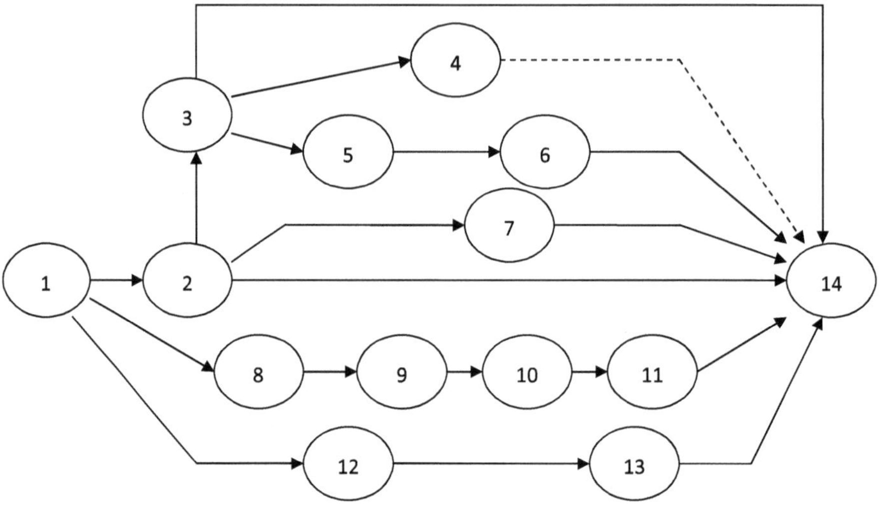

Figure 3.2 Network associated to a multi-attribute utility problem

Table 3.2 Paths in the network

Alternative	Path	Time	Cost	Quality	Safety
A_1	(A,B,C)	92.8	44,817	17	10
A_2	(A,B,D)	86.5	44,533	12	15
A_3	(A,B,E,F,G)	105.2	57,017	25	23
A_4	(A,H,I)	104.0	53,713	14	23
A_5	(A,J)	85.3	52,633	11	9
A_6	(K,L,M,N,O)	102.5	76,875	29	30
A_7	(P,Q,R)	84.2	71,542	21	23

Firstly, in order to assign the weights for each criterion with respect to the goal, the Analytical Hierarchy Process (AHP) developed by Saaty (2000) will be used in accordance with the following steps:

Step 1. A judgemental matrix (pairwise comparison matrix), *A*, is formed and used to compare pairwise criteria with respect to the goal on an integer-value 1–9 scale. The judgements are entered using the fundamental scale of the AHP. An attribute compared with itself is always assigned the value 1 so the main diagonal entries of the pairwise comparison matrix are all 1. The numbers 3, 5, 7, and 9 correspond to the verbal judgements 'moderate importance', 'strong importance', 'very strong importance', and 'absolute importance' (with 2, 4, 6, and 8 for compromise between the previous values). In the matrix, a_{ij}, denotes the comparative importance of attribute i with respect to attribute j. $a_{ij} = 1$ when $i = j$ and $a_{ji} = 1/a_{ij}$. The following pairwise comparison matrix indicates how much more important criterion i is than criterion j:

$$A = \begin{bmatrix} 1 & 2 & 4 & 3 \\ 1/2 & 1 & 2 & 3 \\ 1/4 & 1/2 & 1 & 2 \\ 1/3 & 1/3 & 1/2 & 1 \end{bmatrix}$$

Thus, $a_{14} = 3$ indicates that, when determining the critical path in the network, time is moderately more important than safety.

Step 2. We need to know the vector $W = [w_1, w_2, \ldots, w_n]$ which indicates the weight that each criterion is given in pairwise comparison matrix *A*. To recover the vector *W* from *A* we outline a method in a two-step procedure:

- For each of the *A's* column divide each entry in column *i* of *A* by the sum of the entries in column *i*. This yields a new matrix, called *Anorm* (for normalized) in which the sum of the entries in each column is 1.
- Estimate w_i as the average of the entries in row *i* of *Anorm*.

Step 3. Once we have the pairwise comparisons matrices it is necessary to check it for consistency. Slight inconsistencies are common and do not cause serious difficulties. We can use the following four-step procedure to check for the consistency in the decision-maker's comparisons. From now on, *W* denotes our estimate of the decision-maker's weight.

- Compute $A\,W^T$, where *W* denotes our estimate of the decision-maker's weight.
- Find out the maximum Eigen value ($\lambda_{\max}$):

$$\lambda = \frac{1}{n} \sum_{i=1}^{n} \frac{i_{th} \text{ entry in } A\,W^T}{i_{th} \text{ entry in } A\,W^T} \tag{3.2}$$

- Compute the Consistency Index (*CI*) as follows:

$$CI = \frac{(\lambda_{\max}) - n}{n-1} \tag{3.3}$$

- The smaller the *CI*, the smaller the deviation from the consistency is. If *CI* is sufficiently small, the decision-maker's comparisons are probably consistent enough to give useful estimates of the weights for their objective. For a perfectly consistent decision-maker, the i_{th} entry in $A\,W^T = n$. This implies that a perfectly consistent decision-maker has *CI* = 0.
- Compare the Consistency Index to the Random Index (*RI*) for the appropriate value of *n*, shown in Table 3.3. If $CI/RI < 0.10$, the degree of consistency is satisfactory, but if $CI/RI > 0.10$, serious inconsistencies may exist, and the AHP may not yield meaningful results.

Table 3.3 Random Index (*RI*) for different values of *n*

n	2	3	4	5	6	7	8	9	10	11	12
RI	0	0.58	0.90	1.12	1.24	1.32	1.41	1.45	1.49	1.51	1.48

Following the procedure, the weight vector obtained is $W = [0.47; 0.28; 0.15; 0.11]$, the Consistency Index is 0.03 and $CI/RI = 0.04 < 0.10$. Thus, the pairwise comparison matrix does not exhibit any serious inconsistencies.

Next, utility functions showing the decision-maker's preferences are constructed by the method suggested by Bell et al. (1978), and Keeney and Raiffa (1993). The first step involves the identification of the best and the worst outcomes for each one of the criteria. The decision-maker is free to set these utility values at any level provided that the best outcome has the higher value. The usual method is to assign the worst outcome a utility value of zero and the best outcome a utility value of unity. This establishes the range of utility values from 0 to 1 between the worst and the best possible outcomes. Let us consider the criterion time. The worst outcome (Path 3 with 105.2 days) is assigned a utility value of zero and the best outcome (Path 7 with 84.2 days) a utility value of unity. The utility of the intermediate values is then determined by offering the decision-maker a choice between two lotteries. For example, to determine the utility value of the Path 5 (92.8 days), the decision-maker is offered the options shown in Figure 3.3.

1. Certain option: go to route R_1 for a certain consequence of 92.8 days (Path 5) with a probability $p = 1$;

2. Risk option: go to route R_2 for either a best consequence of 84.2 days (Path 7) with a probability of p or a worst consequence of 105.2 days (Path 3) with a probability of 1-p.

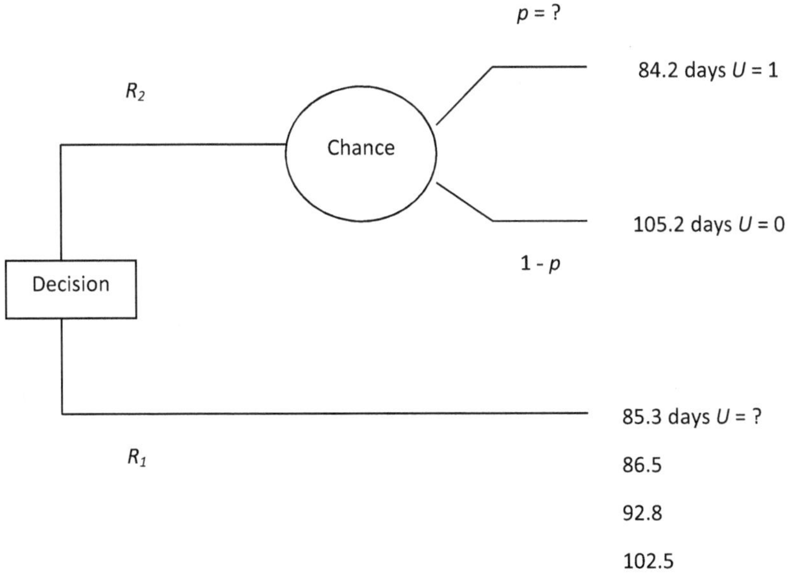

Figure 3.3 Routes to assign utility values

What utility value should the project manager assign to a certain outcome of 92.8 days? For the project manager to make good decision and choose from the two routes, the utility value of 92.8 days must be assessed and compared with the expected utility of the risk option. To do this, the project manager determines a relative preference for a 92.8 days consequence by finding the probability, p, for the best outcome, to which the project manager is indifferent, between the certain route, R_1, for a 92.8 days outcome and the gamble route, R_2, for the two possible outcomes of 105.2 and 84.2 days. Let us assume that there is a probability of 0.3 for getting the best outcome and a probability of 0.7 of getting the worst outcome from the route R_2. Which route would the project manager prefer in this case? Since $p = 0.3$ the chance of getting the best outcome from route R_2 is very small, so in this case a risk-aversion project manager will not gamble. He prefers to choose route R_1 with a 92.8 days certain outcome. However, a risk-seeking project manager will gamble even though the chance of getting the best outcome from route R_2, to complete the project in 84.2 days, is very small.

Now, let us assume that there is a probability of 0.9 for getting the best outcome and a probability of 0.1 for getting the worst outcome from route R_2. Since $p = 0.9$, in this case there is a high chance of getting the best outcome of 84.2 days, so a risk-aversion project manager will gamble and choose route R_2.

Now, let us take a probability of 0.45 of getting the best outcome and a probability of 0.55 of getting the worst outcome from route R_2. Which route does the project manager now prefer? Putting $p = 0.45$ makes the thing difficult to choose for the project manager but a risk-neutral project manager will go for the certain outcome route R_1. Doing some more of these trials and errors, the project manager considers that a probability of 0.5 will make him indifferent between the two routes R_1 and R_2. According to utility theory, by choosing the probability that makes him indifferent between the two routes, the project manager has assigned a utility value for the certain outcome of 92.8 days. It is known from the principles of probabilities that the expected value of any random variable in the space will equal the sum of probability of each variable times its score. In this case, the expected utility for the route R_2 which includes two variables or two outcomes (the best outcome with $u = 1$ and the worst outcome with $u = 0$) will be:

$$
\begin{aligned}
&p\left(\text{utility of best outcome}\right) + \left(1 - p\right)\left(\text{utility of worst outcome}\right) \\
&= 0.5 * U\left(105.2\right) + \left(1 - 0.5\right) * U\left(84.2\right) = 0.5 * 1 + 0.5 * 0 = 0.5
\end{aligned}
$$

Since the project manager is indifferent between 85.3 days for certain and this gamble, the alternatives must have the same utility value, i.e. $U\left(85.3\right) = 0.5$. The same procedure is used for the rest of criteria. Since there are two kinds of criteria; the maximization criteria (the maximum value is desirable for quality and safety) and the minimization criteria (the minimum value is desirable for time and cost) the intermediate utility values are obtained by normalizing the evaluation matrix as follows:

1. For maximization criteria

$$u_j = \frac{A_j - A_{min}}{A_{max} - A_{min}} \tag{3.4}$$

2. For minimization criteria

$$u_j = \frac{A_{max} - A_j}{A_{max} - A_{min}} \tag{3.5}$$

where A_j represents the score assigned to the j_{th} alternative in the evaluation matrix. A_{max} and A_{min} are the maximum and minimum scores assigned for the selected criteria for the identified alternative.

Three different types of utility curves have been used, each one describing different project manager's attitude toward risk. Table 3.4 shows the normalized evaluation matrix and utility for all the criteria in the network using linear utility functions (risk-neutral), and Tables 3.5 and 3.6 show utility values using concave (exhibiting risk-averse behaviour) and convex utility functions (exhibiting risk-seeking behaviour) respectively. The final utility value is found by adding the utilities of the paths on different criteria as follows:

$$\text{Utility} = \sum_{i=1}^{7} w_j u_{ij} \tag{3.6}$$

Table 3.4 Utility values (risk-neutral)

Criteria	Paths						
	A_1	A_2	A_3	A_4	A_5	A_6	A_7
Time	0.587	0.889	0	0.056	0.944	0.127	1
Cost	0.991	1	0.614	0.716	0.750	0	0.165
Quality	0.333	0.056	0.778	0.167	0	1	0.556
Safety	0.048	0.286	0.667	0.667	0	1	0.667

Table 3.5 Utility values (risk-aversion) ($U_i = -1.42x^2 + 2.1x + 0.249$)

Criteria	Paths						
	A_1	A_2	A_3	A_4	A_5	A_6	A_7
Time	0.993	0.994	0.249	0.361	0.966	0.493	0.929
Cost	0.935	0.929	1	1	1	0.249	0.557
Quality	0.791	0.361	1	0.560	0.249	0.929	0.977
Safety	0.346	0.733	1	1	0.249	0.929	1

Table 3.6 Utility values (risk-seeking) ($U_i = 1.20x^2 - 0.42x + 0.05$)

Criteria	Paths						
	A_1	A_2	A_3	A_4	A_5	A_6	A_7
Time	0.215	0.622	0.050	0.030	0.721	0.015	0.827
Cost	0.810	0.827	0.242	0.362	0.407	0.050	0.012
Quality	0.042	0.030	0.447	0.012	0.050	0.827	0.185
Safety	0.032	0.026	0.301	0.301	0.050	0.827	0.301

Table 3.7 shows the final utility values and Table 3.8 a ranked list of the paths for the three situations considered. Paths 1 and 2 are found to be the best outcomes under the three situations. The utility of Path 2 is found to be the highest for a risk-neutral and risk-seeking project manager whereas Path 1 has the highest utility value for a risk-aversion project manager who will need a high probability of getting the best outcome to choose the risky option, other way he will not gamble. On the other hand, a risk-seeking project manager will run the risk of choosing Path 2.

Table 3.7 Final utility values

	Paths						
	A_1	A_2	A_3	A_4	A_5	A_6	A_7
Risk-neutral	0.60	0.73	0.36	0.32	0.65	0.32	0.67
Risk-aversion	0.88	0.85	0.65	0.64	0.80	0.54	0.84
Risk-seeking	0.33	0.53	0.19	0.15	0.46	0.23	0.45

Table 3.8 Ranking list

	Paths						
Risk-neutral	A_2	A_7	A_5	A_1	A_3	A_4	A_6
Risk-aversion	A_1	A_2	A_7	A_5	A_3	A_4	A_6
Risk-seeking	A_2	A_5	A_7	A_1	A_6	A_3	A_4

The VIKOR Method

The VIKOR method is a multi-criteria decision analysis developed to solve decision problems with conflicting and non-commensurable (different units) criteria. The method was originally developed by Duckstein and Opricovic (1980) and the idea of compromise solution was introduced by Yu (1973) and Zeleny (1982).

Assuming that each alternative is evaluated according to each criterion function, the compromise ranking could be performed by comparing the measure of 'closeness' to the 'ideal' solution, F^*. The compromise solution, Fc, is a feasible solution that is the 'closest' to the ideal solution and a compromise means an agreement established by mutual concessions (Opricovic and Tzeng, 2004). The multi-criteria measure for compromise ranking is developed from the Lp-metric used as an aggregating function in a compromise programming method (Yu, 1973; Zeleny, 1982):

$$L_{p,j} = \left\{ \sum_{i=1}^{n} \left[w_i \left(f_i^* - f_{ij} \right) / \left(f_i^* - f_i^- \right) \right]^p \right\}^{1/p}$$

$$1 \leq p \leq \infty \,;\; j = 1,\; 2, \ldots, J \tag{3.7}$$

where $L_{1,j}$ (as S_j in Equation 3.8) and $L_{\infty,j}$ (as R_j in Equation 3.9) are used to formulate ranking measure. The compromise ranking algorithm VIKOR has the following four steps (Opricovic and Tzeng 2004):

Step I Determine the best f_i^* and the worst f_i^- values of all criterion functions from each alternative. If the i_{th} function represents a benefit then $f_i^* = \max_j f_{ij}$ and $f_i^- = \min_j f_{ij}$, while if the i_{th} function represents a cost $f_i^{*} = \min_j f_{ij}$ and $f_i^- = \max_j f_{ij}$.

Step II Compute the values S_j and R_j, $j = 1,\; 2, \ldots, J$ by the relations

$$S_j = \sum_{i=1}^{n} w_i \left(f_i^* - f_{ij}\right) / \left(f_i^* - f_i^-\right) \tag{3.8}$$

$$R_j = \max_i \left[w_i \left(f_i^* - f_{ij}\right) / \left(f_i^* - f_{ij}\right) \right] \tag{3.9}$$

where f_{ij}, is the value of the j alternative for the i criteria, S_j represents the maximum group of utility of the majority (concordance) of alternative j, R_j represents a minimum of individual regret of the opponent (discordance) of alternative j, and w_i are the weights of criteria, expressing the decision-maker's preference as the relative importance of the criteria.

Step III Compute the values Q_j, by the relation

$$Q_j = v\left(S_j - S^*\right) / \left(S^- - S^*\right) + (1 - v)\left(R_j - R^*\right) / \left(R^- - R^*\right) \tag{3.10}$$

where Q_j represents the solution of alternative j, $S^* = \min_j S_j$; $S^- = \max_j S_j$; $R^* = \min_j R_j$; $R^- = \max_j R_j$ and v is introduced as a weight for the strategy of maximum group utility, whereas $(1 - v)$ is the weight of the individual regret. The solution obtained by $min_j S_j$ is with a maximum group utility ('majority' rule), and the solution obtained by $min_j R_j$ is with a minimum individual regret of the 'opponent'. Normally, the value of v is taken as 0.5. However, v can take any value from 0 to 1.

Step IV Rank the alternatives, sorting by the values S, R, and Q. The results are three ranking lists. Propose as a compromise solution the alternative $A^{(1)}$, which is the best ranked by the measure Q (minimum), if the following two conditions are satisfied:

a. Acceptable advantage. $Q\left(A^{(2)}\right) - Q\left(A^{(1)}\right) \geq DQ$, where $DQ = 1/(J - 1)$ and $A^{(2)}$ is the alternative with second position on the ranking list by Q;
b. Acceptable stability in decision-making. The alternative $A^{(1)}$ must also be the best ranked by S or/and R. This compromise solution is stable within a decision- making process, which could be the strategy of maximum group utility (when $v > 0.5$ is needed), or 'by consensus' ($v \approx 0.5$), or with veto ($v < 0.5$).

If one of the conditions is not satisfied, then a set of compromise solutions is proposed, which consists of:

- Alternative $A^{(1)}$ and $A^{(2)}$ if only condition b is not satisfied, or
- Alternatives $A^{(1)}, A^{(2)}, \ldots, A^{(M)}$ if condition a is not satisfied. $A^{(M)}$ is determined by the relation $Q\left(A^{(M)}\right) - Q\left(A^{(1)}\right) < DQ$ for maximum n (the positions of these alternatives are 'in closeness').

The TOPSIS Method

The TOPSIS method is developed by Hwang and Yoon (1981) as an alternative to the ELECTRE method. The basic concept is that the selected alternative should have the shortest distance from the negative-ideal solution. The TOPSIS procedure consists of the following steps:

Step I Calculate the normalized decision matrix. The normalized value (r_{ij}) is calculated as:

$$r_{ij} = f_{ij} \Big/ \sqrt{\sum_{j=1}^{J} f_{ij}^2} \quad j = 1, \ldots, J\,,\ i = 1, \ldots, n \tag{3.11}$$

where j is the number of alternatives, i is the number of criteria and f_{ij} is the value of the j alternative for the i criteria.

Step II Calculate the weight normalized decision matrix. The weighted normalized value v_{ij} is calculated as

$$v_{ij} = w_i r_{ij} \tag{3.12}$$

where w_i is the weight of the i criterion or attribute.

Step III Determine the ideal $\left(A^*\right)$ and negative-ideal $\left(A^-\right)$ solutions

$$A^* = \left\{v_1^*, \ldots, v_n^*\right\} = \left\{\left(\max_j v_{ij} \middle| i \in I'\right), \left(\min_j v_{ij} \middle| i \in I''\right)\right\} \tag{3.13}$$

$$A^- = \left\{v_1^-, \ldots, v_n^-\right\} = \left\{\left(\min_j v_{ij} \middle| i \in I'\right), \left(\max_j v_{ij} \middle| i \in I''\right)\right\} \tag{3.14}$$

where I' is associated with benefit criteria, and I'' is associated with cost criteria.

Step IV Calculate the separation measures, using the n-dimensional Euclidean distance, and the relative closeness to the ideal solution (C_j^*). The separation of each alternative from the ideal solution, from the negative-ideal solution, and the relative closeness of the alternative a_j with respect to A^*, are given by Equations (3.15), (3.16) and (3.17) respectively.

$$D_j^* = \sqrt{\sum_{i=1}^{n} \left(v_{ij} - v_i^*\right)^2} \tag{3.15}$$

$$D_j^- = \sqrt{\sum_{i=1}^{n} \left(v_{ij} - v_i^-\right)^2} \tag{3.16}$$

$$C_j^* = D_j^- \Big/ \left(D_j^* + D_j^-\right) \tag{3.17}$$

Step IV Rank the preference order. Rank the alternatives, sorting by the value C_j^* in decreasing order. Propose as a solution the alternative which is the best ranked (maximum) by the measure.

Both VIKOR and TOPSIS methods are two Multi-criteria decision-making methods based on an aggregating function representing 'closeness to the ideal' which originates in the compromise programming method. However, these two methods introduce different forms of aggregating function for ranking and different kinds of normalization to eliminate the units of criterion function (Opricovic and Tzeng, 2004). Whereas the VIKOR method uses linear normalization and the normalized values do not depend on the evaluation unit of a criterion, the TOPSIS method uses vector normalization, and the normalized value could be different for a different evaluation unit of a particular criterion. As regards the aggregating function, the VIKOR method introduces an aggregating function representing the distance from the ideal solution, considering the relative importance of all criteria, and a balance between total and individual satisfaction. On the other hand, the TOPSIS method introduces an aggregating function including the distances from the ideal point and from the negative-ideal point without considering their relative importance. However, the reference point could be a major concern in decision-making, and to be as close as possible to the ideal is the rationale of human choice (Opricovic and Tzeng, 2004).

Next, the VIKOR and TOPSIS methods will be used in order to determine the critical path of the project shown in Figure 3.4. Four criteria will be considered, time in days, cost in Euros, and quality and safety on a 0–100 scale. The data of the project are shown in Table 3.9. The duration of each path with its time, cost, quality, safety and the weights for each criteria are shown in Table 3.10

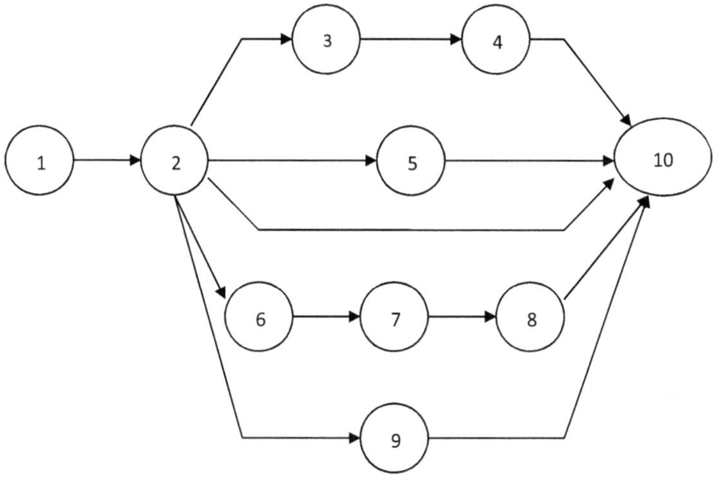

Figure 3.4 Network associated to the VIKOR and TOPSIS application

Table 3.9 Data of the project

Arc (*i,j*)	Task	Time (days)	Cost (€*10³)	Quality	Safety
(1,2)	A	10	60	40	40
(2,3)	B	10	70	20	15
(3,4)	C	15	80	20	15
(4,10)	D	15	70	15	10
(2,5)	E	20	80	27	10
(5,10)	F	30	50	30	10
(2,10)	G	60	100	58	10
(2,6)	H	10	80	10	15
(6,7)	I	5	45	12	10
(7,8)	J	10	55	15	15
(8,10)	K	10	30	22	10
(2,9)	L	30	90	30	20
(9,10)	M	25	50	26	10

Table 3.10 Paths in the network

	Weight	0.47	0.28	0.15	0.10
Alternative	**Path**	**Time**	**Cost**	**Quality**	**Safety**
A_1	(A,B,C,D)	50	280	95	80
A_2	(A,E,F)	60	190	97	60
A_3	(A,G)	70	160	98	50
A_4	(A,H,I,J,K)	45	270	99	90
A_5	(A,L,M)	65	200	96	70

Applying the TOPSIS procedure, the normalized decision matrix and the weight normalized matrix corresponding to steps 1 and 2 are calculated:

$$\text{Normalized matrix} \quad \begin{bmatrix} 0.381 & 0.557 & 0.438 & 0.501 \\ 0.457 & 0.378 & 0.447 & 0.376 \\ 0.533 & 0.318 & 0.452 & 0.313 \\ 0.343 & 0.537 & 0.456 & 0.564 \\ 0.495 & 0.398 & 0.443 & 0.438 \end{bmatrix} \quad \text{Weight normalized matrix} \quad \begin{bmatrix} 0.179 & 0.156 & 0.066 & 0.050 \\ 0.215 & 0.106 & 0.067 & 0.038 \\ 0.250 & 0.089 & 0.068 & 0.031 \\ 0.161 & 0.150 & 0.068 & 0.056 \\ 0.233 & 0.111 & 0.066 & 0.044 \end{bmatrix}$$

The ideal $\left(A^*\right)$ and negative-ideal $\left(A^-\right)$ solutions using Equations (3.13) and (3.14) for the considered attributes are shown in Table 3.11. Table 3.12 shows the values of the separation measures (D_j^* and D_j^-) and the relative closeness to the ideal solution (C_j^*) corresponding to the five paths calculated using Equations (3.15), (3.16), and (3.17), respectively.

Table 3.11 Ideal $\left(A^*\right)$ and negative-ideal $\left(A^-\right)$ solutions

	Time	**Cost**	**Quality**	**Safety**
	Max	Max	Min	Min
v_i^*	0.250	0.156	0.066	0.031
v_i^-	0.161	0.089	0.068	0.056

Table 3.12 Separation measures (D_j^* , D_j^-) and relative closeness to the ideal solution (C_j^*)

	Path 1	Path 2	Path 3	Path 4	Path 5
D_j^*	0.074	0.062	0.067	0.093	0.050
D_j^-	0.069	0.059	0.093	0.061	0.076
C_j^*	0.484	0.489	0.582	0.397	0.605

With regard to the VIKOR method, Table 3.13 shows the best f_i^* and the worst f_i^- values of all criterion functions. The values of S_j, R_j, and Q_j, obtained using Equations (3.8), (3.9), and (3.10), respectively, are shown in Table 3.14.

Table 3.13 Best (f_i^*) and worst (f_i^-) values of all criterion functions

	Time	Cost	Quality	Safety
	Max	Max	Min	Min
f_i^*	70	280	95	50
f_i^-	45	160	99	90

Table 3.14 Values of S_j, R_j, and Q_j

	Path 1	Path 2	Path 3	Path 4	Path 5
S_j	0.451	0.498	0.393	0.743	0.368
R_j	0.376	0.210	0.280	0.470	0.187
Q_j	0.445	0.214	0.197	1.000	0.000

The results obtained by the TOPSIS and the VIKOR methods are shown in Table 3.15. Ranking the alternatives by the TOPSIS method gives Path 5 (A,L,M) as solution. Ranking the alternatives by the VIKOR method also gives, as a compromise solution, Path 5. This alternative is the best ranked by Q. In addition, conditions IV-a and IV-b are satisfied as $Q\left[A^{(2)}\right] - Q\left[A^{(1)}\right] \geq DQ$, and this alternative is also the best ranked by S and R. Being the highest ranked path by the TOPSIS method indicates that Path 5 is the best in terms of the ranking index. In addition, being the highest ranked alternative by the VIKOR method indicates that is the closest to the ideal solution.

Table 3.15 Results obtained by both methods

TOPSIS method		VIKOR method			
	C_j^*		Q_j	S_j	R_j
Path 5	0.605	Path 5	0.000	0.368	0.187
Path 3	0.582	Path 3	0.197	0.393	0.280
Path 2	0.489	Path 2	0.214	0.498	0.210
Path 1	0.484	Path 1	0.445	0.451	0.376
Path 4	0.397	Path 4	1.000	0.743	0.470

Fuzzy PROMETHEE Method

PROMETHEE (Preference Ranking Organization Method for Enrichment Evaluation) is a multi-criteria decision-making method developed by Brans (1982). By 1994, the method had been extended to encompass six ranking formats: PROMETHEE I (partial ranking), PROMETHEE II (complete ranking), PROMETHEE III (ranking based on intervals), PROMETHEE IV (continuous case), PROMETHEE V (net flows and integer linear programming) and PROMETHEE VI (representation of human brain).

Whereas the TOPSIS method is based on the principle that the chosen path should have the shortest distance in geometrical sense from the ideal path and the farthest distance from the negative-ideal one, and the method proposed by Shankar et al. (2010) is based on a metric ranking distance of total fuzzy slack time for each path in the network, the PROMETHEE method deals with the problem from a different perspective. The method uses the outranking methodology to rank the alternatives combined with the ease of use and decreased complexity. Based on extensions of the notion of criterion, the method is well adapted to problem where a finite number of alternative actions are to be ranked considering several criteria. Once a preference function, showing the preferences of the decision-maker between two paths regarding each criterion, has been defined, the decision-maker considers that these two paths can be completely indifferent (or different) as long as the deviation between them does not exceed (exceeds) a certain amount. Six types of functions help the decision-maker to establish his or her preferences regarding each criterion.

PROMETHEE method is implemented in five steps. In the first step, a preference function, showing the preference of the decision-maker for an action *a* with regard to another action *b*, is defined. The second step concerns the comparison of the suggested alternatives in pairs to the preference function. As a third step, the outcomes of these comparisons are presented in an evaluation matrix as the estimated values of every criterion for every alternative. The ranking is realized in the two final steps: a partial ranking in the fourth step and afterwards, a complete ranking of alternatives in the fifth step.

STEP 1. DEFINE PREFERENCE FUNCTION

Given the preference of the decision-maker for an action *a* with regard to *b* of a set of possible actions *K*, the preference function will be defined separately for each criterion; its value will be between 0 and 1. The smaller the function, the greater the indifference of the decision-maker. The closer to 1, the greater his preference. In case of strict preference, the preference function will be 1. The associated preference function *P(a,b)* of *a* with regard to *b* will be defined as (Brans and Vincke 1985):

$$P(a,b)=\begin{cases} 0 & \text{for } f(a)\leq f(b) \\ p\left[f(a),f(b)\right] & \text{for } f(a)\geq f(b) \end{cases} \tag{3.18}$$

For concrete cases, it seems reasonable to choose $p(\cdot)$ functions of the following type:

$$p\left[f(a),f(b)\right]=p\left[f(a)-f(b)\right] \tag{3.19}$$

depending on the difference between the values $f(a)$ and $f(b)$. In order to indicate clearly the areas of indifference in the neighbourhood of $f(a)$ and $f(b)$, we write:

$$x=f(a)-f(b) \tag{3.20}$$

and the function $H(x)$ is graphically represented so that:

$$H(x)=\begin{cases} P(a,b) & x\geq 0 \\ P(b,a) & x\leq 0 \end{cases} \tag{3.21}$$

Six types of functions cover most of the cases occurring in practical applications, namely, usual criterion, quasi-criterion, criterion with linear preference, level criterion, criterion with linear preference and indifference area, and Gaussian criterion:

1. Type I: Usual criterion. Let $p(x)$ be

$$p(x) = \begin{cases} 0 & \text{for } x \leq 0 \\ 1 & \text{for } x > 0 \end{cases} \quad (3.22)$$

In this case, there is indifference between *a* and *b* only when $f(a) = f(b)$. As soon as these values are different the decision-maker has a strict preference for the action having the greatest value.

2. Type II: Quasi-criterion. In this case,

$$p(x) = \begin{cases} 0 & \text{for } x \leq l \\ 1 & \text{for } x > l \end{cases} \quad (3.23)$$

and for this particular criterion, *a* and *b* are indifferent as long as the difference between $f(a)$ and $f(b)$ does not exceed *l*; if not, the preference becomes strict.

3. Type III: Linear preference. Let $p(x)$ be

$$p(x) = \begin{cases} x/m & \text{for } x \leq m \\ 1 & \text{for } x > m \end{cases} \quad (3.24)$$

Such an extension of the notion of criterion allows the decision-maker to prefer progressively *a* to *b* for progressively larger deviations between $f(a)$ and $f(b)$. In this case, the intensity of preference increases linearly until this deviation equals *m*, after this value the preference is strict.

4. Type IV: Level criterion.

$$p(x) = \begin{cases} 0 & \text{for } x \leq q \\ 1/2 & \text{for } q < x \leq q + p \\ 1 & \text{for } x > q + p \end{cases} \quad (3.25)$$

In this case, *a* and *b* are considered as indifferent when the deviation between $f(a)$ and $f(b)$ does not exceed *q*. Between *q* and $q + p$ the preference is weak (1/2), after this value the preference becomes strict.

5. Type V: Linear preference and indifference area. This time we consider for $p(x)$:

$$p(x) = \begin{cases} 0 & \text{for } x \leq s \\ \dfrac{x - s}{r} & \text{for } s < x \leq s + r \\ 1 & \text{for } x > s + r \end{cases} \tag{3.26}$$

In this case the decision-maker considers that *a* and *b* are completely indifferent as long as the deviation between $f(a)$ and $f(b)$ does not exceed *s*. Above this value the preference grows progressively until this deviation equals $s + r$.

6. Type VI: Gaussian criterion. Let $p(x)$ be:

$$p(x) = \begin{cases} 0 & \text{for } x \leq 0 \\ 1 - e^{-\frac{x^2}{2\delta^2}} & \text{for } x > 0 \end{cases} \tag{3.27}$$

If a particular criterion is of the Gaussian type, the preference of the decision-maker still grows with the deviation *x*.

STEP 2. CALCULATE THE PREFERENCE INDEX

Suppose every criterion has been identified as being of one of the six types considered so that the preference functions $P_h(a,b)$ have been defined for each $h = 1,2,\ldots,k$. Next, for each couple of actions, $a,b \in K$, we first define a preference index for *a* with regard to *b* over all the criteria. Let

$$\pi(a,b) = \frac{1}{k}\sum_{h=1}^{K} P_h(a,b) \tag{3.28}$$

be such a preference index, which gives a measure of the preference of *a* over *b* for all the criteria. The closer to 1, the greater the preference.

STEP 3. CONSTRUCT THE VALUED OUTRANKING GRAPH

The values obtained in Step 2 determine the valued outranking graph, the nodes of which are the actions of *K*, so that for all $a,b \in K$, the arc (a,b) has the value $\pi(a,b)$. Let us define, for each node in this valued outranking graph, the outgoing flow:

$$\varphi^{+}(a)=\sum_{x\in K}\pi(a,x) \tag{3.29}$$

and the incoming flow:

$$\varphi^{-}(a)=\sum_{x\in K}\pi(x,a) \tag{3.30}$$

The larger $\varphi^{+}(a)$, the more *a* dominates the other actions of *K*. The smaller $\varphi^{-}(a)$, the less *a* is dominated.

STEP 4. RANKING THE ACTIONS BY A PARTIAL PRE-ORDER

If the decision-maker wants to rank the actions of *K* from the best to the weakest one, the problem consists in using the outranking graph to build a total pre-order on *K*, or a partial one. Let us define the two total pre-orders (P^{+},I^{+}) and (P^{-},I^{-}) such that

$$\begin{cases} aP^{+}b & \text{if } \varphi^{+}(a)>\varphi^{+}(b) \\ aP^{-}b & \text{if } \varphi^{-}(a)<\varphi^{-}(b) \end{cases} \tag{3.31}$$

$$\begin{cases} aI^{+}b & \text{if } \varphi^{+}(a)=\varphi^{+}(b) \\ aI^{-}b & \text{if } \varphi^{-}(a)=\varphi^{-}(b) \end{cases} \tag{3.32}$$

We then obtain the following partial pre-order $\left(P^{(1)},I^{(1)},R\right)$ by considering their intersection:

$$\begin{cases} a \text{ outranks } b \ \left(a\ P^{(1)}\ b\right) & \begin{cases} a\ P^{+}\ b & \text{and} & a\ P^{-}\ b \\ a\ P^{+}\ b & \text{and} & a\ I^{-}\ b \\ a\ I^{+}\ b & \text{and} & a\ P^{+}\ b \end{cases} \\ a \text{ is indifferent to } b \ \left(a\ I^{(1)}\ b\right) & a\ I^{+}\ b \text{ and } a\ I^{-}\ b \\ a \text{ and } b \text{ are incomparable } \left(a\ R\ b\right) & \text{otherwise} \end{cases} \tag{3.33}$$

that is, an action *a* dominates another action *b* by a partial pre-order $P^{(1)}$ if $\varphi^{+}(a)>\varphi^{+}(b)$ and $\varphi^{-}(a)>\varphi^{-}(b)$, or $\varphi^{+}(a)>\varphi^{+}(b)$ and $\varphi^{-}(a)=\varphi^{-}(b)$, or

$\varphi^+(a) = \varphi^+(b)$ and $\varphi^-(a) < \varphi^-(b)$; an action a is indifferent to another action b if $\varphi^+(a) = \varphi^+(b)$ and $\varphi^-(a) = \varphi^-(b)$; and a and b are incompatible otherwise.

STEP 5. RANKING THE ACTIONS BY A TOTAL PRE-ORDER

Suppose a total pre-order (complete ranking without incomparabilities) has been requested by a decision-maker. We then consider for each criterion $a \in K$ the net flow:

$$\varphi(a) = \varphi^+(a) - \varphi^-(a) \tag{3.34}$$

which can easily be used for ranking the actions:

$$\begin{cases} a \text{ outranks } b\left(a\ P^{(2)}\ b\right) & \text{if } \varphi(a) > \varphi(b) \\ a \text{ is indifferent to } b\left(a\ I^{(2)}\ b\right) & \text{if } \varphi(a) = \varphi(b) \end{cases} \tag{3.35}$$

Next, the critical path of the project shown in Figure 3.5 will be determined by using PROMETHEE method. Four criteria will be considered, time in days, cost in Euros, and quality and safety that will be assessed using the fuzzy linguistic variables shown in Table 3.16. The data under the various criteria for the project, expressed as fuzzy triangular numbers (FTNs), are shown in Table 3.17.

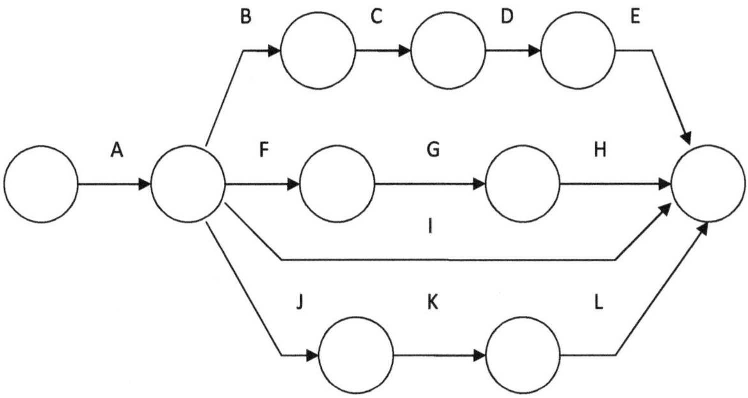

Figure 3.5 Network associated to the fuzzy PROMETHEE application

Table 3.16 Linguistic variables for FTNs

Linguistic variable	FTN
Extremely strong	$\{9;9;9\}$
Intermediate	$\{7;8;9\}$
Very strong	$\{6;7;8\}$
Intermediate	$\{5;6;7\}$
Strong	$\{4;5;6\}$
Intermediate	$\{3;4;5\}$
Moderately strong	$\{2;3;4\}$
Intermediate	$\{1;2;3\}$
Equally strong	$\{1;1;1\}$

Table 3.17 Data of the project

Task	Time	Cost	Quality	Safety
A	$\{0.4;0.5;0.6\}$	$\{700,750,775\}$	$\{4;5;6\}$	$\{2;3;4\}$
B	$\{3;4;5\}$	$\{2,500;3,000;3,600\}$	$\{3;4;5\}$	$\{6;7;8\}$
C	$\{3;4;5\}$	$\{2,900;3,500;4,100\}$	$\{4;5;6\}$	$\{7;8;9\}$
D	$\{8;9;11\}$	$\{12,00;12,500;15,000\}$	$\{7;8;9\}$	$\{9;9;9\}$
E	$\{0,7;1;12\}$	$\{1,000;1,250;1,500\}$	$\{6;7;8\}$	$\{7;8;9\}$
F	$\{11;12;16\}$	$\{4,300;5,000;5,600\}$	$\{6;7;8\}$	$\{5;6;7\}$
G	$\{1;2;3\}$	$\{760;850;925\}$	$\{5;6;7\}$	$\{6;7;8\}$
H	$\{1;2;3\}$	$\{800;850;925\}$	$\{5;6;7\}$	$\{5;6;7\}$
I	$\{15;18;20\}$	$\{7,100;7,500;8,200\}$	$\{7;8;9\}$	$\{9;9;9\}$
J	$\{12.5;16.5;19\}$	$\{5,200;6,000;7,500\}$	$\{6;7;8\}$	$\{7;8;9\}$
K	$\{12;15;20\}$	$\{6,000;6,550;7,400\}$	$\{5;6;7\}$	$\{9;9;9\}$
L	$\{3;4;5\}$	$\{2,500;3,000;3,600\}$	$\{3;4;5\}$	$\{6;7;8\}$

The use of FTNs appears adequate because they require elementary fuzzy algebra and permit to represent the judgements of the experts in a simple and sound manner (Zammori et al., 2009). Other types of fuzzy numbers with different shapes exist, such as trapezoidal fuzzy numbers of bell-shaped fuzzy numbers, and many fuzzy representation methods have been proposed to defuzzy these fuzzy numbers. In this section we use the graded mean integration to represent fuzzy numbers because of its simplicity.

A generic Fuzzy Triangular Number is defined by an ordered triplet $\{a_i, b_i, c_i\}$ representing the *lower*, the *modal*, and the *upper* value respectively. Given any two positive FTNs, $\{a_1, b_1, c_1\}$ and $\{a_2, b_2, c_2\}$, the fuzzy sum of these two FTNs, expressed as:

$$\{a_1 + a_2, b_1 + b_2, c_1 + c_2\} \tag{3.36}$$

is also a FTN.

Equation (3.36) is used to add up the final FTN of each criterion for the four paths of the network which start with the starting event and end with the ending event. These final FTNs are then defuzzied by aim of the graded mean integration (*GM*):

$$GM = \frac{1}{6} \times \left(a_{ij} + 4b_{ij} + c_{ij}\right) \tag{3.37}$$

and the results are shown in Table 3.18. All the successive steps follow the PROMETHEE method.

Different types of preference functions showing the preferences of the project manager regarding each criterion exist. For analytical purposes, the type of preference functions that have been selected for the criteria considered, shown in Table 3.19, are the following:

1. Time: the intensity of preference increases linearly until this deviation equals 15 days, after this value the preference becomes strict.

2. Cost: the decision-maker considers that two paths are completely indifferent as long as the deviation between them does not exceed €2,000, above this value the preference grows progressively until this deviation equals €7,000.

3. Quality: two paths are indifferent as long as the difference between does not exceed 3 points, if not, the preference becomes strict.

4. Safety: the intensity of preference increases linearly until the deviation between two paths equals 5 points, after this value the preference is strict.

Table 3.18 Paths in the network

Alternative	Path	Time	Cost	Quality	Safety
A_1	ABCDE	18.65	21,346	29	35
A_2	AFGH	17	7,431	24	22
A_3	AI	18.33	8,296	13	12
A_4	AJKL	36.08	16,479	22	27

Table 3.19 Type of Preference function and threshold values

Criterion	Time	Cost	Quality	Safety
Preference function	III	V	II	III
Threshold values	$m = 15$	$s = 2{,}000$ $r = 7{,}000$	$l = 3$	$m = 5$

Using Equations (3.18), (3.20), and (3.28) we obtain the preference index for each couple of alternatives. Table 3.20 shows the values $\pi(a,b)$ for every couple of actions.

Table 3.20 Values of $\pi(a,b)$

	Path 1	Path 2	Path 3	Path 4
Path 1	–	0.8	0.53	0.08
Path 2	0.5	–	0	0
Path 3	0.25	0.52	–	0.25
Path 4	0.75	0.75	0.67	–

Let us first suppose that a partial relation would be useful to the project manager. According to Equations (3.29) and (3.30), Table 3.21 is completed with the outgoing and the incoming flow. Next, the pre-orders P^+ and P^- are obtained from Table 3.21, the intersection of which is:

Path 4 $P^{(1)}$ Paths 1, 2, 3; Path 1 $P^{(1)}$ Path 2, 3; and Path 2 $P^{(1)}$ Path 3.

Supposing now that a total pre-order would be useful to the project manager, the net flows shown in Table 3.22 are calculated according to Equation (3.34), so that the total pre-order is:

Path 4 $P^{(2)}$ Path 1; Path 1 $P^{(2)}$ Path 3; and Path 3 $P^{(2)}$ Path 2.

From Table 3.22, the larger net flow $\varphi(A)$ corresponds to Path 4, made up of tasks A-J-K-L, and therefore, is considered the critical path.

Table 3.21 Outgoing and Incoming flow

	Path 1	Path 2	Path 3	Path 4
$\varphi^+(A_i)$	1.41	0.5	1.02	2.17
$\varphi^-(A_i)$	1.5	2.07	1.2	0.33

Table 3.22 Net flows

	Path 4	Path 1	Path 3	Path 2
$\varphi(A)$	1.84	-0.09	-0.18	-1.57

MCDM methods have been widely used to Project Management decisions such as competitive bidding processes (Cagno et al., 2001), contractor's selection (Hatush and Skitmore, 1997; Fong and Choi, 2000; Al Subhi, 2001; Madhi et al., 2002, Topcu, 2004, Cheng and Li, 2004; Lambropoulos, 2007), project selection (Stewart and Mohamed 2002), etc. Zammori et al. (2009) used the TOPSIS method to determine the critical path in a fuzzy network taking into account not only the expected durations of the tasks but also additional parameters such as duration variability, cost, shared resources, risk of major design revisions, and external risk. Amiri and Golozari (2011) used the same method to determine the critical path under fuzzy environments taking into account time, cost, risk, and quality criteria. Shankar et al. (2010) proposed a metric distance ranking method for fuzzy numbers to a critical path method for a fuzzy project network, where the duration time of each activity is represented by a trapezoidal fuzzy number.

Chapter 4

Game Theory

Nowadays, Project Management is facing important problems and challenges. Fragmentation is one of these problems. Since projects are becoming large and complex, involving multiple participants located at different places, the resources and operations of a project are distributed by nature (Yan et al., 2000). Many problems also involve complexity and dynamicity. The construction sector, e.g., represents one of the most dynamic and complex industrial environments requiring the application of different technologies or technical approaches (Abdul-Raman et al., 2006). The components of these large, open, and complex projects are not known in advance, can change over time, and consist of highly heterogeneous agents implemented by different people, at different times and with different software tools and techniques (Ren and Anumba, 2004). Resource discrepancies are also a major cause of change. When the timing of the tasks are not well matched with the available resources, subcontractors may try to change the master schedule in order to accommodate their desires, which may cause conflicts because in tightly couple project schedules any move affects the tasks of other subcontractors. In most cases, these conflicts cannot easily be resolved simply by delaying the succeeding tasks, since task delays could extend the project completion beyond the deadline (Kim et al., 2000). In these cases, subcontractors hinder their own performance as well as that of other subcontractors and ultimately the entire project (Kim, 2001).

In Project Management there are many situations where cooperative behaviour may result in the interest of the firms carrying out a project. For example, is it possible to expedite the project? If this is the case, cooperative game theory answers questions such as: which coalitions can be formed? What is the payoff for each coalition? How can the coalitional gains (costs) be divided in order to secure a sustainable agreement? On the other hand, if the project is delayed, how to divide cost among activities? How much must each firm pay for it?

In these situations the problem arises how to divide among participants the joint costs (and implicitly the cost savings) which result from the cooperation (Tijs and Driessen, 1986). The method adopted for allocating benefits and costs among the members will affect the willingness of various members to remain active in the coalition. The allocation problem may be solved in a variety of ways, but an allocation rule that prescribes, somehow, a solution for the allocation problem should satisfy desirable criteria such as efficiency, fairness and others.

This chapter begins with a review of the existing research on game theory and Project Management, next two solution concepts for cooperative games, the Shapley value and the Core, are presented and illustrated with three examples: allocation of rewards resulting from cooperative behaviour among the firms carrying out a project in order to expedite it; allocation of costs among activities that have caused delays, and finally, float allocation among the non-critical activities in a project.

Game Theory

Negotiation is an important aspect of any project. Negotiation plays an important role in resolving claims, preventing disputes, and keeping a harmonious relationship between project participants (Ren et al., 2003a). However, most project managers consider negotiation as the most time-and energy-consuming activity in claim management (Hu, 1997). In addition, claim negotiation is commonly inefficient due to the diversity of intellectual background, many variables involved, complex interactions, and inadequate negotiation knowledge of project participants (Kraus, 1996; Ren et al., 2003a).

To ensure that interdependencies are properly managed, effective Project Management requires that project participants across the world are able to collaborate and coordinate with each other to perform activities and to gain maximum competence (Yan et al., 2000; Ren and Anumba, 2004). There is a need to develop negotiation methodologies for the project schedule optimization process that identify schedule conflicts, consider alternatives and resolve the conflicts by negotiation among project participants.

To address the complex technical and human issues in negotiation, different negotiation theories and models are available which mainly include game theory, economic theory, and behaviour theory (Ren et al., 2003a). Game theory is divided into two approaches, the axiomatic approach and the strategic approach. Under the latter approach game theorists treat economic theory as a part of game theory. On the other hand, negotiation theorists usually distinguish game theory (mainly referring to the axiomatic approach) from economic theory (Ren et al., 2003b). Game theory seeks to get at the essential of decision-making and the associated strategies in situations where two or more parties are interdependent, and where the outcome of their conflict and competition must be the product of their joint requirements and the interaction of their separate choices (Bacharasch and Lawler, 1981). All the players in games are assumed to be rational, try to maximize their own utilities, and have complete information on the payoff function and utility function (Nash, 1950). In contrast to the classical game theory approach, in economic theory there is no concern for the discovery of once-and-for-all strategies, but rather an intention to examine how the bargainers should interact in terms of their expectations of each other (Young, 1975). Economic models analyse the processes through which the demands of the participants converge in the course of offers and counteroffers toward some specific point on the contract curve (Bacharasch and Lawler, 1981). In behaviour theory much attention is given to the nature of changing expectations and negotiators' tactics, and to the significance of uncertainties of information, perception and evaluation, all matters that tend to be ignored by game theory and economic theory (Zartman, 1977). Behaviour theory attempts to analyse the negotiation processes in which negotiators influence each other's expectations, perceptions, assessments, and decisions during the search of an outcome.

Application of Game theory in Project Management is still in the beginning of its practical applications. Branzei et al. (2002) proposed two coalitional games related to delays cost sharing problems to determine fair shares for each of the agents who contribute to the delay of a project such that the total delay cost is cleared. Bergantinos and Sanchez (2002a) introduced a non-transferable utility game associated to the PERT problem to divide the slacks of time among the different activities. In a second paper, the same authors (Bergantinos and Sanchez, 2002b) presented two different approaches, one based on serial cost sharing problems and the other in game theory, to distribute the cost caused by the delay of a project among the firms which are responsible for it.

Game theory can be defined as the study of mathematical models of conflict and cooperation between intelligent rational decision-makers (Myerson, 1991). In a broad sense, game theory can be classified into two categories: non-cooperative game approaches, where a decision-making unit treats the others as competitors, and cooperative approaches where a group of decision-makers decide to undertake a project together in order to achieve their joint business objectives. In game theory individuals or groups become players when their respective decisions, coupled with the decisions made by other players, produce an outcome. The options available to players to bring about particular outcomes are called strategies. Strategies are linked to outcomes by a mathematical function that specifies the consequences of the various combinations of strategy choices by all of the players in a game. A coalition refers to the formation of subsets of players' options under coordinated strategies.

A n-person game is a game with more than three players. Let $N = \{1, 2, \ldots, n\}$ be the set of players (or a set of contractors involved in a given project), for each subset S of N, the characteristic function V of a game gives the amount $V(S)$ that the members of S can be sure of receiving if they act together and form a coalition. Thus, $V(S)$ can be determined by calculating the amount that members of S can get without any help from players who are not in S.

Consider any subsets of sets A and B such that A and B have no players in common ($A \cap B = \phi$). Then, for any n-person game, the characteristic function must satisfy the following property:

$$V(A \cup B) \geq V(A) + V(B) \tag{4.1}$$

This property is called superadditivity and implies that $V(A \cup B)$ must be at least as large as $V(A) + V(B)$. In other words, it is more beneficial for A and B to collaborate than to act independently.

A solution concept for any n-person game should indicate the reward that each player will receive. More formally, let $x = \{x_1, x_2, \ldots, x_n\}$ be a vector such that player i receives a reward x_i, we call such a vector a reward vector. A reward vector is not a reasonable candidate for a solution unless x satisfies two properties: individual rationality and group rationality:

a) *Individual rationality*

$$x_i \geq V(i) \; \forall \; i \in N \tag{4.2}$$

Equation (4.2) implies that player i must receive a reward at least as large as what he can get for himself.

b) *Group rationality*

$$V(N) = \sum_{i=1}^{n} x_i \tag{4.3}$$

Equation (4.3) states that any reasonable reward vector must give all the players an amount that equals the amount that can be attained by the supercoalition consisting of all players. If x satisfies both Equations (4.2) and (4.3), we say that x is an imputation.

The Shapley Value

In situations where one player's decision may affect the other player's decision and decision-makers are assumed to have rational behaviour, game theory may be efficiently employed to analyse conditions for the best beneficial decisions and, consistent with the definition of cooperative games, if the profit gained by a cooperation player exceeds that which would be gained when acting independently, that player will certain seek to establish a coalition (Curiel, 1997). Then, players can negotiate how to distribute resulted benefits. The Shapley value (1953) is one of the best known solution concepts which fit the aforementioned criteria.

The Shapley value is an alternative solution concept for n-person games which in general gives more equitable solutions than the Core value does. The Shapley value describes one approach to fair allocation of gains obtained by cooperation among several actors who form a coalition. Since some actors may contribute more to the coalition than others, the question arises how to distribute fairly the gains among the actors, or what payoff can they reasonably expect?

To formalize this situation, let us consider that, for any characteristic function, there is a unique reward vector $x = (x_1, x_2, \ldots, x_n)$ satisfying the following axioms:

- Axiom 1. Relabeling of players interchanges the players' rewards.
- Axiom 2. Group rationality $\sum_{i=1}^{n} x_i = V(n)$
- Axiom 3. If $V(S - \{i\}) = V(S)$ holds for a coalition S, then the Shapley value has $x_i = 0$. If player i adds no value to any coalition, then player i receives a reward of zero from the Shapley value.

- Axiom 4. Let x be the Shapley value vector for game V and y be the Shapley value vector for game $\bar{V}$. Then, the Shapley value vector for the game $(V+\bar{V})$ is the vector $(x+y)$.

Given any n-person game with the characteristic function V, there is a unique reward vector $x=(x_1,x_2,\ldots,x_n)$ satisfying Axioms 1–4. The reward of the i_{th} player x_i is given by:

$$x_i=\sum p_n(S)\left[V(S\cup\{i\}-V(S))\right]=\sum\frac{|S|!(n-|S|-1)\,!}{n!}\left[V(S\cup\{i\}-V(S))\right] \quad (4.4)$$

where $p_n(S)$ is the probability that when player i arrives, the players in the coalition S are present. If player i forms a coalition with the players who are present when he arrives, then player i adds $V(S\cup\{i\})-V(S)$. Equation (4.4) implies that player i's reward should be the expected amount that player i adds to the coalition made up of the players who are present when he or she arrives.

Allocation of Benefits Resulting from Cooperative Behaviour Using the Shapley Value

Faster completion of projects has always been an important goal in virtually all project environments (Liberatore and Pollack-Johnson, 2006). In this section, the Shapley value is applied in order to allocate the benefits resulting from cooperative behaviour among the firms carrying out a project, which decide to expedite it. Table 4.1 shows the tasks to undertake the project, the immediate predecessors, the normal duration and the crash time corresponding to these tasks. Figure 4.1 shows the network associated to the project. Solving the network through the critical path method algorithm, the normal time to undertake the project is 23 days.

Let us consider that each path of the network is a player, so we have three players:

- Player 1 (path 1): tasks *A*, *B* and *C*;
- Player 2 (path 2): tasks *D*, *E*, and *F*; and
- Player 3 (path 3): tasks *G*, *H*, and *I*.

These three players decide to cooperate in order to expedite the project. Let us consider that each day the project is reduced a saving of €5,000 is obtained. Reducing the time to undertake the project to the crash time, the project can be completed in 17 days. This implies the cooperation among the three players (paths) and a total saving of €30,000 can be achieved. The aim of this section is to allocate these benefits among the players in a way such that do not affect their willingness to participate active in the coalition.

Table 4.1 Tasks, predecessors, normal duration and crash time

Task	Time (days)	
	Normal	Crash
A	6	5
B	9	7
C	8	5
D	8	7
E	7	6
F	5	4
G	7	6
H	5	4
I	10	7

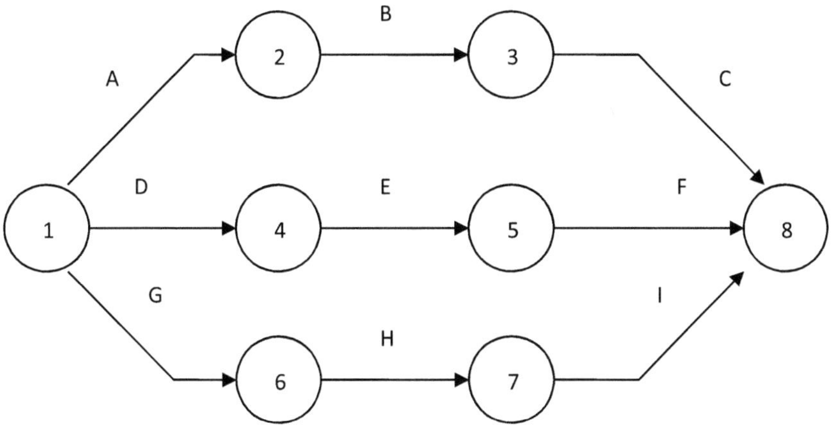

Figure 4.1 Network associated to the Shapley value application

Table 4.2 shows the possible coalitions and the benefits obtained. Players 2 and 3 do not do anything by themselves, whereas player 1 (tasks *A*, *B* and *C*), on his own, can reduce the project one day (€5,000). The coalitions formed by players 1 and 2 (tasks *A*, *B*, *C* and tasks *D*, *E*, *F*), and 2 and 3 (tasks *D*, *E*, *F* and tasks *G*, *H*, *I*) cannot reduce the project. However, the coalition formed by player 1 and 3 (tasks *A*, *B*, *C* and tasks *G*, *H*, *I*) can reduce the project three days (€15,000). Finally, if the three players decide to cooperate together, the project can be completed in 17 days and the total saving of €30,000 (6 days) can be achieved.

Table 4.2 Coalitions and gains for Paths 1, 2, and 3

$V(1) = 5{,}000$	$V(1,2) = 0$	$V(1,2,3) = 30{,}000$
$V(2) = 0$	$V(1,3) = 15{,}000$	
$V(3) = 0$	$V(2,3) = 0$	

Applying Equation (4.4), the Shapley value for each player is as follows:

$S_1 = €14{,}167$

$S_2 = €4{,}167$

$S_3 = €11{,}666$

Thus, the Shapley value concept suggests that player 1 (tasks *A*, *B*, and *C*), that has to make the highest reduction in time (6 days), receives €14,167. Player 3, that has to reduce the time of the path *G*, *H*, and *I* in 5 days receives €11,666, and finally, player 2 reducing the path *D*, *E*, and *F* in 3 days, receives €4,167.

The Core

In Game theory, the Core is the set of feasible allocations that cannot be improved upon by a coalition. An imputation, $x = \{x_1, x_2, \ldots, x_n\}$, is in the core of an n-person game if and only if for each subset S of N:

$$\sum_{i=1}^{n} x_i \geq V(S) \tag{4.5}$$

Equation (4.5) states that an imputation, x, is in the core (that x is undominated) if and only if for every coalition S, the total of the received by the players in S (according to x) is at least as large as $V(S)$. The Core can also be defined as the set C, of stable imputations:

$$C:\left\{x=\left(x_1,\ldots,x_n\right):\sum_{i\in N} x_i = V\left(N\right) \text{ and } \sum_{i\in S} x_i \geq V\left(S\right), \forall S\subset N\right\} \tag{4.6}$$

If $V\left(S\right)>\sum_{i\in S} x_i$, we say that the imputation x is unstable through a coalition S, and we say x is stable otherwise. The core can consist of many points, but the core can also be empty. It may be impossible to satisfy all the coalitions at the same time. The size of the core can also be taken as a measure of stability, or how likely it is that a negotiated agreement is prone to be upset.

To determine the least amount of transferable utility which is necessary for an allocation so that no coalition can improve upon it Naharahi (2009) uses the following linear programming problem:

$$\begin{aligned} &\text{Minimize} && \left(x_1+x_2+\ldots+x_n\right) \\ &\text{subject to} && \sum_{i\in C} x_i \geq V\left(C\right)\forall C\subset N \\ & && \left(x_1+x_2+\ldots+x_n\right)\in R^n \end{aligned} \tag{4.7}$$

Note that the above linear programming problem definitely has a solution because all the inequalities are 'greater than or equal to' and also there is a structure which makes it feasible. Let $\left(x_1^*+x_2^*+\ldots+x_n^*\right)$ be an optimal solution of this problem, then:

$$\sum_{i\in C} x_i^* \geq V\left(C\right)\forall C\subseteq N \tag{4.8}$$

In particular, $x_1^*+x_2^*+\ldots+x_n^*\geq V\left(N\right)$. There are two possibilities:

1. $x_1^*+x_2^*+\ldots+x_n^*=V\left(N\right)$. In this case, all solutions of the linear programming problem will constitute the core. In fact, the core will consist precisely of the solution of this problem.

2. $x_1^*+x_2^*+\ldots+x_n^*>V\left(N\right)$. In this case, the core is empty.

A Cost-Allocation Method Based on the Core

A vital section specified in any contract is the performance period of time of project execution. However, the real duration of the activities in a project is usually extended and the time required to complete it is frequently greater than the time specified in the contract. These overruns on time extension give rise to delays. Delays may be defined as an act or event that extends the time required to perform the tasks under a constraint (Stumpf, 2000). They occur in every project and their magnitude varies considerably from project to project (Alaghbari, 2007). Strikes, rework, poor organization, material shortage, equipment failure, change orders, act of God, are the main factors causing delays.

Delays are disruptive and expensive. There is a universal agreement that construction delay is acknowledged as the most common, costly, complex, and risky problem, representing an area of leakage in the construction industry worldwide (Abdul-Raman et al., 2008, Aibinu and Odeyinka, 2005). In addition, delays are interconnected making the situation even more complex and the problem can be more evident in traditional type of contract which is awarded to the lowest bidder (Odeh and Battaineh, 2002).

Because of the overriding importance of time for both the owner (in terms of performance) and the contractor (in terms of money), it is the source of frequent disputes and claims among owners, clients, and consultants leading to lawsuits (Alaghbari, 2007). Such situations usually involve questioning the facts, causal factors, contract interpretations, quantum of the claims, mistrust, arbitration, cash-flow problems, loss of productivity and even total abandonment or termination of contract (Aibinu and Jagboro, 2002).

When a project is delayed questions that emerge are: does a particular delay warrant an extension of project duration and/or an extra cost? If an activity, whose real duration is greater than the planned duration, makes use of the expedition created by other activities, is this activity responsible for the delay? What is the maximal amount that an activity can be held responsible for? How can costs be divided among the activities?

The purpose of this section is to determine the maximum delay that an activity of a project can be held responsible for, and next, to share the penalty associated with the total delay of the project among the activities that have caused this delay. With this aim, the following assumptions are considered: 'a coalition is defined as the activity or set of activities of the network that represent a sub-path within a path. Each coalition is considered a player. The activities that form a coalition and are in the same path of the network cannot be held responsible for more than the net delay of the path as a consequence of the delay of activities in the path and the expedition of activities in the coalition. A delayed activity cannot be held responsible for more than the total delay of the project. Any activity or coalition that form a sub-path and cause a delay in the project, will be held responsible for at least, the delay caused by these activities individually.'

To explain the proposed approach, the project shown in Figure 4.2 is presented. As we can see, in the network there are four coalitions (*AB*; *CDE*; *GH*; and *F*) and three paths.

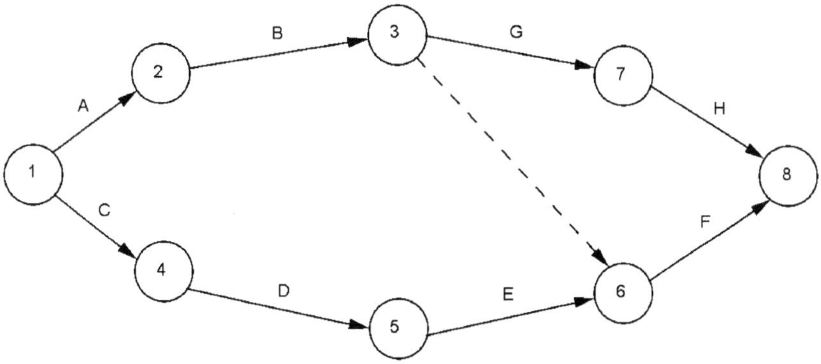

Figure 4.2 Network associated to the cost allocation problem

In order to calculate the delay and expedition of the activities, and real duration of the project the following equations are used (Estevez-Fernandez, 2012):

$$d(i) = \max[r(i) - p(i), 0] \tag{4.9}$$

$$e(i) = \max[p(i) - r(i), 0] \tag{4.10}$$

where $p(i)$ and $r(i)$ represent the planned and real time, and $d(i)$ and $e(i)$ represent the delay and expedition functions of activity i respectively.

The planned, real duration and slack of the paths are calculated as follows:

$$D\left(N_\alpha, p\right) = \sum_{i \in N_\alpha} p\left(i\right) \tag{4.11}$$

$$D\left(N_\alpha, r\right) = \sum_{i \in N_\alpha} r\left(i\right) \tag{4.12}$$

$$Slack\left(N_\alpha, p\right) = D\left(l\right) - D\left(N_\alpha, p\right) \tag{4.13}$$

where $D\left(N_\alpha, p\right)$ and $D\left(N_\alpha, r\right)$ are the planned and real duration of a path N_α, $D(l)$ is the planned duration of the project (i.e., the maximum of $D\left(N_\alpha, p\right)$), and $Slack\left(N_\alpha, p\right)$ is the maximum time that the path N_α can be delayed without altering the duration of the project. If a path has slack zero, then we say that this path is critical.

Table 4.3 shows the planned and real time (in days), and delay and expedition of the activities after the realization of the project. Table 4.4 shows the planned, real duration, and slack of the paths. The planned duration of the project is 170 days but the real duration is 195 days, thus the total delay of the project is $D(r)$-$D(p)$=25 days. The delay of the coalition *AB* is 35 days (20+15), and the delay of *F* is 10 days (20 minus a slack of 10). However, these coalitions cannot be held responsible for more than 25 days, the total delay of the project, because other activities of the project have been expedited. Thus, coalition *AB* is responsible for 35 days on its own but when forming a coalition with *GH*, they are only responsible for 25 days because they take advantage of the expedition of activities *G* and *H* (10 days). Table 4.5 shows the delay for the rest of the coalitions in the network calculated in a similar way, and the cost, $C_y(S)$, associated to each coalition considering that the penalty for each day the project is delayed is €500.

Table 4.3 Planned time, real time, delays and expeditions

Task	$p(i)$	$r(i)$	$d(i)$	$e(i)$
A	20	35	15	0
B	40	60	20	0
C	30	25	0	5
D	40	30	0	10
E	20	18	0	2
F	70	90	20	0
G	70	65	0	5
H	40	35	0	5

Table 4.4 Planned time, real duration, and slacks of the paths

Path	Coalition	$D(N_\alpha, p)$	Slack (N_α, p)	$D(N_\alpha, r)$
N_1	AB-GH	170	170-170 = 0	195
N_2	AB-F	130	170-130 = 40	185
N_3	CDE-F	160	170-160 = 10	163

Table 4.5 Coalitions, delays (days) and costs associated to each coalition

Coalition	Delay	Cost	Coalition	Delay	Cost	Coalition	Delay	Cost
$\{AB\}$	35	17,500	$\{AB, CDE\}$	35	17,500	$\{AB, CDE, GH\}$	25	12,500
$\{CDE\}$	0	0	$\{AB, GH\}$	25	12,500	$\{AB, CDE, F\}$	35	17,500
$\{GH\}$	0	0	$\{AB, F\}$	35	17,500	$\{AB, GH, F\}$	25	12,500
$\{F\}$	10	5,000	$\{CDE, GH\}$	0	0	$\{CDE, GH, F\}$	15	7,500
			$\{CDE, F\}$	0	0	$\{N\}$	25	12,500
			$\{GH, F\}$	0	0			

Once we have the coalitions that can be created in the project and the total delay that these coalitions can be held responsible for, the next step is to allocate the total penalty among the delayed coalitions and activities. Using model (4.7) and the assumptions considered at the beginning of this section, we have:

$$\text{Minimize} \quad \left(x_{AB} + x_{CDE} + x_{GH} + x_F\right)$$

$$\text{subject to} \quad x_{AB} \geq 7,500$$

$$x_F \geq 5,000$$

$$x_{AB} \leq 17,500$$

$$x_{AB} + x_{CDE} \leq 17,500$$

$$x_{AB} + x_{GH} \leq 12,500$$

$$x_{AB} + x_F \leq 17,500$$

$$x_{AB} + x_{CDE} + x_{GH} \leq 12,500$$

$$x_{AB} + x_{CDE} + x_{F} \leq 17,500$$

$$x_{AB} + x_{GH} + x_{F} \leq 12,500$$

$$x_{CDE} + x_{GH} + x_{F} \leq 7,500$$

$$x_{AB} + x_{CDE} + x_{GH} + x_{F} \leq 12,500$$

$$x_{AB}, x_{CDE}, x_{GH}, x_{F} \geq 0$$

where the first inequalities are based on the assumption that any activity or set of activities that form a sub-path and cause a delay in the project, will be held responsible for at least, the delay caused by these activities individually. Thus, the coalition *AB* will be held responsible for, at least, 15 days caused by activity *A* (€7,500) and task *F* will be held responsible for, at least 10 days (€5,000). The last inequality establishes that the maximum penalty to allocate among the coalitions is €12,500.

The solution to the above linear programming problem is x_{AB} =7,500; x_{CDE} = 0; x_{GH} =0; and x_F = 5,000. The last step is to share the cost allocated to a coalition (player) among the activities that form this coalition. This is the case of activities *A* and *B*, responsible for a cost of €7,500. This amount will be shared proportionally according to the delay of these activities (15 and 20 days respectively) to the total delay of the coalition (35 days). Thus, the cost allocated to activity *A* is €3,225 and to activity *B* is €4,275.

Float Allocation Using Game Theory

Next, the concept of the Core of a game is applied to a project in order to allocate the floats among the non-critical activities. The concept of float is central to the analysis of activity networks in Project Management. Float is a byproduct of the critical path method calculations representing the length of time an activity's finish date may be delayed without affecting the completion date of the entire project (De la Garza et al., 1991). It is an indicator of the extent to which the schedule can absorb delays in the completion of the activity without affecting its committed dates (Raz and Marshall, 1996). Float is often considered to be a 'safe harbour' for resource allocations and other purposes without causing a negative impact on the project's duration (Gong, 1997). The concept of float ownership, raised by Householder and Rutland (1990), is one of the controversial issues at the core of most delay claims. Construction time-based claims have added another meaning to the particular expression 'time is money', namely, 'float is money' (De la Garza et al., 1991).

The inappropriate consumption of float time early in the project can lead to difficult challenges in the management of the remaining float time at later stages of the project (Al-Gahtani, 2009). Due to the dynamics of schedules, an activity that originally has float may later have zero or negative float as a result of delays to preceding activities and become critical (De la Garza et al., 2007). In these situations, do not allocate the float of each activity will provide a significant increase in the total cost and/or in the probability of delay of the project (Castro et al., 2012).

The question of who owns the float has multiple valid answers and the answer one gets depends on who is asked (De la Garza et al., 1991). Some authors believe that total float does not belong to a particular party and therefore can be used by any of the project parties (Al-Gahtani, 2009). The current practice of apportioning the utilization of float as 'first came, first served' basis together with the Common Law's Proximate Cause principle favours the party who uses float first to mitigate the potentially negative effect of delaying events at the expense of another party who delays critical activities in the later stages of the project (De la Garza et al., 2007).

On fixed-price contracts, wherein the contractor has the ultimate risk or benefit from project costs, the presence of float in the schedule allows the contractor for flexibility in the arrangement and performance of the non-critical activities, thereby producing the most economical use of resources. The contractor's ability to shift resources and perform his work with maximum efficiency is severely impaired if he loses this flexibility. If the owner forces the contractor to wait to commence the activity until the last start time by claiming the float, the activity becomes critical. If anything occurs during the performance of the activity that extends its duration, the project completion date is extended (Householder and Rutland, 1990). On cost-plus contracts wherein the owner has the ultimate risk or benefit from project costs, the owner may decide that other considerations outside the scope of the project are more important and affect a trade-off by impacting the schedule and thereby potentially increasing the cost of the project to the owner (Householder and Rutland, 1990).

Contractors have reacted to owners' tendency to use float time to accommodate changes in the original project concept by using total float sequestering techniques like artificial lead/lags, unprecedentedly long activity durations, preferential logic and other methods (Ponce de León, 1984). This has resulted in schedule submittals showing unreal logic sequences and activity durations that, in turn, make it impossible to use submitted critical path method as the means for monitoring construction progress (De la Garza et al., 1991).

The core gives a set-valued solution that covers a wide variety of project situations that can have different needs depending, e.g., on the float clauses in contract documents. For analytical purposes, the following assumptions are considered: 'each activity with a slack greater than zero is considered a player. A coalition is defined as the set of activities (players) that share a common float between two critical nodes. In a coalition the activity with the lowest float is considered to be the first to enter into the coalition. Two or more activities that form a coalition can act as players in others coalitions.'

Let $\left\{N_1, N_2, \ldots, N_m\right\}$ the collection of paths in the project. The duration of the project will be the maximum duration of its paths:

$$D(l) = \max_{1\leq\alpha\leq m}\left\{D\left(N_\alpha, l\right)\right\} \tag{4.14}$$

The float (F_α) of a path is the maximum time that the path N_α can be delayed without altering the duration of the project:

$$F_\alpha = D(l) - D\left(N_\alpha, r\right) \tag{4.15}$$

We say that a path is critical if it has float zero. Figure 4.3 shows the network associated to the project and Table 4.6 the tasks to undertake the project and their duration. Table 4.7 shows the earliest start (*ES*), earliest finish (*EF*), latest start (*LS*), latest finish (*LF*), and the float time. The duration and slack of each path, and the coalitions formed are shown in Table 4.8.

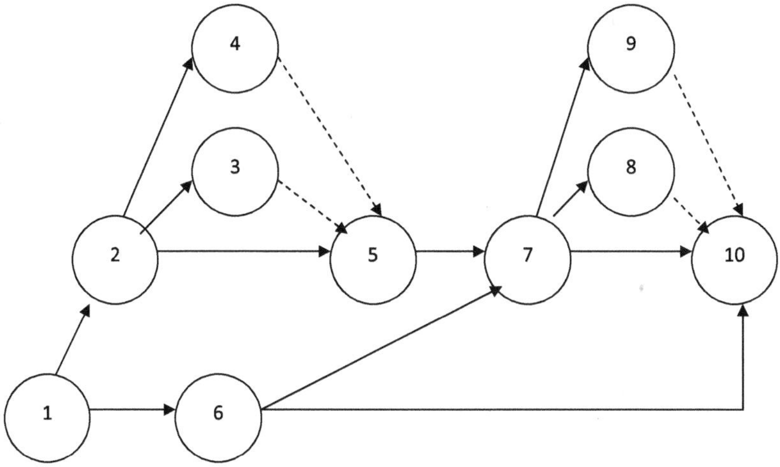

Figure 4.3 Network associated to a float allocation problem.

Table 4.6 Tasks to undertake the project

Node	Task	Time (Weeks)
1–2	A	27
2–4	B	15
2–3	C	20
2–5	D	29
1–6	E	36
6–7	F	25
5–7	G	39
7–9	H	17
7–8	I	22
7–10	J	25
6–10	K	29

Table 4.7 Earliest start, earliest finish, latest start, latest finish and float time

Task	*ES*	*EF*	*LS*	*LF*	**Float (*F*)**
A	0	27	0	27	0
B	27	42	41	56	14
C	27	47	36	56	9
D	27	56	27	56	0
E	0	36	34	70	34
F	36	61	70	95	34
G	56	95	56	95	0
H	95	112	103	120	8
I	95	117	98	120	3
J	95	120	95	120	0
K	36	65	91	120	55

Table 4.8 Paths, durations, floats, and coalitions

Path (N_α)	**Duration $\left(N_\alpha, l\right)$**	**Float (F_α)**	**Coalitions**
A-D-G-J (critical)	120	0	
A-BC-G-J	111	9	B and C
A-D-G-HI	117	3	H and I
A-BC-G-HI	108	12	BC and HI
E-F-J	86	34	E and F
E-F-HI	83	37	H and I
E-K	65	55	E and K

According to the assumptions at the beginning of this section, activities *B* and *C*, *H* and *I*, *E* and *F*, and *E* and *K*, form the coalitions *BC*, *HI*, *EF*, and *EK* respectively. In the coalition *BC*, activity *B* provides a slack of 14 weeks and activity *C* provides a slack of 9 weeks. In the coalition *HI*, activity *I* provides a slack of 3 weeks and activity *H*, provides a slack of 8 weeks. As activities *E* and *F* have the same slack (34 weeks) and form the coalition *EF* between nodes 1 and 7, a slack of 18 weeks is assigned to each activity. In the coalition *EK* with a slack of 55 weeks between nodes 1 and 10, activity *E* provides a slack of 18 weeks and activity *K* provides a slack of 37 weeks. In order to ensure that any activity consumes part of its slack, all the activities must be assigned with an amount greater than or equal to 10 per cent of their slack.

Applying model (4.7) the following linear programming problem determines the least amount of transferable utility which is necessary for an allocation so that no coalition can improve upon it:

Minimize $\left(F_B + F_C + F_E + F_F + F_H + F_I + F_K\right)$

subject to $F_A + F_B + F_C + F_G + F_J \leq 9$

$$F_A + F_D + F_G + F_H + F_I \leq 3$$

$$F_A + F_B + F_C + F_G + F_H + F_I \leq 12$$

$$F_E + F_F + F_J \leq 34$$

$$F_E + F_F + F_H + F_I \leq 37$$

$$F_E + F_K \leq 65$$

$$F_B + F_C \geq 9$$

$$F_H + F_I \geq 3$$

$$1.4 \leq F_B \leq 14; 0.9 \leq F_C \leq 9;\ 0.8 \leq F_H \leq 8$$

$$0.3 \leq F_I \leq 3; 3.4 \leq F_E \leq 18; 3.4 \leq F_F \leq 18$$

$$5.5 \leq F_K \leq 55$$

$$F_B + F_C + F_E + F_F + F_H + F_I + F_K = 55$$

$$F_A + F_D + F_G + F_J = 0$$

$$F_B, F_C, F_E, F_F, F_H, F_I, F_K \geq 0$$

The solution to the above linear programming problem is $F_B = 8.1$; $F_C = 0.9$; $F_E = 18$; $F_F = 3.4$; $F_H = 2.7$, $F_I = 0.3$; and $F_K = 21.6$. This means that a slack of 8.1 weeks is assigned to activity *B* and 0.9 weeks to activity *C*. Activities *E* and F are assigned a slack of 18 and 3.4 weeks respectively. Activity *H* is assigned a slack of 2.7 weeks, 0.3 weeks are assigned to activity *I*, and activity *K* is assigned the greatest slack, 21.6 weeks. The method adopted for allocating the costs and the floats, the Core, ensures that the activities that form a coalition remain active in the coalition.

Chapter 5
Dynamic Programming

Of all mathematics techniques employed in Operations Research, dynamic programming is perhaps the simplest in concept and one of the most difficult to apply. One of the difficulties in applying dynamic programming is the lack of a clear-cut formulation and solution algorithm (Shamblin and Steven, 1974). As a result, each problem requires basic decisions for formulation. Dynamic programming is a technique that can be used to solve many optimization problems that require interrelated solutions, i.e., decisions which must be made in a sequence and which influence future decisions in that sequence. In most applications, dynamic programming obtains solutions by working backwards from the beginning, thus breaking a large, unwieldy problem into a series of smaller, more tractable problems. In this chapter, we begin by introducing the dynamic programming recursion and apply it to a multi-project investment problem. Next, the time-cost trade-off problem will be revisited using dynamic programming.

Dynamic Programming

The following characteristics are common to most applications of dynamic programming (Shamblin and Steven, 1974; Winston, 2003):

1. The problem can be divided into stages with a decision required at each stage. The stage is the amount of time that has elapsed since the beginning of the problem.

2. Each stage has a number of states associated with it. By a state we mean the information that is needed at any stage to make an optimal decision.

3. The decision chosen at any stage describes how the state at the current stage is transformed into the state at the next stage. In many problems, a decision does not determine the next stage's state with certainty; instead,

the current decision only determines the probability distribution of the state at the next stage.

4. Given the current state, the optimal decision for each of the remaining stages must not depend on previously reached states or previously chosen decisions. This idea is known as the principle of optimality.

5. If the states for the problem have been classified into one of T stages, there must be a recursion that relates the cost (or reward) incurred during stages $t, t+1, \ldots, T$ to the cost (or reward) incurred from stages $t+1, \ldots, T$. In essence, the recursion formalizes the working-backwards procedure:

$$f_t(i) = \min_j \left\{ c_{ij} + f_{t+1}(j) \right\} \tag{5.1}$$

In many dynamic programming problems a given stage simply consists of all the possible states that the system can occupy at this stage. If this is the case, then the dynamic programming recursion (for a minimization problem) can often be written in the following form (Winston, 2003):

$$f_t(i) = \min \left\{ (\text{cost during stage } t) + f_{t+1}(\text{new state at stage } t+1) \right\} \tag{5.2}$$

where $f_t(i)$ is the minimum cost incurred from stage t to the end of the problem (the problem ends after stage T), given that at stage t the state is i. The minimum in (5.1) is over all decisions that are allowable, or feasible, when the state at stage t is i. Equation (5.1) reflects that fact that the minimum cost incurred from stage t to the end of the problem, must be attained by choosing at stage t an allowable decision that minimizes the sum of the costs incurred during the current stage (stage t) plus the minimum cost that can be incurred from stage $t+1$ to the end of the problem.

Correct formulation of Equation (5.1) requires that we identify three important aspects of the problem:

1. What are the allowable or feasible decisions for the given state and stage? These decisions depend on both t and i.

2. What is the cost (or net profit) incurred (earned) during the current time period t?

3. What will be the state during stage $t+1$?

The cost incurred during the current time period and the state at stage t +1 depends on both the state at stage t, and the decision chosen at stage t.

A Multi-Project Investment Problem

In order to illustrate the dynamic programming formulation, the following multi-project investment problem is considered.

A company has €5 million to invest, and three projects are available. If x_j dollars are invested in project j (the amount planned in each investment must be an exact multiple of €1 million), then a net present value of $n_j\left(x_j\right)$ is obtained. The $n_j\left(x_j\right)$'s for each project are as follows.

Project 1 $n_1\left(x_1\right) = 5x_1 + 3$

Project 2 $n_2\left(x_2\right) = 6x_2 + 7$

Project 3 $n_3\left(x_3\right) = 7x_4 + 5$

$$n_1\left(0\right) = n_2\left(0\right) = n_3\left(0\right) = 0$$

How should the company allocate the €5 million in order to maximize the net present value of the investment? To formulate this problem as a dynamic programming problem we begin by defining the stage and the state. We define stage t to represent a case where funds must be allocated to investments $t, t+1, \ldots, 3$. The stage should be chosen so that when one stage remains the problem is easy to solve. At any stage, the state is the amount of money available for investments $t, t+1, \ldots, 3$. Since we can never have more than €5 million available, the possible states at any stage are 0, 1, 2, 3, 4, and 5. Let $f_t\left(d_t\right)$ be the maximum net present value that can be obtained by investing d_t million dollars in investments $t, t+1, \ldots, 3$, and $x_t\left(d_t\right)$ be the amount that should be invested in investment t to obtain $f_t\left(d_t\right)$. We start by computing $f_3\left(0\right), f_3\left(1\right), \ldots, f_3\left(5\right)$ and then determine $f_2\left(0\right), f_2\left(1\right), \ldots, f_2\left(5\right)$. We terminate the computations by computing $f_1\left(5\right)$.

STAGE 3

We first determine $f_3\left(0\right), f_3\left(1\right), \ldots, f_3\left(5\right)$, investing all available money (d_3) in project 3 as shown in Table 5.1

Table 5.1 Computations for $f_3(d_3)$

x_3	$f_3(d_3)$	$n_3(x_3) = 7x_4 + 5$
0	$f_3(0)$	$n_3(0) = 0$
1	$f_3(1)$	$n_3(1) = 12$
2	$f_3(2)$	$n_3(2) = 19$
3	$f_3(3)$	$n_3(3) = 26$
4	$f_3(4)$	$n_3(4) = 33$
5	$f_3(5)$	$n_3(5) = 40$

STAGE 2

Since x_2 is the amount invested in project 2, a net present value of $n_2(x_2)$ will be obtained from project 2, and a net present value of $f_3(d_2 - x_2)$ will be obtained from project 3. The computations for $f_2(d_2)$ are given in Table 5.2.

Table 5.2 Computations for $f_2(d_2)$

d_2	x_2	$n_2(x_2) = 6x_2 + 7$	$f_3(d_2 - x_2)$	NPV	$(f_2(d_2); x_2(d_2))$
0	0	$n_2(0) = 0$	$f_3(0) = 0$	0	$(0;0)$
1	0	$n_2(0) = 0$	$f_3(1) = 12$	12	
1	1	$n_2(1) = 13$	$f_3(0) = 0$	13	$(13;1)$
2	0	$n_2(0) = 0$	$f_3(2) = 19$	19	
2	1	$n_2(1) = 13$	$f_3(1) = 12$	25	$(25;1)$
2	2	$n_2(2) = 19$	$f_3(0) = 0$	19	
3	0	$n_2(0) = 0$	$f_3(3) = 26$	26	
3	1	$n_2(1) = 13$	$f_3(2) = 19$	32	$(32;1)$

Table 5.2 *Concluded*

3	2	$n_2(2) = 19$	$f_3(1) = 12$	31	
3	3	$n_2(3) = 25$	$f_3(0) = 0$	25	
4	0	$n_2(0) = 0$	$f_3(4) = 33$	33	
4	1	$n_2(1) = 13$	$f_3(3) = 26$	39	$(39;1)$
4	2	$n_2(2) = 19$	$f_3(2) = 19$	38	
4	3	$n_2(3) = 25$	$f_3(1) = 12$	37	
4	4	$n_2(4) = 31$	$f_3(0) = 0$	31	
5	0	$n_2(0) = 0$	$f_3(5) = 40$	40	
5	1	$n_2(1) = 13$	$f_3(4) = 33$	46	$(46;1)$
5	2	$n_2(2) = 19$	$f_3(3) = 26$	45	
5	3	$n_2(3) = 25$	$f_3(2) = 19$	44	
5	4	$n_2(4) = 31$	$f_3(1) = 12$	43	
5	5	$n_2(5) = 37$	$f_3(0) = 0$	37	

STAGE 1

Since the amount invested in project 1 is x_1, a net present value of $n_1(x_1)$ will be obtained from project 1, and a net present value of $f_2(d_1 - x_1)$ will be obtained from project 2. The computations for $f_1(5)$ are given in Table 5.3.

Table 5.3 Computations for $f_1(5)$

d_1	x_1	$n_1(x_1) = 5x_1 + 3$	$f_2(d_1 - x_1)$	NPV	$(f_1(5); x_1(5))$
5	0	$n_1(0) = 0$	$f_2(5) = 46$	46	
5	1	$n_1(1) = 8$	$f_2(4) = 39$	47	$(47;1)$
5	2	$n_1(2) = 13$	$f_2(3) = 32$	45	
5	3	$n_1(3) = 18$	$f_2(2) = 25$	43	
5	4	$n_1(4) = 23$	$f_2(1) = 13$	36	
5	5	$n_1(5) = 28$	$f_2(0) = 0$	28	

Since $x_1(5) = 1$, the company invests €1 million in project 1. This leaves €5 - €1 = €4 million for project 2 and 3. Then, the company should invest $x_2(4) = 1$ million in project 2 and €3 million in project 3, $x_3(3) = 3$. Therefore, the company can obtain a maximum net present value of $f_1(5) = \$47$million.

Dynamic Programming Formulation of the Time-Cost Trade-off Problem

One cannot find many models regarding dynamic project scheduling in the literature. Actually, as the classical definition of project indicates, it is a one-time job which consists of several activities. Therefore, most of the models representing the project scheduling in the literature are static (Azaron and Tavakkoli-Moghaddam, 2006).

Butcher (1967) presents a dynamic programming model to solve the time-cost trade-off when the project networks are pure series and pure parallel. The recursive equations for the series and parallel cases are respectively:

$$g_i(z) = \min\{g_{i-1}(z - z_i) + h_i(z_i)\} \tag{5.3}$$

and

$$g_i(z) = \min\{\max\{g_{i-1}(z - z_i), h_i(z_i)\}\} \tag{5.4}$$

where z_i ($z = 0,\ldots,b$) is the budget allocated to activity i; $h_i(z_i)$ is the least time in which activity i can be executed with budget z_i; and $g_i(z)$ is the least time to execute activities 1 through i with budget z.

Robinson (1975) presents the following conceptual dynamic programming framework for solving the time-cost trade-off problem in general project networks:

$$g(z) = \min\left\{\max_{1\le p\le q}\left\{\sum_{i\in L(p)} h_i(z_i)\right\}\right\};\ \forall\ z = 0,\ldots,b \tag{5.5}$$

where q is the number of complete paths through the project network; $L(p)$ is the set of nodes of path p; and $g(z)$ is the least time in which the project can be executed with budget z. Robinson (1975) provides a sufficient condition under which the problem in Equation (5.5) will recursively decompose into a single-dimensional problem as in Equation (5.3) and Equation (5.4). However, the author recognizes the multidimensionality problem which arises when Equation (5.5) does not decompose. The work of Bein et al. (1992) on optimal reduction of two-terminal directed acyclic networks provides an alternative way to implement Robinson's dynamic programming framework (Elmaghraby, 1993; De et al., 1995).

Hinderlang and Muth (1979) provide a complete dynamic programming formulation. The basic recursion of the model is given by:

$$e_i(s) = \min_{1\le j\le a(i)}\left\{\left[\sum_{k\in S_{(i)}} e_k\left(s + t_{ij}\right)\right] + c_{ij}\right\};\ \text{for } \underline{s}_i \le s \le \overline{s}_i \tag{5.6}$$

where $e_i(s)$ is the minimum cost of realizing node i and all of its successors such that node i starts at time s and that all nodes complete by time d.

Panagiotakopoulos (1977) presents a different approach focusing primarily on problem simplification. Given a due date, the approach makes repeated passes through the network, updating the estimates of the activity start and finish times, until the number of feasible alternatives for the activities cannot be reduced any further. Azaron and Tavakkoli-Moghaddam (2006) develop a multi-objective model for the time-cost trade-off problem in a dynamic PERT network. The authors consider a service centre serving various projects with the same structure. Each dynamic PERT network is represented as a network of queues, where the service times represent the durations of the corresponding activities and the arrival stream to each node follows a Poisson process with the generation rate of new projects.

Next, the dynamic programming model presented by De et al. (1995) to solve the time-cost trade-off is shown and illustrated with an example. Let a $(k+1)$-tuple, φ_k, (a list of $k+1$ elements enclosed with $\langle$ and $\rangle$), represents the stage of the dynamic program when the node k is being considered (call it stage k). For each node i, $i < k$, that has an immediate successor r such that $r > k$, let the finish time f_i of i be recorded in the $i_{\text{-th}}$ element in φ_k. Let the finish time f_k of k be recorded in the $k_{\text{-th}}$ element and the minimum cost e_k of executing activities 1 through k, given the first k elements of φ_k be recorded in the $(k+1)_{-st}$ element; all other elements of φ_k are unspecified (and represented by $\bullet$). Let Ω_k represent the set of all tuples φ_k at stage k. Initialize the dynamic program with $\Omega_0 \equiv \{\langle 0,0 \rangle\}$ and for stages $k = 1,\ldots,n+1$, do as follows: for each tuple $\varphi_{k-1} \in \Omega_{k-1}$, create $m(k)$ new tuples such that the first k-1 elements of the $j_{\text{-th}}$ tuple φ_k are the same as those of φ_{k-1} and the $k_{\text{-th}}$ and element $(k+1)_{-st}$ elements are computed as

$$f_k = \max_{i \in P(k)} \{f_i\} + t_{kj} \tag{5.7}$$

and $e_k = e_{k-1} + c_{kj}$ respectively. For each newly created tuple, φ_k, retain each element i, $i = 1,\ldots,k-1$, that is necessary for the state description at stage k. Once all new tuples are created at stage k, iteratively eliminate any tuple φ_k' for which there is another tuple φ_k such that $f_i \le f_i'$ for all $i = 1,\ldots,k$ at which the $i_{\text{-th}}$ element is specified, and $e_k \le e_k'$ (break ties arbitrarily). The set of tuples Ω_{n+1} retained at the end of stage $n+1$ delivers Ω, the solution to the time-cost trade-off problem.

The network shown in Figure 5.1 is used to illustrate the method. Table 5.4 shows the sets of time-cost alternatives for the activities of the project and the set of tuples that has survived at the end of stage k in the example is shown in Table 5.5 for all k ($k = 0, 1,\ldots,n+1$). Note that a tuple at stage 2 is given by $\langle \cdot, f_1, f_2, e_2 \rangle$, whereas at stage 3 is given by $\langle \cdot, \cdot, f_2, f_3, e_3 \rangle$.

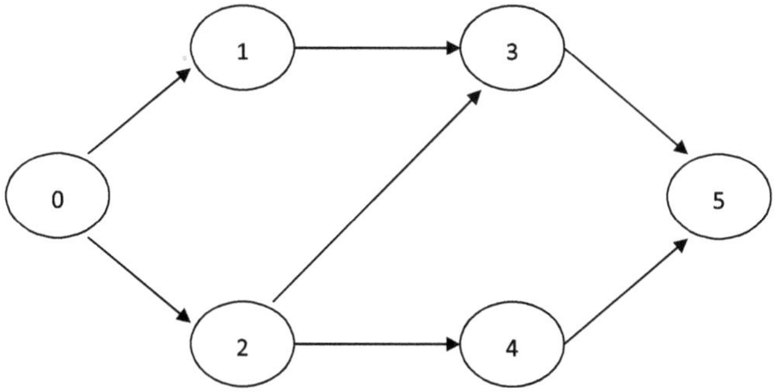

Figure 5.1 **Network associated to the project**

Table 5.4 **Sets of time-cost alternatives ($\langle \text{Time, Cost} \rangle$) for the activities**

Node	Alternative 1	Alternative 2
0	$\langle 0,0 \rangle$	$\langle 0,0 \rangle$
1	$\langle 1,20 \rangle$	$\langle 2,10 \rangle$
2	$\langle 2,6 \rangle$	$\langle 3,3 \rangle$
3	$\langle 1,12 \rangle$	$\langle 3,6 \rangle$
4	$\langle 3,10 \rangle$	$\langle 4,6 \rangle$
5	$\langle 0,0 \rangle$	$\langle 0,0 \rangle$

Take the tuple $\langle \cdot,1,2,26 \rangle$ from stage 2. At stage 3 from this tuple, we will first create the tuples:

$$\langle \cdot,1,2,\max\{1,2\}+1,26+12 \rangle$$

and

$$\langle \cdot,1,2,\max\{1,2\}+3,26+6 \rangle$$

corresponding to the set of time-cost alternatives $\langle 1,12 \rangle$ and $\langle 3,6 \rangle$ for activity 3. Since f_1 is no longer needed for the state description at stage 3, we will rewrite the newly created tuple as $\langle \cdot,\cdot,2,3,38 \rangle$ and $\langle \cdot,\cdot,2,5,32 \rangle$. Similarly, from $\langle \cdot,2,2,16 \rangle$, and $\langle \cdot,2,3,13 \rangle$, we will later create the tuples $\langle \cdot,\cdot,2,3,28 \rangle$, $\langle \cdot,\cdot,2,5,22 \rangle$

, $\langle \cdot,\cdot,3,4,25 \rangle$, and $\langle \cdot,\cdot,3,6,19 \rangle$. Note that these tuples force the elimination of the tuples $\langle \cdot,\cdot,2,3,38 \rangle$, $\langle \cdot,\cdot,2,5,32 \rangle$, $\langle \cdot,\cdot,3,4,35 \rangle$, and $\langle \cdot,\cdot,3,6,29 \rangle$ respectively.

Table 5.5 Set of tuples at the end of stage 1, 2, 3, 4, and 5

Stage	Tuple representation	Completely representative set of non-dominated tuples		
0	$\langle f_0, e_0 \rangle$			
		$\langle 0,0 \rangle$	$\langle 0,0 \rangle$	
1	$\langle f_0, f_1, e_1 \rangle$			
	$\langle 1,20 \rangle ; \langle 2,10 \rangle$	$\langle 0,1,20 \rangle$	$\langle \cdot,1,20 \rangle$	
		$\langle 0,2,10 \rangle$	$\langle \cdot,2,10 \rangle$	
2	$\langle \cdot, f_1, f_2, e_2 \rangle$			
	$\langle 2,6 \rangle ; \langle 3,3 \rangle$	$\langle \cdot,1,2,20+6 \rangle$	$\langle \cdot,1,2,26 \rangle$	
		$\langle \cdot,1,3,20+3 \rangle$	$\langle \cdot,1,3,23 \rangle$	
		$\langle \cdot,2,2,10+6 \rangle$	$\langle \cdot,2,2,16 \rangle$	
		$\langle \cdot,2,3,10+3 \rangle$	$\langle \cdot,2,3,13 \rangle$	
3	$\langle \cdot,\cdot, f_2, f_3, e_3 \rangle$			
	$\langle 1,12 \rangle ; \langle 3,6 \rangle$	$\langle \cdot,1,2,\max\{1,2\}+1,26+12 \rangle$	$\langle \cdot,1,2,3,38 \rangle$	$\langle \cdot,\cdot,2,3,38 \rangle$
		$\langle \cdot,1,2,\max\{1,2\}+3,26+6 \rangle$	$\langle \cdot,1,2,5,32 \rangle$	$\langle \cdot,\cdot,2,5,32 \rangle$
		$\langle \cdot,1,3,\max\{1,3\}+1,23+12 \rangle$	$\langle \cdot,1,3,4,35 \rangle$	$\langle \cdot,\cdot,3,4,35 \rangle$
		$\langle \cdot,1,3,\max\{1,3\}+3,23+6 \rangle$	$\langle \cdot,1,3,6,29 \rangle$	$\langle \cdot,\cdot,3,6,29 \rangle$
		$\langle \cdot,2,2,\max\{2,2\}+1,16+12 \rangle$	$\langle \cdot,2,2,3,28 \rangle$	$\langle \cdot,\cdot,2,3,28 \rangle$
		$\langle \cdot,2,2,\max\{2,2\}+3,16+6 \rangle$	$\langle \cdot,2,2,5,22 \rangle$	$\langle \cdot,\cdot,2,5,22 \rangle$

Table 5.5 *Concluded*

Stage	Tuple representation	Completely representative set of non-dominated tuples		
		$\langle \cdot, 2, 3, \max\{2,3\} + 1, 13 + 12 \rangle$	$\langle \cdot, 2, 3, 4, 25 \rangle$	$\langle \cdot, \cdot, 3, 4, 25 \rangle$
		$\langle \cdot, 2, 3, \max\{2,3\} + 3, 13 + 6 \rangle$	$\langle \cdot, 2, 3, 6, 19 \rangle$	$\langle \cdot, \cdot, 3, 6, 19 \rangle$
4	$\langle \cdot, \cdot, \cdot, f_3, f_4, e_4 \rangle$			
	$\langle 3, 10 \rangle ; \langle 4, 6 \rangle$	$\langle \cdot, \cdot, 2, 3, 2 + 3, 28 + 10 \rangle$	$\langle \cdot, \cdot, 2, 3, 5, 38 \rangle$	$\langle \cdot, \cdot, \cdot, 3, 5, 38 \rangle$
		$\langle \cdot, \cdot, 2, 3, 2 + 4, 28 + 6 \rangle$	$\langle \cdot, \cdot, 2, 3, 6, 34 \rangle$	$\langle \cdot, \cdot, \cdot, 3, 6, 34 \rangle$
		$\langle \cdot, \cdot, 2, 5, 2 + 3, 22 + 10 \rangle$	$\langle \cdot, \cdot, 2, 5, 5, 32 \rangle$	$\langle \cdot, \cdot, \cdot, 5, 5, 32 \rangle$
		$\langle \cdot, \cdot, 2, 5, 2 + 4, 22 + 6 \rangle$	$\langle \cdot, \cdot, 2, 5, 6, 28 \rangle$	$\langle \cdot, \cdot, \cdot, 5, 6, 28 \rangle$
		$\langle \cdot, \cdot, 3, 4, 3 + 3, 25 + 10 \rangle$	$\langle \cdot, \cdot, 3, 4, 6, 35 \rangle$	$\langle \cdot, \cdot, \cdot, 4, 6, 35 \rangle$
		$\langle \cdot, \cdot, 3, 4, 3 + 4, 25 + 6 \rangle$	$\langle \cdot, \cdot, 3, 4, 7, 31 \rangle$	$\langle \cdot, \cdot, \cdot, 4, 7, 31 \rangle$
		$\langle \cdot, \cdot, 3, 6, 3 + 3, 19 + 10 \rangle$	$\langle \cdot, \cdot, 3, 6, 6, 29 \rangle$	$\langle \cdot, \cdot, \cdot, 6, 6, 29 \rangle$
		$\langle \cdot, \cdot, 3, 6, 3 + 4, 19 + 6 \rangle$	$\langle \cdot, \cdot, 3, 6, 7, 25 \rangle$	$\langle \cdot, \cdot, \cdot, 6, 7, 25 \rangle$
5	$\langle \bullet, \bullet, \bullet, \bullet, \bullet, f_5, e_5 \rangle$			
	$\langle 0, 0 \rangle$	$\langle \cdot, \cdot, \cdot, 5, 5, \max\{5,5\} + 0, 32 + 0 \rangle$	$\langle \cdot, \cdot, \cdot, 5, 5, 5, 32 \rangle$	$\langle \cdot, \cdot, \cdot, \cdot, \cdot, 5, 32 \rangle$
		$\langle \cdot, \cdot, \cdot, 6, 6, \max\{6,6\} + 0, 28 + 0 \rangle$	$\langle \cdot, \cdot, \cdot, 6, 6, 6, 28 \rangle$	$\langle \cdot, \cdot, \cdot, \cdot, \cdot, 6, 28 \rangle$
		$\langle \cdot, \cdot, \cdot, 6, 7, \max\{6,7\} + 0, 25 + 0 \rangle$	$\langle \cdot, \cdot, \cdot, 6, 7, 7, 25 \rangle$	$\langle \cdot, \cdot, \cdot, \cdot, \cdot, 7, 25 \rangle$

Chapter 6
Forecasting Models

Forecasting is a critical component of Project Management. The effectiveness of project control relies on the capability of project managers to make reliable forecasts in a timely manner. Project managers must be able to make reliable predictions about the final outcome of projects and such predictions need to be constantly revised and compared with the project's outcomes. Currently available methods, such as the Critical Path Method or the Earned Value Management are deterministic and fail to account for the inherent uncertainty in forecasting and project performance. In this chapter we begin presenting two forecasting methods, the linear regression method and the grey method. Then, the Earned Value management method is introduced.

Forecasting

As anyone has no doubt experienced, it seems that almost all projects, especially large projects, tend to be completed late and over-budget. For controlling both completion time and cost, project managers must be able to make reliable predictions in a timely manner about the final duration and cost of projects. Such predictions need to be revised and compared with the project's objective to obtain early warnings against potential problems to provide effective corrective actions.

When project durations and costs are forecasted before the project begins, the process is carried out as a part of project planning, once the project get started the process is carried out as a part of project tracking. Such predictions need to be revised and compared with scheduled completion and the available budget in order to complete the project on time and within budget. There is not a viable alternative to forecasting in Project Management, so we need to try to make the best, most cost-effective forecasts possible, keeping efficiency and quality in mind (Pollack-Johnson, 1995).

The limits of deterministic approaches and the need for probabilistic models in engineering and management decision-making have been repeatedly addressed over the last four decades (Ang and Tang, 1975; Barraza et al., 2004; Hertz, 1979; Spooner, 1974). Traditional approaches such as CPM and PERT are deterministic and do not provide forecasting methods that are consistently applicable to both schedule and cost predictions. CPM ignores uncertainty of the duration of the activities, which is more likely to cause overall delays. PERT provides a semi-probabilistic evaluation of project duration. However, PERT has been criticized for systematic underestimation due to neglecting the influence of near-critical paths. Unfortunately, in the most common version of PERT only the path(s) of critical activities (using expected durations) are analysed probabilistically, and so, possible dependencies between activities are ignored.

Forecasting in Project Management is motivated by several reasons (Kim, 2007): (i) the presence of uncertainty in both future project performance and current performance measure, (ii) the lack of reliable and consistent forecasting tools available to project managers, and (iii) the lack of a comprehensive and integrative forecasting framework which integrates all the information relevant to project performance predictions such as detailed project plans, subjective knowledge from project managers' hand-on experiences, and measurement errors.

Typically, three alternatives are available for project managers to update the original estimates, depending on the decision-maker's perception of the relationship between past and future performance (PMI Box Guide, 2004): (i) forecasting based on the original estimate; (ii) forecasting based on a new estimate; and (iii) forecasting based on the original estimate modified by past performance information. The first two approaches referred to as 'estimate forecasting' are valid only when any actual performance data observed from a project is considered irrelevant to the future performance of remaining jobs. In such cases, the remaining work is considered a separate project. In the third case, referred to as projective forecasting, project duration and cost at completion are updated using both the original estimate and actual performance data up to the time of forecasting.

Linear Regression

Simple linear regression can be used to estimate the value of a dependent variable, i.e. time, from the value of an independent variable, i.e. cost. In this section, simple linear regression technique will be used for the verification of the Bromilow's time-cost relationship. Bromilow (1974) developed a model which predicts project time in form of the formula:

$$T = KC^B \tag{6.1}$$

where T is the duration of construction period (dependent variable); C is the final cost of building in millions of euros (independent variable); K is a constant describing the general level of time performance for a 1 million euros project; and B is a constant describing how the time performance is affected by project size as measured by cost. Different versions of the time-cost model are shown in Table 6.1.

Table 6.1 Bromilow's, Ireland's, and Chan's time-cost models

Bromilow's model (1974)	Ireland's model (1983)	Chan's model (1999)
$T = 313C^{0.3}$	$T = 219C^{0.47}$	$T = 269C^{0.32}$

In order to model the linear relationship between T and C, Equation (6.1) is rewritten in the natural logarithmic form as:

$$LnT = LnK + BLnC \tag{6.2}$$

Table 6.2 shows time and cost data obtained from a total of 44 projects that will be used to estimate the values of K and B.

Figure 6.1 shows a scatter plot of LnT and LnC relationships. Since a scatter plot is a good means for judging how well a straight line fits the data, there appears to be a strong linear relationship between LnT and LnC, so we can conclude that a straight line fits the data reasonably well.

Table 6.2 Time and cost data obtained from the projects

(Time;Cost)	(Ln*T*;Ln*C*)	(Time;Cost)	(Ln*T*;Ln*C*)	(Time;Cost)	(Ln*T*;Ln*C*)
(351;1.050)	(5.86;0.0487)	(376;1.300)	(5.93;0.262)	(380;1.600)	(5.94;0.470)
(340;1.100)	(5.83;0.095)	(388;1.300)	(5.96;0.262)	(354;1.600)	(5.87;0.470)
(358;1.100)	(5.88;0.095)	(354;1.350)	(5.87;0.300)	(372;1.650)	(5.92;0.501)
(376;1.100)	(5.93;0.095)	(372;1.400)	(5.92;0.336)	(392;1.700)	(5.97;0.531)
(369;1.100)	(5.91;0.095)	(392;1.450)	(5.97;0.372)	(407;1.700)	(6.01;0.531)
(340;1.150)	(5.83;0.140)	(358;1.450)	(5.88;0.372)	(369;1.750)	(5.91;0.560)
(365;1.20)	(5.90;0.182)	(384;1.500)	(5.95;0.405)	(384;1.800)	(5.95;0.560)
(351;1.20)	(5.86;0.182)	(369;1.500)	(5.91;0.405)	(399;1.900)	(5.99;0.588)
(380;1.900)	(5.94;0642)	(407;1.900)	(6.01;0.642)	(392;2.000)	(5.97;0.693)
(372;2.000)	(5.92;0.693)	(407;2.100)	(6.01;0.742)	(380;2.100)	(5.94;0.742)
(395;2.200)	(5.98;0.788)	(420;2.200)	(6.04;0.788)	(372;2.200)	(5.92;0.788)
(388;2.300)	(5.96;0.833)	(416;2.400)	(6.03;0.875)	(428;2.400)	(6.06;0.875)
(441;2.400)	(6.09;0.875)	(392;2.500)	(5.97;0.916)	(420;2.600)	(6.04;0.956)
(441;2.600)	(6.09;0.956)	(395;2.700)	(5.98;0.993)	(433;2.800)	(6.07;1.030)
(412;2.900)	(6.02;1.065)	(437;3.000)	(6.08;1.099)		

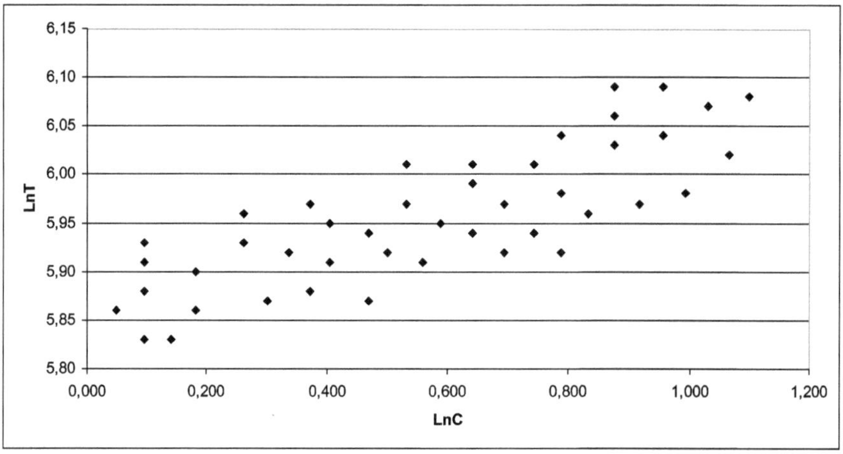

Figure 6.1 Scatter plot of *LnT* and *LnC*

Equation (6.2) is similar to the linear model:

$$Y_i = \beta_0 + \beta_1 X_i \quad (6.3)$$

Suppose we estimate $\beta_0(LnK)$ using $\hat{\beta}_0$ and estimate $\beta_1(B)$ by using $\hat{\beta}_1$. Then, our prediction for $Y_i(LnT)$ is given by:

$$\hat{Y}_i = \hat{\beta}_0 + \hat{\beta}_1 X_i \tag{6.4}$$

the least square regression line. Next, we define e_i, the error or residual for data point i:

e_i = (actual Y_i)- (predicted Y_i) = $Y_i - \hat{\beta}_0 - \hat{\beta}_1 X_i$

We now choose $\hat{\beta}_0$ and $\hat{\beta}_1$ to minimize $\sum e_i^2$

$$F\left(\hat{\beta}_0, \hat{\beta}_1\right) = \sum e_i^2 = \sum \left(Y_i - \hat{\beta}_0 - \hat{\beta}_1 X_i\right)^2 \tag{6.5}$$

The values $\hat{\beta}_0$ and $\hat{\beta}_1$ minimizing $\sum e_i^2$ are called the least squares estimates of β_0 and β_1. We find $\hat{\beta}_0$ and $\hat{\beta}_1$ by setting

$$\frac{\partial F}{\partial \hat{\beta}_0} = \frac{\partial F}{\partial \hat{\beta}_1} = 0 \tag{6.6}$$

The resulting values of $\hat{\beta}_0$ and $\hat{\beta}_1$ are given by:

$$\hat{\beta}_1 = \frac{\sum \left(X_i - \bar{X}\right)\left(Y_i - \bar{Y}\right)}{\sum \left(X_i - \bar{X}\right)^2} \tag{6.7}$$

$$\hat{\beta}_0 = \bar{Y} - \hat{\beta}_1 \bar{X} \tag{6.8}$$

where $\bar{X}$ is the average value of all $x_{i's}$ and $\bar{Y}$ is the average value of all $y_{i's}$. From the data in Table 6.2 we have:

$\bar{X} = \sum x_i = 0.57$ and $\bar{Y} = \sum y_i = 5.96$

$$\hat{\beta}_1 = \frac{\sum \left(X_i - \bar{X}\right)\left(Y_i - \bar{Y}\right)}{\sum \left(X_i - \bar{X}\right)^2} = \frac{0.733}{4.065} = 0.1802$$

$$\hat{\beta}_0 = \bar{Y} - \hat{\beta}_1 \bar{X} = 5.96 - 0.1802 * 0.57 = 5.854$$

Then, our least square line is

$$\hat{Y} = 5.854 + 0.1802X$$

$$LnT = LnK + BLnC \Rightarrow \begin{cases} LnK = 5.854 \Rightarrow K = 348.6 \\ B = 0.1802 \end{cases} \Rightarrow T = 348.6C^{0.1802}$$

which means that it takes 348.6 days to complete a project with a contract sum of €1 million.

An important part of this statistical procedure that derives models from empirical data is to indicate how well the model actually fits, or its goodness of fit. A commonly used measure of the goodness of fit of a linear model is R^2, or the coefficient of determination. This coefficient of determination is defined by

$$R^2 = \frac{SSR}{SST} \tag{6.9}$$

percentage of variation in the dependent variable (Y) explained by the independent variable (X).

$$1 - R^2 = \frac{SSE}{SST} \tag{6.10}$$

percentage of variation in the dependent variable (Y) not explained by the independent variable (X).

where

SSE is the sum of square error $= \sum e_i^2 = \sum \left(Y_i - \hat{Y}_i\right)^2$. A small SSE indicates that the least square line fits the data well.

SST is the sum of square total $= \sum \left(Y_i - \bar{Y}\right)^2$. It measures the total variation of Y_i about its mean.

SSR is the sum of square regression $= \sum \left(\hat{Y}_i - \bar{Y}\right)^2$

$$SST = SSR + SSE \tag{6.11}$$

If all the observations fall on the regression line, R^2 is 1. If there is no linear relationship between the dependent and independent variable, R^2 is 0. For our problem,

$SSE = 0.072$; $SST = 0.204$; and $SSR = 0.132$

$$R^2 = \frac{0.132}{0.204} = 0.647$$

$$1 - R^2 = \frac{0.072}{0.204} = 0.353$$

We can conclude that the cost of the project explains 64.7 per cent of the variation in the time to undertake this project.

The standard error of the estimate (*Se*) is also a measure of the accuracy of predictions made with a regression line. If we let *n* = number of observations, the standard error of the estimate (*Se*) is given by

$$Se = \sqrt{\frac{SSE}{n-2}}$$

Approximately 68 per cent of the values of Y_i should be within *Se* of the predicted value $\hat{Y}_i$, and approximately 95 per cent of the values of Y_i will be within 2*Se* of the predicted value $\hat{Y}_i$. Any observation for which Y_i is not within 2*Se* of the predicted value is called an outlier. For our example:

$$Se = \sqrt{\frac{0.072}{44-2}} = 0.0414$$

Using a *t*-test regression we can test the significance of a linear relationship between LnT and LnC. We test:

$H_0 : \beta_1 = 0$ no significance relationship between LnT and LnC

$H_0 : \beta_1 \neq 0$ significance relationship between LnT and LnC

At a level of significance α, we compute the *t*-statistic given by

$$t = \frac{\hat{\beta}_1}{stdErr\left(\hat{\beta}_1\right)}$$

where $stdErr\left(\hat{\beta}_1\right)$ measures our uncertainty in our estimate of β_1. We reject H_0 if $|t| \geq t_{(\alpha/2, n-2)}$. For our example,

$$stdErr\left(\hat{\beta}_1\right) = \frac{Se}{\sqrt{\left(X_i - \overline{X}\right)^2}} = \frac{0.0414}{2.016} = 0.0205$$

Then,

$$t = \frac{0.1802}{0.0205} = 8.79$$

Using $\alpha = 0.01$, we can find from the tables of the t-Distribution $t_{(0.005,42)} = 2.704$, so we reject H_0 and conclude that there is a strong linear relationships between LnC and LnT.

Since the t-value is greater than the table value of t al level of significance of 0.01, therefore the null hypothesis of no relationships is rejected. It is concluded that statistically the time-cost relationship for all the data sampled can be expressed in the form:

$$T = 348.6C^{0.1802}$$

Grey Methodology

The grey system theory, originally presented by Deng (1982, 1989), focuses on model uncertainty and information insufficiency in analysing and understanding systems seeking mathematical relations and movement rules. The grey system puts each stochastic variable as a grey quantity that changes within a given range. It does not rely on statistical method to deal with the grey quantity. It deals directly with original data, and searches the intrinsic governing laws from the available data (Mao and Chirwa, 2006). In the grey system theory there are three systems classified by the degree of information completed. A white system is defined as the case where information in it is fully known; while a black system is defined as the case where information is unknown or nothing in the system is clear. A system with partial information known and partial information unknown is defined as a grey system.

Among the various forecasting models that have been developed, the Grey prediction model requires fewer data and less complicated mathematical calculation. This characteristic is the core of the Grey system theory (Cheng et al., 2011), which has been successfully applied to many fields including wafer fabrication, opto-electronics, electricity costs, integrated circuits, and meteorology (Wu et al., 2012). Additionally, a lot of refined models and combination of other methodologies have been proposed to improve the prediction accuracy and extent of the original grey prediction model.

The GM (1,1) Model

The most commonly used grey forecasting model is GM (1,1) (Deng, 1989), which indicates one variable is employed in the model and the first differential equation is adopted to match the data generated by the accumulation generating operation (AGO). The AGO reveals the hidden regular pattern in the system development and converts a series lacking obvious regularity into a monotonously increasing series to reduce the randomness of the series, and increase the smoothness of the series.

The grey dynamic prediction model should be operated in accordance with the principle of keeping the same dimension of data series. The minimum number of data must be four in consecutive order without bypassing any data (Deng, 1989). That is to say, a new data is attached on tail end of the original data series and the first data in the original data series should be removed before the next forecasting operation. This operation could be performed step-by-step to get a new predicted value for each subsequent period.

Step 1. The raw data series of number $X^{(0)}$ is assumed to be

$$X^{(0)} = \left\{x^{(0)}\left(1\right), x^{(0)}\left(2\right), \ldots, x^{(0)}\left(n\right)\right\} \tag{6.12}$$

where n is the total number of modelling data. This series of number can be selected from the experimental and/or statistical data. These data are fluctuating in a definite range. Some of the factors which cause the variation of the data are known, but some of the factors are unknown.

Step 2. In order to find out the regular patterns, the series of data is treated by 1-AGO:

$$x^{(1)}\left(k\right) = \sum_{i=1}^{k} x^{(0)}\left(i\right) \tag{6.13}$$

so

$$\begin{aligned} x^{(1)}(1) &= x^{(0)}(1) \\ x^{(1)}(2) &= x^{(0)}(1) + x^{(0)}(2) \\ \ldots & \quad \ldots \\ x^{(1)}(n) &= x^{(0)}(1) + x^{(0)}(2) + \ldots + x^{(0)}(n) \end{aligned} \tag{6.14}$$

then, a series of number $X^{(1)}$ is formed

$$X^{(1)} = \left\{x^{(1)}(1), x^{(1)}(2), \ldots, x^{(1)}(n)\right\} \tag{6.15}$$

Step 3. The GM (1,1) model can be constructed by establishing a first order differential equation for $x^{(1)}(k)$ as:

$$\frac{dX^{(1)}}{dt} + aX^{(1)} = u \tag{6.16}$$

where parameters *a* and *u* are called the developing coefficient and grey input, respectively. Equation (6.16) is the GM (1,1) model differential equation with one order and one variable.

$$\frac{dX^{(1)}}{dt} = x^{(1)}(t + \Delta t) - x^{(1)}(t) = x^{(1)}(k) - x^{(1)}(k-1) = x^{(0)}(k) \tag{6.17}$$

In practice parameters *a* and *u* are not calculated directly from Equation (6.16) but the Grey differential equation instead

$$x^{(0)}(k) + aZ^{(1)}(k) = u\,;\; k \geq 2 \tag{6.18}$$

Step 4. Combine $x^{(1)}(k)$ and $x^{(1)}(k-1)$ in the $X^{(1)}$ with the background value and obtain

$$\begin{gathered} Z^{(1)}(k) = \alpha x^{(1)}(k) + (1-\alpha)x^{(1)}(k-1) \\ k \geq 2;\; 0 \leq \alpha \leq 1 \end{gathered} \tag{6.19}$$

where $\alpha = 0.5$ is the most commonly used value.

Step 5. Define the suitable α (see Figure 6.2) with the bisection method and golden section method.

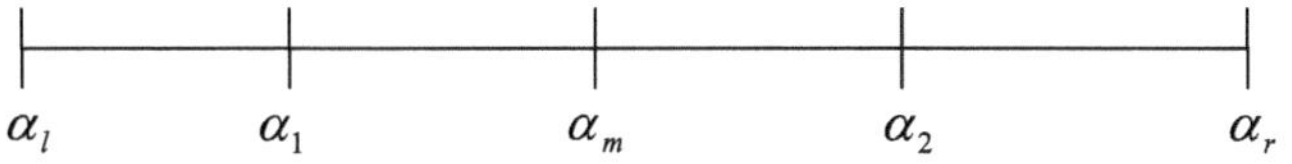

Figure 6.2 **α values**

(i) Set objective: Min Error

$$e^{(0)}(k) = \frac{x^{(0)}(k) - \hat{x}^{(0)}(k)}{x^{(0)}(k)} \quad (6.20)$$

where $e^{(0)}(k)$ is the error rate, $x^{(0)}(k)$ is the actual value, and $\hat{x}^{(0)}(k)$ is the predicted value.

(ii) Decide for the three periods of the *S*-curve the suitable α

Bisection method

$$\alpha_m = \frac{(\alpha_l + \alpha_r)}{2} \quad (6.21)$$

where $\alpha_l = 0$, and $\alpha_r = 1$

Set

$$\alpha_1 = \alpha_l + 0.5 * (\alpha_m - \alpha_l) \quad (6.22)$$

$$\alpha_2 = \alpha_r - 0.5 * (\alpha_r - \alpha_m) \quad (6.23)$$

a) Golden section method

Set

$$\alpha_1 = \alpha_l + 0.382 * (\alpha_m - \alpha_l) \quad (6.24)$$

$$\alpha_2 = \alpha_r - 0.382 * (\alpha_r - \alpha_m) \quad (6.25)$$

Step 6. *a* and *u* can be estimated by the least squares error method as:

$$\hat{a} = \left[a, u\right]^{(T)} = \left(B^T B\right)^{-1} B^T Y \tag{6.26}$$

where

$$B = \begin{bmatrix} -Z^{(1)}\left(2\right) & 1 \\ -Z^{(1)}\left(3\right) & 1 \\ \vdots & \vdots \\ -Z^{(1)}\left(n\right) & 1 \end{bmatrix} \tag{6.27}$$

and

$$Y_N = \left(x^{(0)}\left(2\right), x^{(0)}\left(3\right), \ldots, x^{(0)}\left(n\right)\right)^T \tag{6.28}$$

Step 7. The solution of the differential equation (6.16) is

$$\overline{x}^{(1)}\left(k+1\right) = \left(x^{(0)}\left(1\right) - \frac{u}{a}\right) \exp\left(-ak\right) + \frac{u}{a} \tag{6.29}$$

Then, according to the inverse accumulated generating operation (IAGO), we can get the modelling calculated values $\hat{X}^{(0)}$

$$\hat{X}^{(0)} = \left\{\hat{x}^{(0)}\left(1\right), \hat{x}^{(0)}\left(2\right), \ldots, \hat{x}^{(0)}\left(n\right)\right\} \tag{6.30}$$

where

$$\hat{x}^{(0)}\left(k\right) = x^{(1)}\left(k\right) - x^{(1)}\left(k-1\right), \left(k = 2, 3, \ldots, n\right) \tag{6.31}$$

and

$$\hat{x}^{(1)}\left(1\right) = x^{(0)}\left(1\right) \tag{6.32}$$

Step 8. Calculate the error rate.

If Error α_1 > Error α_2 > takes $\begin{cases} \alpha_l = \alpha_1 \\ \alpha_r = \alpha_r \end{cases}$

If Error α_1 < Error α_2 > takes $\begin{cases} \alpha_l = \alpha_l \\ \alpha_r = \alpha_2 \end{cases}$

Repeat items 5 to 8 until the error rate is less than 0.0001 or the iterations reach 100, and then record the proper α for this interval

Step 9. Continue to calculate the forecasting value, error rate, and α for the subsequent interval

Step 10. Calculate the average α for each case

$$\alpha_{case} = \frac{1}{h}\sum_{p=1}^{h} \alpha_p \tag{6.33}$$

where α_{case} is the average α of each case, and $\alpha_p = \alpha$ of each interval in each case.

An error measure is used to assess the accuracy in terms of closeness of fit as well as to provide a basis for model performance evaluation. The evaluation criterion to measure the per cent of prediction accuracy is the mean absolute percentage error (MAPE):

$$MAPE = \frac{1}{n}\sum_{k=1}^{n} \frac{\left| x^{(0)}(k) - \hat{x}^{(0)}(k) \right|}{x^{(0)}(k)} \tag{6.34}$$

Lower MAPE values are better because they indicate that smaller percentage errors are produced by a forecasting model. Following Lewis (1982), less than 10 per cent is highly accurate forecasting. Values between 10 per cent and 20 per cent, between 20 per cent and 50 per cent, and higher than 50 per cent are considered indicators of high, average, and low prediction accuracy, respectively.

The proposed model can be a useful tool for project managers in controlling and revising the gap between the estimated and actual S-curve during the course of a project. It is assumed that the profile of the cumulative cost versus elapsed time on projects takes the shape of an S-curve. The reason is that projects start slowly when the resources necessarily need to set up, and then projects start to accelerate once all resources have been acquired (Kaka, 1999; Kenley and Wilson, 1986). S-curves are usually taken as expression of project progress and have become a requisite tool for engineering managers through their execution phase (Lin et al., 2012).

Various mathematical formula forms for S-curves have been developed (Berny and Howes, 1982; Miskawi, 1989; Tuker, 1988; Lin et al., 2012). Kenley and Wilson (1986) proposed an ideographic methodology to build individual construction project cash flows model based on the logit transformation approach. Skitmore (1998) utilized three approaches, analytic, synthetic, and hybrid, in combination with six alternative models to determine the best approach/model combination for the available data and forecasts for future expenditure flows. Kaka (1999) used a stochastic model based on historical data with logit transformation technique to incorporate variability and inaccuracy in their forecasts and decision-making. Barraza et al., (2000) developed stochastic S-curves to provide probability distributions of budgeted cost and planned elapsed time for a given percentage of progress in order to evaluate cost and time variations. Hwee and Tiong (2002) developed an S-curve profile model from cost-schedule integration equipped with progressive construction-data feedback mechanisms. Mavrotas et al., (2005) modelled cash flows based on a bottom-up approach from a single contract to the entire organization with an S-curve based on a conventional non-linear regression model. Blyth and Kaka (2006) proposed a model that standardized activities to produce an individual S-curve for an individual project using a multiple linear regression model. Chao and Chien (2009) proposed an empirical method for estimating project S-curves that combined a succinct cubic polynomial function and a neural network model based on existing S-curve formulas and attributes of the project. Cheng and Roy (2011) proposed an evolutionary fuzzy decision model for cash flow prediction using time-dependent support vector machines and S-curves. Cheng et al., (2011) proposed a progress payment forecasting approach using S-curves for the construction phase. The authors improve the traditional grey prediction model by applying the golden section and bisection method to build a short-interval cost-forecasting model. Maravas and Pantouvakis (2012) developed an S-surface cash flow model based on fuzzy set theory to predict the working capital requirements of projects. Lin et al., (2012) proposed a construction project progress forecasting approach which combines the grey dynamic prediction model and the residual modified model to forecast the current project progress during the construction phase. Chen et al., (2013) estimated project's profitability at completion using a multivariate robust regression model to test how well the key variables in project initiation and planning phases predict project profitability.

The literature review suggests that S-curves can be used for several purposes, as a target against which the actual progress of the project can be evaluated at any point in time to monitor whether the project is on schedule (Cheng et al., 2011), to forecast the likely duration of the project once the contract price and cumulative expenditure are known, and even to manage cash flow, current performance status, future necessary cost/duration, etc. for running projects (Tuker, 1988; Barraza et al., 2000; Blyth and Kaka, 2006; Lin et al., 2012).

The common methodology for predicting S-curve forecasting models has been based on classifying projects into groups and producing a standard curve for each group simply by fitting one curve into historical data using the multiple linear regression technique (Blyth and Kaka, 2006; Kaka, 1999; Kaka and Price, 1993; Skitmore, 1998). Given that the total value and duration of the projects to be constructed are known, these models could be used to forecast the cumulative monthly value/cost of that project (Blyth and Kaka, 2006). However, previous attempts to forecast S-curves have not been accurate for two reasons (Blyth and Kaka, 2006; Lin et al., 2012). First, every project is unique and the progress of work varies greatly from one project to another, hence attempts to standardize the cost/value relationship is likely to fail (Kenley and Wilson, 1986; Kaka, 1999). Secondly, the individual characteristics of a group may vary from situation to situation and could display a variety of S-curves due to uncertain factors.

There are limitations that existed in the previous studies at developing models to forecast S-curves. Traditional regression models taken to fit individual projects could not be well fitted. These methods require a large amount of data and make many strict assumptions regarding statistical distribution of data. Few data, extreme values, emerging changes, classifications of projects, uncertainties and uniqueness always exist in the project engineering environment. They could be the biggest weakness and unfortunately bring forecasts to failure or unsatisfied results (Lin et al., 2012). The grey system theory is well suited to study the behaviour of a system with incomplete information or limited amount of discrete data. Ease of use and accuracy, two significant criteria to project managers when choosing a forecasting model, are considered two additional attributes of the grey system theory.

Next, the GM(1,1) model is applied to the project shown in Table 6.3 in order to control the gap between the estimated and actual S-curve during the course of the project. The planned duration was 34 days, with a budget at completion of € 1,030,322. The project was finished 16 days later than expected but within budget. Table 6.4 shows the actual cost, the forecasted value and the corresponding MAPE values.

Table 6.3 Tasks to undertake the project, duration and cost

Task	Predecessor	Duration (days)	Cost (€)
A	-	1	3,146
B	A	1	55,353
C	B	1	2,000
D	B	19	11,276
E	B	5.5	43,200
F	C	31	124,809
G	C	17	33,843
H	A	28	103,761
I	B	4	41,271
J	I	19	381,014
K	J	4	48,507
L	E	1	31,250
M	C	1	35,080
N	M	1	3,146
O	N	2	112,674

Table 6.4 Actual cost, forecasted value and MAPE values

Date	Actual cost (€)	Forecast	MAPE
5 Jan	73,246		
8 Jan	194,430		
12 Jan	254,583		
16 Jan	357,716		
20 Jan	567,671	477,229	4.39
23 Jan	767,628	822,194	3.60
27 Jan	835,336	1,092,032	8.31
30 Jan	876,053	1,021,479	6.20
4 Feb	893,587	939,802	1.52
8 Feb	935,944	927,860	0.54
12 Feb	967,298	963,620	0.43
16 Feb	999,256	1,008,153	0.35
20 Feb	1,030,322	1,032,465	0.05

In order to obtain the values shown in Table 6.4, we will proceed as follows:

with the data from 5 Jan to 16 Jan, a series of number $X^{(0)}$ is formed:

$$X^{(0)} = \{73,246;194,430;254,583;357,716\}$$

This series of number is treated by 1-AGO (Equations. 6.13 and 6.14). Then, we get a new series of number:

$$X^{(1)} = \{73,246;267,676;522,259;879,975\}$$

Applying Equations (6.16), (6.17), and (6.18) we can get $\hat{a}$

$$\hat{a} = [a,u]^T = [-0.309;138,278]$$

where

$$B = \begin{bmatrix} -170,461 & 1 \\ -394,967 & 1 \\ -701,117 & 1 \end{bmatrix}$$

and

$$\bar{Y} = [194,430;254,583;357,716]^T$$

The solution of the differential equation (6.16) is therefore

$$\bar{x}^{(1)}(k+1) = 520,144\exp(0.309k) - 446,898$$

Then, a series of calculated data $\hat{X}^{(0)}$ is given by inverse accumulated generating operation

$$\hat{X}^{(0)} = [73,246;188,621;257,022;350,226;477,229]$$

Operating in accordance with principle of keeping the same dimension of data series, i.e., attaching a new data on tail end of the original data series and removing the first data, a new predicted value is obtained for each subsequent period. Performing this operation step-by-step, the forecast values and their corresponding MAPE values shown in Table 6.4, are obtained.

Most MAPE values, except the two predicted values on 27 Jan and 30 Jan are lower than 5 per cent. In addition, the last four MAPE values for are lower than 1 per cent, which indicates the small percentage error produced by the forecasting model at the final stage of the project, as can be seen in Figure 6.3. According to Lewis' (1982) interpretation, these results show that the accuracy of the GM (1,1) model to forecast the cost and the cost at completion of the project is highly efficient.

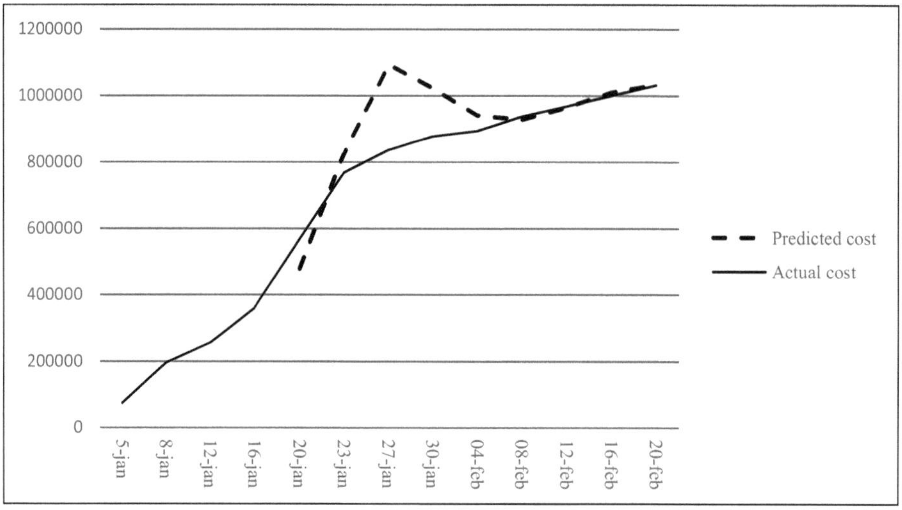

Figure 6.3 Actual cost and predicted value

Earned Value Management

Based on the classification described in Anbari (2003), during the execution a project the following situations can be considered:

1. The final project duration is considered to be on plan, regardless of the past performance. This situation does not require any forecasting.

2. Due to changing conditions, the original project assumptions are no longer valid. The performance indicators are obsolete and a new schedule for the remaining work needs to be developed.

3. Performance problems are irreversible and a lot of extra work is needed to fix these problems. The planned duration of the remaining work is very high and a new schedule needs to be developed.

4. Past performance is not a good predictor of future performance. Problems/opportunities of the past will not affect the future, and the planned duration of the remaining work will be done according to plan.

5. Past performance is a good predictor of future performance. Problems/opportunities of the past will affect future performance and the remaining work will be corrected for the observed efficiencies or inefficiencies, using schedule performance index.

6. Past cost and schedule problems are good indicators for future performance and the planned duration of the remaining work will follow current schedule and cost index.

One of the best methods to provide reliable early warning signals for schedule and cost performance forecasting in Project Management is the Earned Value (*EV*) method (Fleming and Koppelman, 2006). The *EV* method integrates the project's scope, cost and schedule by using a resource-loaded project schedule and provides a systemic way of measuring, analysing, communicating, and controlling the actual performance of a project (Kim, 2007). It has the advantage of being universally applicable over a wide range of project types and sizes, because every project, no matter how large or complex is, is represented by three functions: the Planned Value (*PV*), the *EV* and the Actual Cost (*AC*). To summarize, the terms and equations developed for *EV* management are shown in Table 6.5.

Table 6.5 Terms and equations developed for *EV* management

Planned Value (*PV*)	Approved budget for accomplish the project related to the schedule. The graph of the cumulative *PV* is often referred to as the S-curve
Budget at Completion (*BAC*)	Highest value of the *PV* and the last point of the cumulative *PV* curve
Earned Value (*EV*)	Amount budgeted for performing the work that was accomplished by a given point in time. To obtain the *EV*, multiply the total budget by its completed proportion
Actual Time (*AT*)	Duration at which the *EV* accrued is recorded
Actual Cost (AC)	Real cost incurred at the actual time (*AT*)
Cost Variance (*CV*)	It measures the budgetary conformance of the actual cost of work performance. It indicates how much over- or under-budget the project is: $$CV = EV - AC$$ • $CV > 0$. The project is under-budget • $CV < 0$. The project is over-budget
Schedule Variance (*SV*)	It is a measure of the conformance of actual progress to the schedule. It indicates how much ahead or behind schedule the project is: $$SV = EV - PV$$
Cost Performance Index (*CPI*)	It is a measure of the budgetary conformance of actual cost of work performed. It shows the efficiency of the utilization of the resources of the project. $$CPI = \frac{EV}{AC}$$ • $CPI > 1$. The efficiency in utilizing the resources is good • $CPI < 1$. The efficiency in utilizing the resources is not good
Schedule Performance Index (*SPI*)	It is a measure of the conformance of actual progress to the schedule. It shows the efficiency of the time utilized on the project $$SPI = \frac{EV}{PV}$$

Table 6.5 *Concluded*

Critical Ratio (*CR*)	It is an indicator of the overall project health. $$CR = CPI * SPI$$ • *CR* = 1. The overall project performance is on target • *CR* < 1. The overall project performance is poor • *CR* > 1. The overall project performance is excellent
Variance at Completion (*VAC*)	Difference between what the project was originally expected (baselined) to cost, versus what it is now expected to cost
Time Estimate at Completion (*TEAC*)	$$TEAC = \frac{SAC}{SPI}$$
Time Variance at Completion (*TVAC*)	It gives an indication of the estimated amount of time that the project will be completed ahead or behind schedule. $$TVAC = SAC - TEAC$$ • *TVAC* = 0. The project is expected to be completed on schedule • *TVAC* > 0. The project is expected to be completed ahead of schedule • *TVAC* < 0. The project is expected to be completed behind schedule

The schedule forecasting method using the *EV* performance indicators *SV* and *SPI* have been criticized for systematic distortion in results by different authors (Leach, 2005; Lipke, 2003; Short, 1993; Sparrow, 2005; Vandevoorde and Vanhoucke, 2006):

1. The *SV* is measured in monetary units and not in time units, which makes it difficult to understand and is often a source of misinterpretations.

2. A *SV* = 0 (or a *SPI* = 1) could mean that the task is completed, but could also mean that the task is running according to plan.

3. Towards the end of the project, the *SV* always converges to 0 (and the *SPI* always converges to 1) indicating a perfect performance even if the project is late.

In order to have a better understanding of *EV* management, several studies were performed from the cancellation of the US Department of Defense project for development of a Navy aircraft. The results of these studies can be summarized as follows (Lipke et al., 2009):

1. The $EAC = BAC/CPI$ indicator is a reasonable running estimate of the low value for final cost.

2. The cumulative value of *CPI* stabilizes by the time the project is 20 per cent complete which means that the final *CPI* does not vary by more than plus or minus 0.10 from the value at 20 per cent complete.

3. The range for final cost is obtainable from finding 2: $EAC = BAC/(CPI_{20\%} \pm 0.10)$

4. The value of *CPI* tends only to worsen from the point stability until project completion.

It is questionable whether these findings can be generally applicable to all types of projects, spanning from extremely large multi-billion projects lasting more than a decade, to small projects requiring less than a year of completion (Fleming and Koppelman, 2006). Lipke (2005) reports than findings 2 and 3, which require stability of *CPI* at 20 per cent complete, are likely applicable only for extremely large projects of long duration. Managers of small projects, however, report that they very seldom observe the findings for *CPI* stability. Without knowledge of *CPI* stability behaviour for small projects, these managers have limited ability to produce reliable forecasts of project cost outcome (Lipke et al., 2009).

At a certain point in time during project execution, the *SPI* and *SVI* lose their predictive ability and become unreliable indicators. This usually occurs over the last third of the project, the most critical period when the forecasts need to be accurate, since upper management wants to know when they can move up to the next project stage (Anbari, 2003). In order to overcome the anomalies with the *EV* schedule performance indicators, Lipke (2006) introduced the concept of Earned Schedule (*ES*). The *ES* indicator translates the *EV* into time increments and measures the real project performance in comparison to its expected time performance. From the two measures *ES* and *AT*, the following schedule performance indicators can be calculated:

- The schedule variance time: $SV(t) = ES - AT$

- The schedule performance index time $SPI(t) = ES/AT$

The behaviour of $SV(t)$ over time results in a final $SV(t)$ that equals exactly the real time difference at completion, in contrast to the *SV* indicator that always ends at zero. A $SV(t) < 0$ (>0) indicates the number of time units that the project lags (is ahead of) its expected performance. The same holds for the *SPI* indicator, which has a final value reflecting the final project schedule performance, while the *SPI* always equals 1 (Vandevoorde and Vanhoucke 2006). With these two time-based indicators it is possible to compare where the project is time-wise with where it should be in accordance to the *S*-curve.

Chapter 7
Simulation Models

A major problem faced by project managers is the uncertainty affecting project's outcomes. Traditionally, uncertainty has been mainly considered as the randomness of duration of activities. However, other factors such as the amount of resources required by each activity can be affected by uncertainty.

Simulation is a very powerful and widely used management technique for the analysis and study of complex systems. Simulation may be defined as a technique that imitates the operation of a real-world system as it evolves over time. This is normally done by developing a simulation model, which takes the form of a set of assumptions about the operation of the system, expressed as mathematical or logical relations between the objects of interests in the system. In contrast to the exact mathematical solutions available with most analytical models, the simulation process involves running the model through time to generate representative samples of the measures of performance. In this respect, simulation may be seen as a sampling experiment on the real system, with the results being sample points (Winston, 2003).

When projects become large or complex, computer simulation techniques can be used to improve overall Project Management, providing the tools required to design and analyse project processes regardless of complexity or size. In general, building a simulation model involves four phases (AbouRizk, 2010):

1. product abstraction phase (specifying the product to be built);
2. process abstraction and modelling phase (where processes, resources, environment, etc., required to build the product are abstracted and reduced to models);
3. experimentation phase (where the simulation is carried out); and
4. decision-making phase.

In this chapter we begin with a simulation model with random numbers, and then we present two research areas of Artificial Intelligence that can enhance current automation efforts in the Project Management industry, namely expert systems and artificial neural networks.

A Simulation Model with Random Numbers

Consider the project network shown in Figure 7.1 (Winston, 2003) in activity-on-arc form. Table 7.1 shows the data of the project.

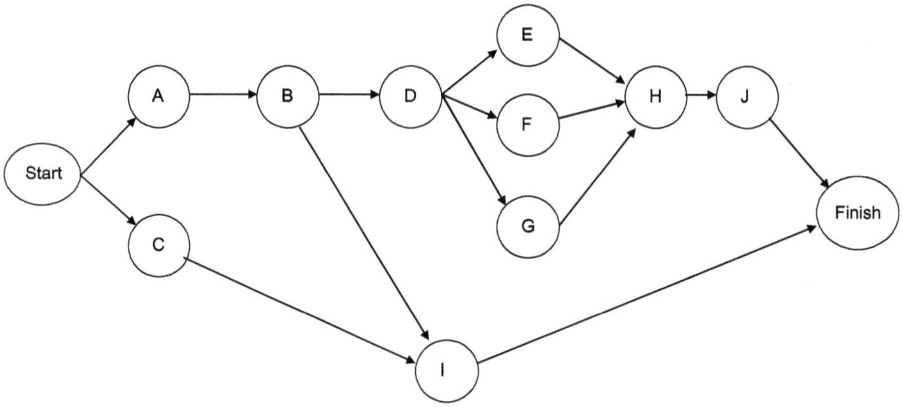

Figure 7.1 Network associated to a simulation model

Table 7.1 Data of the project

Task	Minimum time (days) (*a*)	Maximum time (days) (*b*)	Mean
A	1.5	8.5	5
B	3	5	4
C	7	19	13
D	2	6	4
E	3	7	5
F	2	6	4
G	2	6	4
H	2.5	3.5	3
I	0.5	1.5	1
J	1.5	2.5	2

In order to propose a simulation model with random number, the adopted model in this section assumes that the duration of each activity is uniformly distributed (other laws have been proposed to model the distribution of the duration of the activities in a project, i.e., the beta distribution, the lognormal, etc.). Consider a random variable x, that is uniformly distributed on the interval $\left[a,b\right]$. The probability density function of this function is:

$$f\left(x\right)=\begin{cases}\dfrac{1}{b-a} & \text{for } a\leq x\leq b\\ 0 & x<a \text{ or } x>b\end{cases} \tag{7.1}$$

where a and b are its minimum and maximum values. The cumulative distribution function is:

$$F\left(x\right)=\begin{cases}0 & \text{for} \quad x<a\\ \dfrac{x-a}{b-a} & \text{for} \quad a\leq x\leq b\\ 1 & \text{for} \quad x>b\end{cases} \tag{7.2}$$

and its inverse is:

$$F^{-1}\left(p\right)=a+p\left(b-a\right) \text{ for } 0<p<1$$

To use the inverse transformation method in order to generate observations from a uniform distribution, we first generate a random number, r, and then set $F\left(x\right)=r$ to solve for x. This gives

$$\frac{x-a}{b-a}=r \tag{7.3}$$

Solving for x yields

$$x=a+\left(b-a\right)r \tag{7.4}$$

as the process generator for the uniform distribution

The earliest an activity can finish is the earliest time it can start plus its duration. In general, if d_j is the duration of activity j, we have:

$$EF_j = ES_j + d_j \tag{7.5}$$

Activity j cannot start until all of its immediate predecessors have finished, so the earliest time activity j can start is the maximum of the earliest finish time of its immediate predecessors:

$$ES_j = \max\left(EF_i\right) \tag{7.6}$$

The project completion time is the earliest time of the finish node. The latest time activity j can finish without increasing the project completion time is LF_j. Again, we have analogous to Equation (7.5):

$$LS_j = LF_j - d_j \tag{7.7}$$

where LS_j is the latest time activity j can start. The latest time activity i can finish is the minimum of the latest start times of all its successors:

$$LF_i = \min\left(LS_j\right) \tag{7.8}$$

Applying Equations (7.5), (7.6), and (7.8) the data shown in Table 7.2 are obtained and we can conclude that the time to complete the project is 23 days.

Table 7.2 Start and finish times

Task	Earliest start time	Earliest finish time	Latest finish time	Latest start time	slack
Start	0	0	0	0	
A	0	5	5	0	0
B	5	9	9	5	0
C	0	13	22	9	9
D	9	13	13	9	0
E	13	18	18	13	0
F	13	17	18	14	1
G	13	17	18	14	1
H	18	21	21	18	0
I	13	14	23	22	9
J	21	23	23	21	0
Finish	23	23	23	23	

After performing 1,000 simulations the histogram in Figure 7.2 shows the distribution of the duration of the activities in the project. Looking at Table 7.3, which shows the relative and cumulative frequency of the data, it is clear that the highest probability (36.7 per cent) corresponds to 23–25 days.

Table 7.3 Relative and cumulative frequency

Time (days)	n° of observations	Relative frequency	Cumulative frequency
17–19	28	2.8	2.8
19–21	89	8.9	11.7
21–23	194	19.4	31.1
23–25	367	36.7	67.8
25–27	167	16.7	84.4
27–29	133	13.3	97.8
29–31	22	2.2	100

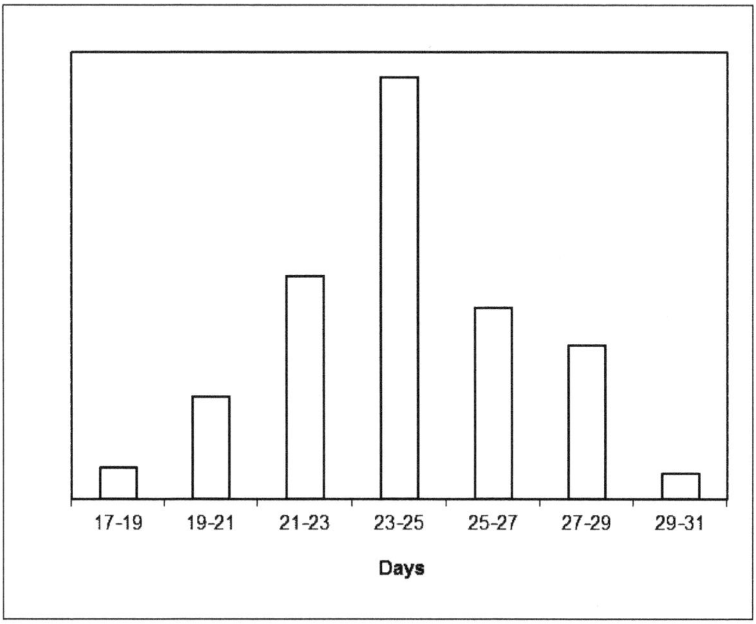

Figure 7.2 Distribution of the duration of the activities

Artificial Intelligence

Expert systems and artificial neural networks are among current Artificial Intelligence (AI) research areas of interest that can enhance current automation efforts in the Project Management industry. Unlike the AI-based systems, traditional decision analysis techniques, such as probabilistic methods, multi-attribute utility theory, fuzzy sets theory, etc., generally require advanced mathematics, making them less acceptable for practising construction personnel (Ahmad and Minkarah, 1990). Artificial Intelligence is concerned with building computer systems that solve the problem intelligently by emulating the human brain (Ko and Cheng, 2007). Since AI technology provides techniques for the computer program to carry out a variety of tasks, at which humans are currently better, AI paradigms are appropriate for solving Project Management problems (Haykin, 1999; Ko and Cheng, 2007). Project Management can be considered a fertile field for many AI applications due to the fact that expert knowledge, judgement and experience are the key requirements for the resolution of most construction engineering and management tasks.

Expert Systems

Expert systems are procedural software systems that attempt to model the intelligent reasoning and the problem-solving capabilities of the human brain. Based on heuristics and empirical knowledge, expert systems use domain specific knowledge to simulate the reasoning of an expert in order to perform intelligent tasks. The success of any expert system relies mainly on the ability to formalize and represent the knowledge within a discipline. There are several components which are common to most expert systems (McGartland and Hendrickson, 1985). They are: (1) The knowledge base; (2) the short-term memory; (3) the inference engine; (4) the explanation module; and (5) the knowledge acquisition module.

1. The knowledge base contains general information as well as heuristic or judgemental knowledge. For rule-based systems, this knowledge is represented in the form of IF (condition) THEN (action) rules. Rules may be in the form of situation/action, premise/conclusion or antecedent/consequent relationships. For example:

   IF: activity has no float time

   THEN: activity is on the critical path

The combination of these rules represents the reasoning of an expert in the field and contains the specific knowledge required to solve problems with the domain of the system. Experts systems can also be constructed to recognize the uncertainty inherent in decision-making. For example,

IF: activity has a cost overrun and activity is labour intensive and productivity has been adequate

THEN: the reason for the overrun is probably a poor estimate of the effort required for the activity

WITH: probability = 0.7

Sometimes, determination of the exact probability of a conclusion based upon a long and complicated string of such rules is difficult. In these cases, expert systems can use some combinatorial expressions to account for conditional probabilities.

2. The context of a short-term memory is often referred to as the fact base, which represents the current state of the system. As the actions of the rules are executed, the facts in the short-term memory are changed to reflect these actions. Thus, if the rule

IF: new material is stored in inventory

THEN: inventory level = present amount + new amount

is executed, the fact base records this by setting this new inventory level to the revised value.

3. Inference engine or executor is responsible for the execution of the system through manipulation of the rule base and the short-term memory. In general, the inference engine selects an 'active' rule (one in which the premise is satisfied) and executes or performs the indicated action. Three types of interrelated components may be used to locate active rules: (i) a change monitor which detects changes in the short-term memory that may require action; (ii) a pattern matcher that compares the short-term memory with the knowledge base; and (iii) a scheduler that decides which action is the most appropriate. The combination of these various components forms the matching section of the inference engine. Once a

rule is selected, two other components are used to perform the required actions:

a) the processor executes the required actions.

b) the knowledge modifier makes changes in the knowledge base as specified by the performed actions.

The inference engine uses a combination of these components to manipulate the rule base and the context in order to locate and execute active rules. Two processing strategies are generally used in existing systems:

a) Antecedent driven or forward chaining (also known as bottom up processing). System begins with all the required facts and searches to find the best conclusion that fits the facts.

b) Consequent driven or backward chaining (also known as top down processing). System begins with a hypothesis and works backward checking to see if the facts support the hypothesis.

4. Explanatory module. An explanation of the system's actions is actually contained in the rules that are fired. As a minimum, the explanation module should be capable of repeating the last rule. Then, if the user required additional explanation, the module would successively list previous rules which were evaluated.

5. Knowledge acquisition module. It is now possible to construct a knowledge base that contains all the knowledge for a specific discipline. As the system is demonstrated and put into practice, experts will contribute additional rules and suggestions to augment the knowledge base.

Let us consider an expert system in the area of time and cost control for project monitoring (McGartland and Hendrickson 1985). During the life of the project, time, and cost control include comparison of estimation data, activity schedules and accounting reports. A data base would contain schedules and estimates. For each activity, the following data items might be input each week:

1. estimated per cent complete;
2. expenditures to date;
3. actual quantities of labour (man-hr);
4. actual quantities of material;
5. actual quantities of equipment (hr).

In addition, the following two items are input once for each activity:

1. actual start time (AST); and
2. actual finish time (AFT).

An initial expert system could be established to verify these weekly inputs to the data base. The system would analyse the other information in the data base and based on the rules contained in the system's knowledge base, determine whether or not the new accounting information is reasonable. If the expert system decided that an input was questionable, it would request new input information of the current value. The system would automatically be executed whenever new data are entered into the data base.

When analysing the actual start time (AST) or the actual finish time (AFT) of an activity, the system would compare the new values with:

1. previous values of AST or AFT for this activity;
2. values of AFT for predecessor activities;
3. scheduled activity times;
4. estimated durations; and
5. previous and current estimated per cent complete.

When verifying values for estimated per cent complete and expenditures to date, the system would consider:

1. previous values of per cent complete and cost to date;
2. activity schedules;
3. estimated durations;
4. unit costs and expended quantities for manpower, material and equipment;
5. estimated cost; and
6. previous quantities for manpower, material and equipment.

When comparing actual expended quantities (labour, equipment, and material), the system would use:

1. estimated quantities;
2. percent complete;
3. expenditures to date; and
4. activity schedules.

A typical rule in the system knowledge base could be of the following form:

IF: per cent complete > 0

and AST is not initialized

THEN: one of the two values must be wrong

A more advanced expert system would be capable of recognizing cost overruns or time slippage problems and diagnosing potential causes. This system would also be executed automatically whenever new accounting data is entered into the data base. Based on a predetermined level, the system would spot individual activities with cost overruns or time delays. The system would not be limited to completed activities but would also function for activities in progress. In order to determine potential overruns for activities in progress, rules could be established based on the type of activity and comparing the AST, cost to date and per cent complete with estimated cost, estimated duration. Thus, the expert system would provide early warning on potential overruns and time delays before the problem became critical. Rules can concentrate on comparing estimated data with actual project data. For example:

IF: (per cent complete*estimated cost * adjustment values) > (expenditures to date* 1.15)

and AST is not initialized

THEN: when complete, activity will probably have a significant cost overrun

An adjustment value is added to the equation to account for the normal fluctuations in productivity during an activity. In general, productivity is lower towards the beginning and end of an activity, as represented by the S-curves, which forecast expenditures over the span of an activity (see Figure 7.3).

For example, a project manager may expect that the relationship between per cent complete and per cent of total cost expended to date is as shown in Table 7.4. To include this knowledge in the expert system, the adjustment values shown in the third column would then be used

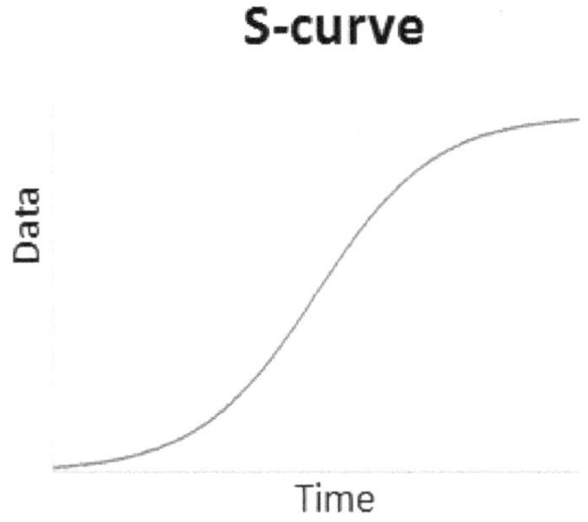

Figure 7.3 S-curve

Table 7.4 Adjustment values

Percent complete	Expenditures (per cent of total)	Adjustment value
0	0	
20	25	(25/20) = 1.25
30	45	(45/30) = 1.50
45	55	(55/45) = 1.22
70	65	(65/70) = 0.93
95	80	(80/95) = 0.84
100	100	1.00

A typical activity specific rule for defining an activity's adjustment value might be:

IF: per cent complete = 100 per cent

THEN: only consider final values, do not consider rules concerning activities in progress.

Several functions that can be included in more advanced systems could be:

1. Analyse the proposed project schedule and suggest improvements based on previous experiences and past trend.
2. When the project is partially complete, the system could be requested to update the remaining schedule to reflect progress to date.
3. Predict and anticipate problems that may occur during the course of a project.
4. Suggest remedies for predicted problems.
5. Revise proposed project schedule to allocate resources based on current availability while minimizing overall time and cost (resource levelling).
6. Suggest possible activity duration or cost changes based on past trends.

A typical rule in the knowledge base may be similar to:

IF: activity is on critical path

and activity is labour intensive

and sufficient labour is available

THEN: it may be possible to shorter activity duration and reduce overall project time

Artificial Neural Networks

Artificial neural networks, commonly referred to as 'neural networks', are massively parallel-distributed processors made up of simple processing units (neurons), which perform computations and store knowledge (Haykin, 1999). The arrangement of a number of processing elements in different meaningful configurations leads to different neural network models. Neural networks are introduced as hardware or software systems analogous to biological neural systems both in structure and functionality that attempt to model the brain learning, thinking, storage and retrieval of information, as well as associative recognition (Moselhi et al., 1991; Wassermann, 1989).

Neural networks are suitable for solving complex cognitive problems. It has been claimed that problems with non-conservative domains can be better solved by neural networks than by conventional methods (Dutta and Shekhar, 1988). Neural networks can fit such problems because of their adaptivity owing to their structure, i.e., hidden layers and the non-linear activation function (Chao and Skibniewski, 1994).

Figure 7.4 shows a feed-forward multilayer neural network which consists of input layers, to which data are presented to the network, output layers, which hold the response of the network to a given input, and hidden layers, that are layers distinct from the input layers and the output layers. Designing network architecture includes determining the number of input and output variables (i.e., neurons in input and output layers) and selecting the number of hidden layers and neurons in each hidden layer.

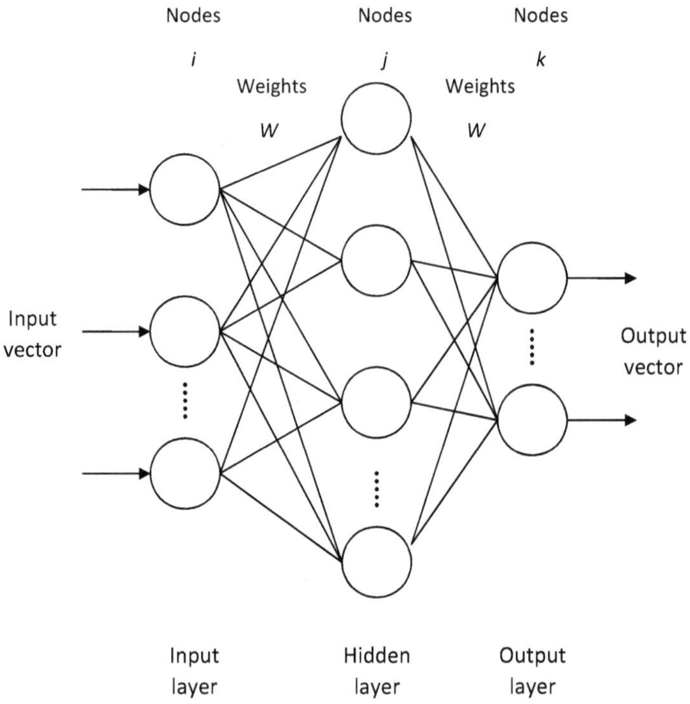

Figure 7.4 A feed-forward neural network

In the general form of a neural network, the unit analogous to the biological neuron is referred to as processing element. The network consists of many of these elements usually organized into a sequence of layers or slabs with full or partial connections between successive layers specifically designated. A neural network model can be described by the number of layers, the number of nodes in each layer, the node interconnection pattern, and the node activation function. Each interconnection in the network has an associated weight and each node has an assigned threshold. These weights and thresholds are called the parameters of a neural network model. Initially, the parameters of a neural network are given random values. When the network is subject to the training process, it self-organizes its parameters such that it can perform a useful function (Kamarthi et al., 1992).

The training of a neural network typically involves the application of the input and the corresponding known output vectors while adjusting the network parameters according to a predetermined training algorithm. Each pair of input and output vectors used in the training process is called a training example or a training pair. When a set of training examples are presented to a neural network, it learns the implicit knowledge, expertise, or rules implied by the training examples. Once the training or the learning is complete, a neural network can provide the desired output for a given input stimulus. A trained neural network acts as a transfer function relating the inputs and the outputs. Once a neural network is trained with a set of training examples to respond in a certain manner, the network continues to give the desired response even if the input stimulus contains a certain level of noise (Kamarthi et al., 1992).

Neural networks enjoy several characteristics that distinguish them from others Artificial Intelligence traditional architectures (Wassermann, 1989; Pao, 1989; Gallant 1988; Castelaz et al., 1987). Some of these characteristics include:

1. They are particularly suited for pattern recognition tasks where large number of attributes must be considered in parallel.

2. Unlike expert systems, neural networks learn many example patterns and their associations, i.e., desired outputs or conclusions. These examples could be elicited from experts without the need for asking how and why they came to those conclusions.

3. Due to their parallel structure, neural networks produce fast responses, irrespective of their requirement of large computer time for learning.

4. They could extract classification (clustering) characteristics from a large number of input examples, as in the case of unsupervised learning. If, e.g., a large number of field data are collected from a construction site, a suitable network can identify the different clusters (groups or classes) that characterize the whole population.

5. Neural networks have distributed memory; the connections weights are the memory units of the network. The value of the weights represents the current state of knowledge of the network. A unit of knowledge, represented e.g. by an input/desired-output pair, is distributed across all the weighted connections of the network.

6. They have associative memory. The network responds in an accretive or interpolative way to noisy, incompetent, or previously unseen data. An auto-associative network, where input is equal to desired output, can produce a full output if presented with a partial input. This property is called 'generalization'.

7. They are fault-tolerant. Since memory is distributed, failure of some processing elements will slightly alter the overall behaviour of the network. However, failure of any small part in a traditional computing system will stop its performance. This characteristic is very well suited to applications where reliable systems need to be developed from less reliable components.

8. Neural networks could represent uncertainty. A measure of 'belief' could be incorporated by modifying the problem pattern in two ways: (i) by selecting input values to represent a measure of belief in the attribute; and (ii) by adding another attribute representing the measure of belief in the input example.

9. They require a lesser amount of storage memory, since there is only one set of network weights capable of representing a large space of stored patterns.

Chapter 8
Markov Models

Contrary to the key assumption used in CPM-PERT networks that activities, and hence their durations, are independent, there is a general acceptance among project managers that the way in which early activities are performed has a great impact on the later stages of the project. It is widely accepted that the quality of specification and the quality of design affect both the time and cost of implementation on subsequent activities (Shepperd, 1990; Cooper and Kleinschmidt, 1994).

Projects do not progress in linear predetermined sequences from one end to the other. Projects are systems which continually loop back to earlier stages, and the later that a problem is identified and rectified the greater the cost and delay involved. When a problem occurs, it is necessary to identify the stage at which the problem was created, and reactivate that activity so that the problem can be fully resolved (Hardie, 2001).

Traditionally, the progress of a project is measured by the stage which has been reached. However, when loops occur, progress is not represented by the furthest stage which the project has reached, for there is a significant probability that the project will revert to an earlier stage at some subsequent time. The whole nature of a project becomes more probabilistic, and it becomes much less easy to determine how long it will be to finish a project. The sequence of activities is no longer determined. The current stages of a project no longer represent a reliable measure of progress and the overall timescale of the project depends on how often loops occur.

Unfortunately, existing project duration prediction models such as PERT and CPM do not recognize the impact of earlier problems on later delays. Since these planning systems define all activities as independent, delay is assumed to be caused by the current activity and the blame is allocated to the people currently involved (Hardie, 2001). These models are based on a few critical basic assumptions like: 'A Project can be fragmented into a set of discrete and logically sequenced activities which are statistically independent of each other.' The implications of these assumptions are (Kandathil, 2003):

1. The progress of a project can be predictable from knowing the activities completed and the percentage completion of the currently ongoing activities.

2. The distribution of completion time is a normal distribution around the most likely time.

As far as R&D projects is concerned (software development projects, aerospace projects, etc.,) it is obvious that at any point of time anomalies/problems in the earlier activities can be identified in the later stages (during testing, e.g.) and can affect the future activities, and thereby the total duration of the project. Thus, there is a likelihood that from any activity or stage, reversion (going back) can occur to earlier activities or stages. Experience says that reversion or looping back is an essential or rather more critical parameter, which affects the length of duration of each activity as well as the total duration of the project. Moreover, it is reasonable to consider activities with comparable durations having more reversion chance as more critical, than the activities having just more duration alone as more critical as in CPM (Kandathil, 2003). To get closer to the reality, the occurrences of reversion in any project is to be accommodated and therefore, better prediction models which take into account this reality are required.

Various scientific methods have been tried to improve the performance of project prediction and control, such as concurrent engineering (Carter and Baker, 1991), stage-gate systems, in which projects must meet specified criteria before they pass from one stage to the next (Cooper, 1991), and GERT (Wiest and Levey, 1977). Among these models, concurrent engineering emphasized on project controlling and practising facets more than on project duration prediction, while GERT was the most accepted one, especially for its probabilistic branching feature, although looping back to previous stages was not permitted in this technique. Boehm's spiral model of software accepted the possibility of reverting to the previous stages for rework (Boehm, 1988; Wolff, 1989) but reversion to earlier stages was discouraged. Recent analysis has proposed networks with reversions back over several stages (Dawson and Dawson, 1998) but has admitted that the computation is very complex.

Fortunately, there exists a powerful tool which can be used to analyze the behaviour of projects: the Markov chain. The limitation of CPM/PERT model due to reversion and the computational complexities of other models, where reversion is allowed, can be surmounted if Markov chain analysis is suitably adapted for modelling (Kandathil, 2003).

Markov Chain

Markov modelling is a classical technique used for assessing the time-dependent behaviour of many dynamic systems. A Markov model is a mathematical system characterized with the property of memoryless: the next state depends only on the current state and not on the sequence of events that precede it. It is used for describing systems that follow a chain of linked events. Where what happens next depends only on the current state of the system.

Control of projects in the Markov model is very different to control in other models like PERT. In the reversion model, control of projects with respect to the schedule means taking the decision on when to stop the incremental effort of an activity or when to finish the activity and take up the next activity (Kandathil, 2003). At the end of an activity, examine how well the activity has been performed and estimate the probability of reversion to it from ever future dependent activity. If the reversion probability is high, further work on this activity needs to be done to reduce the reversion probability. If it is acceptably low, next activity can be taken up. The finalization of the acceptance probability is a trade-off between the time spent on the current activity, refining and reviewing it, and the risk of coming back to the current activity at later stage (Kandathil, 2003).

The assumption made in PERT about the distribution of completion time as a normal distribution around the most likely time ignores the impact of the past activities on future activities. In the Markov model, however, since this impact has already been accounted in reversion probabilities, it can be safely assumed that the population of duration for each activity would approximate to normal distribution (Kandathil, 2003).

Let $\{X_n, n = 1,2,\ldots\}$ be a stochastic process that assumes values in a discrete (finite or countable) state space S. If $X_n = i$, then the process is said to be in state i at time n. We say that $\{X_n, n = 1,2,\ldots\}$ is a Markov chain if (Sujiao, 2009):

$$P\{X_{n+1} = j \mid X_n = i, X_{n-1} = i_{n-1}, \ldots, X_1 = i_1\} = P\{X_{n+1} = j \mid X_n = i\} \quad (8.1)$$

for all state $i_1, \ldots, i_{n-1}, i, j$ and all $n \geq 1$. Eq. (8.1) may be interpreted as stating that, for a Markov chain, given the past state $i_1, \ldots, i_{n-1}$ and the present state *i*, the conditional distribution of any future state *j* is independent of the past states and depends only on the present state. If $P\{X_{n+1} = j | X_n = i\}$ does not depend on *n*, we call the Markov chain stationary or time homogeneous.

The behaviour of a Markov chain is described by a transition matrix which specifies the transition probabilities between any two states. Let *P* denotes the matrix of one-step transition probabilities, with elements P_{ij} as probability of transition from state *i* into state *j*, so that:

$$P = \begin{bmatrix} P_{11} & P_{12} & \cdots & P_{1j} & \cdots \\ P_{21} & P_{22} & \cdots & P_{2j} & \cdots \\ \vdots & \vdots & & \vdots & \\ P_{i1} & & \cdots & P_{ij} & \cdots \\ \vdots & \vdots & & \vdots & \end{bmatrix} \tag{8.2}$$

There are three rules that determine the transition probabilities:

1. The probability of forward jumps in activities is zero, i.e., from activity 1 to activity 4, $P_{14} = 0$. It means that the probability of transition from state *i* into state $i + n = 0$ for values $n > 1$, where *n* is the number of stages in the project. Thus, progress must always be made by following the proper sequence.

2. The sum of all transition probabilities for a particular activity is 1. Thus, for any activity *i*, $\sum P_{ij} = 1$.

3. When the project ends satisfactorily, it stays in a completed state and cannot move to any other state. Thus, $P_{n+1,n+1} = 1$, $P_{n+1,x} = 0$ (*x* not equal to *n*+1).

The probability of a project moving from one activity to the next one planned is, therefore, one minus the sum of the probabilities of all reversions:

$$\begin{aligned} P_{12} &= 1 - P_{11} \\ P_{23} &= 1 - P_{22} - P_{21} \\ P_{34} &= 1 - P_{33} - P_{32} - P_{31} \end{aligned} \tag{8.3}$$

We write $P_{ij} = P\{X_{n+1} = j | X_n = i\}$ and refer to it as one-step transition probability of X_n, which represents the probability that the process will make a transition from state i into state j. By multiplying the transition matrix itself n times, the probabilities of over nT period (future states) can be obtained.

Next, the following example shows how a Markov chain can be used to describe a project in which transition can occur in three ways (Hardie, 2001):

1. normal transition to the next sequential activity;
2. transition to earlier activities which need rectification; and,
3. transition back to the start of the current activity when this needs to be repeated (rework of the activity).

Thus, if we define a single project which requires a number of activities to be performed in sequence for its completion, we can establish a transition matrix for that project by examining the reversion probabilities between activities. The following simplifying assumptions are made in the initial analysis:

1. Activity durations are all equal.
2. Repeating an activity (rework) takes the same time as the original activity.
3. The problem is a linear one with no branches.

Using the stochastic ability of Markov chain analysis, the model presented above is applied for predicting the duration of the project shown in Table 8.1, assuming the transition probabilities are known. Figure 8.1 shows the linear network associated to the project.

Table 8.1 Activity durations

Activity	**Duration (days)**
Analysis	21
Design and Planning	25
Implementation and Development	32
Testing and Validation	22
Shipment	20
Total	120
Average activity duration	24

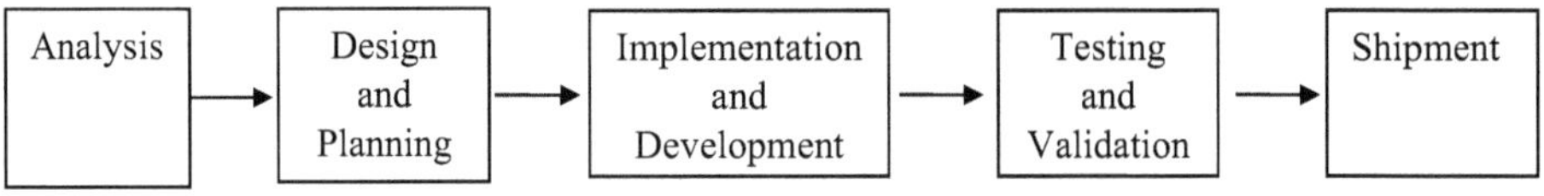

Figure 8.1 Linear network associated to the project

The transition matrix that defines the probabilities of going forward, staying still, or regressing, for any current stage of the project, is shown in Table 8.2. The probability of any reversion to the same activity is 0.05 and to an earlier one is 0.1. Thus, there is a probability P_{12} = 0.95 of moving from stage 1 (Analysis) to stage 2 (Design and Implementation), but there is also a probability P_{11} = 0.05 of having to repeat stage 1. At the end of stage three, during which activity Implementation and Development is being performed, there is 75 per cent probability (P_{34} = 0.75) of moving into stage four (Testing and Validation), a 10 per cent probability (P_{31} = 0.10) of reverting back to stage one (Analysis), a 10 per cent probability (P_{32} = 0.10) of reverting back to stage two (Design and Planning), and a 5 per cent probability (P_{33} = 0.05) of reverting to the same stage.

Table 8.2 Transition matrix for a 4-stage project with each activity duration = 24 days

	Analysis	Design and Planning	Implementation and Development	Testing and Validation	Shipment
Analysis	0.05	0.95			
Design and Planning	0.1	0.05	0.85		
Implementation and Development	0.1	0.1	0.05	0.75	
Testing and Validation	0.1	0.1	0.1	0.05	0.65
Shipment	0	0	0	0	1

The probability of transition over two time periods is obtained by multiplying this matrix by itself giving the matrix shown in Table 8.3. By successive multiplications of the matrix, the probability of completing the project in various time periods can be found. For example, the transition matrix for 4*T* period, obtained by multiplying the transition matrix for *T* period three times, is shown in Table 8.5. Thus, the probability of completing the project (moving to Analysis stage to Shipment stage) in the minimum time is 39 per cent.

Table 8.3 Transition matrix for a 4-stage project. $T = 2$

	Analysis	**Design and Planning**	**Implementation and Development**	**Testing and Validation**	**Shipment**
Analysis	0.10	0.10	0.81	0	0
Design and Planning	0.10	0.18	0.09	0.64	0
Implementation and Development	0.10	0.18	0.16	0.08	0.49
Testing and Validation	0.03	0.12	0.10	0.08	0.68
Shipment	0	0	0	0	1

Table 8.4 Transition matrix for a 4-stage project. $T = 3$

	Analysis	**Design and Planning**	**Implementation and Development**	**Testing and Validation**	**Shipment**
Analysis	0.10	0.18	0.12	0.61	0
Design and Planning	0.10	0.17	0.22	0.10	0.41
Implementation and Development	0.05	0.12	0.17	0.13	0.54
Testing and Validation	0.03	0.05	0.11	0.08	0.73
Shipment	0	0	0	0	1

Table 8.5 Transition matrix for a 4-stage project. $T = 4$

	Analysis	Design and Planning	Implementation and Development	Testing and Validation	Shipment
Analysis	0.10	0.17	0.22	0.12	0.39
Design and Planning	0.05	0.13	0.17	0.17	0.48
Implementation and Development	0.04	0.08	0.13	0.13	0.62
Testing and Validation	0.03	0.05	0.06	0.09	0.78
Shipment	0	0	0	0	1

Table 8.6 Transition matrix for a 4-stage project. $T = 9$

	Analysis	Design and Planning	Implementation and Development	Testing and Validation	Shipment
Analysis	0.02	0.05	0.07	0.07	0.79
Design and Planning	0.02	0.04	0.05	0.05	0.84
Implementation and Development	0.01	0.03	0.04	0.04	0.89
Testing and Validation	0.01	0.02	0.02	0.02	0.94
Shipment	0	0	0	0	1

Calculations using transition matrices can be made for subsequent time periods obtaining the graph of cumulative completion probability against time shown in Figure 8.2. As the graph shows, there is never certainty that the project will be finished within a specified time. The probability of completion increases with time, but there is always a finite chance that the project will continue. In the graph shown for a project which has nominally four time periods, there is still a 21 per cent (1-.79) of probability on non-completion after nine periods.

It is observed, especially in large projects with more number of stages, that project delays are generally more affected by reversion than the slowness in individual activities. Since, the overall project duration is a function of the

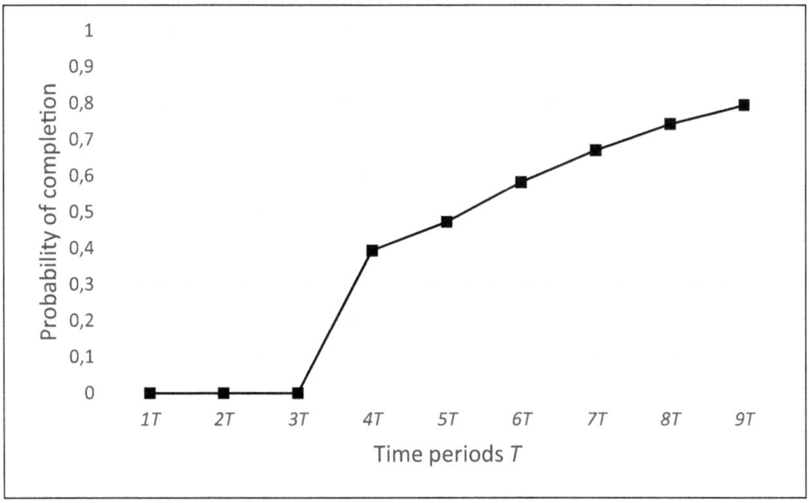

Figure 8.2 Prediction curve of cumulative probabilities for a 4-stage project

probability or reversion (P), the higher the value of P, the longer the project is likely to take because reversion will lead to more frequent loops back to earlier stages. So, to reduce the project length and thus, to avoid project delay, reversion probability should be reduced (Hardie, 2001; Kandathil, 2003).

The way in which project length varies with different values of reversion probabilities can be easily calculated from the transition matrix. Figure 8.3 shows the completion probability for a four-stage project with different reversion probabilities. That is, when the probability of reversion to the same activity or to an early one is 0.02, 0.05, 0.08, 0.10, and 0.15. The comparison between completion probability and reversion probability shows that, for a four-stage project, the probability of completion is 0.633 over six periods when $P = 0.08$ and is 0.700 over five periods when $P = 0.05$. Thus, if spending extra time on every activity is able to reduce the reversion probability, the project is likely to be finished more quickly. Similarly, as can be shown in the figure, for the same number of time periods, T, the lower the probability of reversion, the higher the probability of completion.

The Markov model presented in this chapter relies on three basic assumptions: (i) the project is linear with no branches; (ii) approximately equal duration for each activity; and (iii) rework of activities. Seldom one gets a network project without branches and with activities of approximately equal duration. To transform complex networks with many activities and

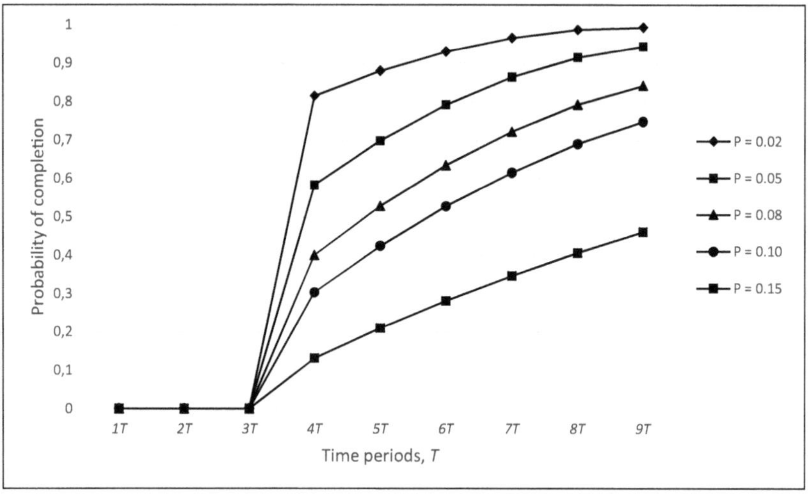

Figure 8.3 Probability of completion of a 4-stage project with varying reversion probabilities

branches into simpler and more synthetic networks, several approaches have been proposed (Tavares, 2002): the method of modular decomposition and the method of network reduction. The method of modular decomposition is based on the identification of modules which can be synthesized by equivalent macro-activities (Muller and Spinrad, 1989). The method of network reduction (Bein et al., 1992) is based on three different types of reduction: series, parallel, and network reduction. Through series reduction, a sequence of activities is substituted by an equivalent activity; using parallel reduction, a set of parallel activities is substituted by an equivalent activity, and using node reduction, a set of arcs converging to a node with just one out-arc, or a set of arcs diverging from a node just receiving one arc can be substituted by a set of equivalent arcs.

The second assumption of approximately equal duration for each activity also may not be practically possible. When some activities are of much greater lengths than others, those activities of incomparable length can be broken down into component activities with length of duration similar to other activities. A zero reversion probability can be assigned for the component activities so that it works out as a single activity.

Regarding the third assumption on rework activities, if the duration of the rework is not approximately equal to the duration of the original activity, the duration of the rework can be represented as a percentage of the original model (Kandathil, 2003)

Risk Analysis Based on Markov Chains

Project risks change continuously due to the rapid changes in project environment (Nigel et al., 2006; Bunni, 1985). Because future progress of a project depends mainly on the present project environment but has to do little with past conditions, project risks have the Markov property and can be modelled by Markov chains. According to Sujiao (2009), risk analysis of construction projects based on Markov chains may be implemented through the following procedure:

Let $R_1, R_2, \ldots, R_i$, denote certain risk levels. Let us suppose that, at the initial stage of the project, T experts are interviewed to assess project risks. If there are T_i experts who determine the risk level as R_i, the probability of this project exposed to risk level R_i can be calculated as:

$$S_i^{(0)} = \frac{T_i}{T} \tag{8.4}$$

In this way, we obtain the initial distribution of risk probabilities:

$$S^{(0)} = \left(S_1^{(0)}, S_2^{(0)}, \ldots, S_i^{(0)}, S_j^{(0)}, \ldots\right) \tag{8.5}$$

At a later stage of the project, T_{ij} experts think that the overall project risk change from level R_i to R_j, then, the corresponding transition probability from state i into state j is:

$$P_{ij} = \frac{T_{ij}}{T_i} \tag{8.6}$$

and we can obtain the one-step transition probability matrix as in (8.2). The risk distribution at the second stage is

$$S^{(1)} = S^{(0)} * P \tag{8.7}$$

Generally, the risk distribution after K-step transition from the initial stage is:

$$S^{(k)} = S^{(0)} * P^k \tag{8.8}$$

Next, a project case is used to illustrate the method presented above. Let us consider that, at pre-construction stage and early construction stage, ten experts are interviewed to assess the risk level. The results of this assessment are shown in Table 8.7.

Table 8.7 Project risk assessment

		Assessment at the second stage			Total
	Risk level	**Low**	**Medium**	**High**	
Assessment at the first stage	Low	2	1	0	3
	Medium	3	1	0	4
	High	1	1	1	3
Total		6	3	1	10

Then, the initial risk distribution can be derived as:

$$S^{(0)} = \left(0.3, 0.4, 0.3\right)$$

and the one-step transition probability matrix is:

$$P = \begin{bmatrix} 0.67 & 0.33 & 0.00 \\ 0.75 & 0.25 & 0.00 \\ 0.33 & 0.33 & 0.33 \end{bmatrix}$$

By using Equation 8.7, the risk distribution at the second stage is:

$$S^{(1)} = S^{(0)} * P = \left(0.3, 0.4, 0.3\right) * \begin{bmatrix} 0.67 & 0.33 & 0.00 \\ 0.75 & 0.25 & 0.00 \\ 0.33 & 0.33 & 0.33 \end{bmatrix} = \left(0.60, 0.30, 0.10\right)$$

and the risk distribution at the next stage is:

$$S^{(2)} = S^{(1)} * P = \left(0.60, 0.30, 0.10\right) * \begin{bmatrix} 0.67 & 0.33 & 0.00 \\ 0.75 & 0.25 & 0.00 \\ 0.33 & 0.33 & 0.33 \end{bmatrix} = \left(0.66, 0.31, 0.03\right)$$

and the risk distribution after 4-step transition from the initial stage is:

$$S^{(4)} = S^{(3)} * P = \left(0.68, 0.31, 0.01\right) * \begin{bmatrix} 0.67 & 0.33 & 0.00 \\ 0.75 & 0.25 & 0.00 \\ 0.33 & 0.33 & 0.33 \end{bmatrix} = \left(0.69, 0.31, 0.00\right)$$

The results show that, after four periods, the probabilities of project risk at low, medium, and high level are 69 per cent, 31 per cent, and 0 per cent respectively. It can be shown that, by comparison to the risk level at the initial stage, the project risks have diminished during the process.

Chapter 9

Data Envelopment Analysis Models

In today's competitive business environment, companies need to continuously invest in both consecutive and simultaneous projects to guarantee healthy and profitable growth. Companies are being forced to improve their effectiveness and efficiency looking for effectively comparing the performance of various projects at a given time period. (Vitner et al., 2006). Planning for these projects typically involves scheduling, budgeting, and fundraising. Some of these projects need to be completely funded while some of them can be partially funded in a particular year (Gabriel et al., 2006).

Virtually, contractors and construction companies run several projects simultaneously and R&D organizations and high-technology companies are characterized by having many ongoing projects. Since projects compete for resources and typically, there are always less resources available than demand, these organizations are often confronted with having more projects to choose from than the resources to carry them out. To select from an array of projects those better adapted to the organization's objectives and determining the priority in which these projects will be worked on is a challenging managerial task that motivates project managers and their teams and creates an improvement environment (Schmidt, 1993; Vitner et al., 2006). Determining which projects are to be funded is a complicated process and can involve examining various needs or opportunities (Guido and Clements, 2003). One must evaluate the benefits, drawbacks, and consequences of each possible choice, and these comparisons can be quantitative and/or qualitative as well as tangible and/or intangible depending on the specifics of each project (Gabriel et al., 2006).

The literature on project selection contains many types of models including (Tavana et al., 2013): scoring methods, ad hoc methods, comparative methods, economic methods, and mathematical optimization methods:

1. Scoring methods. These methods use a relatively small number of quantitative criteria to specify project desirability. The merit of each project is determined with respect to each criterion, and then scores are combined to yield an overall performance for each project.

2. Ad hoc methods. These methods are a special form of scoring methods. Using these types of methods, limits are set for the various criteria levels and any projects which fail to meet these limits are eliminated.

3. Comparative methods. They use both quantitative and qualitative attributes. The weights of these different attributes are determined and projects are compared on the basis of their contributions to these attributes. Once the projects have been arranged on a comparative scale, the decision-maker selects projects from the top of the list until available resources are exhausted.

4. Economic methods. These methods use financial ratios to calculate the monetary payoff of each project. Using two dimensions such as the expected monetary value and the likelihood of success, a representative mix of projects with respect to these dimensions is selected.

5. Mathematical optimization methods. This type includes a wide range of methods such as linear, non-linear, integer, dynamic, goal and stochastic mathematical programming. In order to select a project or group of projects these methods employ mathematical programming to facilitate the optimization process taking into account project interactions such as resource dependencies and constraints, technical and market interactions, etc.

The selection among firms of projects applying for financial support from a restricted budget constitutes a typical ranking problem where the decision-maker is called to single out the most attractive alternatives by taking into account different aspects of the firms' or projects' efficiency (Mavrotas et al., 2006). Ranking and selecting projects is a difficult task with typically more than one dimension for measuring project impacts and more than one decision-maker. As part of the selection process, the evaluation involves multiple and often conflicting goals and criteria, including maximizing net present value, achieving regulatory compliance, enhancing (or reducing) environmental impacts, minimizing risk and cost, minimizing total completion time, not exceeding a given budget, intangible benefits, relevance to the organization's mission, probability of technical and commercial success, availability of resources, etc. Moreover, the list of proposed projects invariably exceeds budgetary allocation. Thus, the decision problem becomes one of ranking projects in order of preference and selecting the best ones (Buchanan and Vanderpooten, 2007). Based on the evaluation, management has to decide which project proposal should be selected or which resource level should be associated with each selected project. Cooper et al. (1997) recognized three broad objectives that usually dominate this decision process:

1. Effectiveness. The alignment of the mix of projects in the portfolio with the strategic goals of the organization.

2. Efficiency. The value of the portfolio in terms of long-term profitability, return-on- investment, likelihood of success, or other relevant performance measures.

3. Balance. The diversification of the projects in the portfolio in terms of various trade-offs such as high risk versus sure bets, internal versus outsourced work, even distribution across industries, etc.

Selecting projects to develop from the many projects that are usually possible, or 'project portfolio selection', is a crucial decision in many organizations, where efforts must be made to estimate, evaluate and choose optimal sets of projects to be undertaken. Portfolio selection problems can be decomposed into two major classes: dynamic versus static problems (Eilat et al., 2006). In the dynamic class, at every decision point there are projects that have already started, denoted as active projects, and a set of proposed projects, known as candidate projects. The static class addresses situations in which all the projects considered at the decision point are candidates. The major difficulties associated with project portfolio selection are (Ghasemzadeh et al., 1999):

1. There may be multiple and often conflicting objectives.

2. Some of the objectives are qualitative, as opposed to quantitative, in nature.

3. There is usually uncertainty associated with project parameters such as risk and cost.

4. Some projects are high interdependent in nature.

5. Constraints such as finance, workforce, and equipment, must be considered in the decision-making process.

6. A portfolio should be balanced in terms of certain factors, such as risk and time to completion, that are of importance to decision-makers.

7. The number of feasible portfolio is often enormous.

The importance of project selection stems from the fact that projects are a core element of corporate renewal, heavily influence a firm's market success or failure, if no properly chosen and trimmed, and may waste large amount of resources or even ruin the enterprise. Wrong decisions in project selection have two negative consequences. On the one hand, resources are spent on unsuitable projects and, on the other hand, the organization loses the benefits it may have gained if those resources had been spent on more suitable project (Martino, 1995).

Data Envelopment Analysis

Data Envelopment Analysis (DEA) is a mathematical programming technique that provides the correct method for project evaluation and selection (Charnes et al., 1994; Charnes et al., 1978). DEA calculates the relative efficiency of multiple decision-making units (DMUs) on the basis of observed inputs and outputs which can be expressed with different types of metrics. The DEA approach is used for evaluating the performance of projects in a multi-project environment where each project is considered a decision-making unit having its own inputs and outputs, where the inputs represent the resources to perform the project, and the outputs represent all of dimensions by which the project is measured. Following Cooper et al. (2006), DEA is used to:

1. identify the best alternative;

2. rank the alternatives; or

3. establish a shortlist of the better alternatives for detailed review.

Given a group of projects, all projects should be able to operate at an optimal efficiency level which is determined by the efficient projects in the group. These efficient projects determine the benchmark, usually referred to as the efficient frontier, against which the relative performance of projects is measured. The projects that form the efficient frontier use a minimum quantity of inputs to produce the same quantity of outputs. The distance to the efficient frontier provides a measure for the efficiency or its lack thereof. The existing gap from any DMUs to the efficiency frontier shows how far the DMUs should be further improved to reach the optimal efficiency level. DEA produces detailed information on the efficiency of the unit, to be measured without any assumptions regarding the functional form of the production function, not only relative to the efficiency frontier, but also to specific efficient units which can be identified as role models. Thus, DEA can be used by inefficient organizations to benchmark efficient and 'best-practice' organizations.

The technique was first proposed by Charnes et al. (1978) and later extended by Banker et al. (1984). The two basic DEA models are named after the respective researchers who first introduced them: the Charnes Cooper Rhodes (CCR) and the Banker Charnes Cooper (BCC) models. DEA models can be either input-oriented or output-oriented. Input orientations implies that an efficient DMU may be made efficient by reducing the proportions of its inputs but keeping the output proportions constant. Output orientation implies that an inefficient DMU may be made efficient by increasing the proportions of its outputs while keeping the input proportions constant.

The two models are generally distinguished by the type of their envelopment surfaces and orientation. The envelopment surfaces are depicted by either a constant-return-to-scale (CRS) or a variable-return-to-scale (VRS) represented in the CCR and BCC models, respectively. CRS models provide the most conservative measure of efficiency. Under CRS, all units are compared against a frontier defined by units operating under the most productive scale size. Units operating under any diseconomies of scale, therefore, cannot be 100 per cent efficient. On the other hand, VRS models allow units operating under diseconomies of scale to form part of the frontier, as long as they perform better than their most similar peers (Farris et al., 2006). Choosing which model to use will depend on both the case under study and the characteristics of the data set.

DEA has been used very successfully in Project Management in the context of technology selection or R&D project evaluation. Examples of software project applications include Mahmood et al. (1996), Chatzoglou and Soteriou (1999), Banker et al. (1987, 1991), Paradi et al. (1997), Parkan et al. (1997), Banker and Kemerer (1989), Banker et al. (1994), Banker and Slaugher (1997), Stensrud and Myrtveit (2003), Yang and Paradi (2004). R&D project applications focused on selecting the best set of projects to receive funding include Kauffmann et al. (2000), Oral et al. (1991), Cook et al. (1996), Green et al. (1996), Linton et al.

(2002), Thore and Lapao (2002), Thore and Rich (2002), Liu and Chen (2004), Eilat et al. (2006). Verma and Sinha (2002), Yuan et al. (2002), and Revilla et al. (2003) have used DEA to measure the efficiency of completed or ongoing R&D projects. Other application areas that did not include either software projects or R&D projects have focused on the selection of projects (Chai and Ho, 1998; Thore and Pimentel, 2002) or on assessing performance of completed projects (Linton and Cook, 1998; Busby and Williamson (2000).

The first step in specifying the DEA model is to identify the input and output variables of interest necessary to capture important differences between projects. There exist a wide variety of measures that describe the outcomes of a project and the input characteristics and factors which impact project outcomes (Cooke-Davies, 2002; Dvir et al., 1998; Kerzner, 1987; Pate-Cornell and Dillon, 2001; Pinto and Mantel, 1990; Pinto and Slevin, 1987, 1989). The most commonly cited project outcome measures include cost, schedule, technical performance outcomes and client satisfaction (Might and Fischer, 1985; Pinto and Slevin, 1988). The Project Management Institute (PMI, 2004) identified 10 dimensions of project performance measures for studying in benchmarking efforts including, cost, schedule performance, staffing, alignment to strategic business goals, and customer satisfaction. Belassi and Tukel (1996) also identified four overall groups of project success factors:

1. factors related to the project (e.g., size, urgency);
2. factors related to the project manager and team members (e.g., technical background, competence);
3. factors related to the organization (e.g., top management support);
4. factors related to the external environment (e.g., client, market).

While it is important that the input variables that most impact project outcomes are identified, if too many variables are included, the DEA model loses discriminatory power, i.e., all or most units become efficient due to their unique levels of inputs and outputs (Farris et al., 2006). The recommended maximum number of input and output variables is equal to one-half the number of DMUs in any given category or analysis (Dyson et al., 2001). Since the case study we are going to use as an example concerns 12 projects, the maximum number of input and output variables that could be included in the DEA model is six. Therefore, in addition to two input variables, project duration and quality, four output variables are identified for inclusion in the model for a total of six variables. The four input variables are: effort, project staffing, priority, and level of monitoring. Table 9.1 defines the variables and the unit of measurement.

Table 9.1 Variables and unit of measurement

Variable	Definition	Unit
Duration	Work days to complete the project	Days
Quality	Quality of the project	1 = lowest priority 9 = highest priority
Effort	Work content of the project	Person/Day
Project staffing	Number of people on project/effort	People/Day
Priority	Urgency of the project	1 = lowest priority 9 = highest priority
Level of monitoring	Technical difficulty and uncertainty of the project	1 = lowest priority 9 = highest priority

OUTPUT VARIABLES

In Project Management, time, cost, quality, safety, technical performance, and satisfaction represent a key category of project performance measures. In this case study, project duration and quality are used as the output variables in the DEA model.

- Project duration is a measure of the length of the project in working days.
- Quality of the project means delivering precisely what is promised. It is a measure of how well the project meets the purposes for which it has been created. Quality can be rated on a scale from 1 to 9, with 1 representing the lowest level of quality and 9 representing the highest level of priority.

INPUT VARIABLES

- Effort. In Project Management, cost is considered a dimension of project performance, as is project scope or size. Effort describes the total work content allocated for the project including the planning stage. Since there is always a minimum level of effort that must be completed to meet the objectives of the project, effort can be viewed as a cost measure related to the project scope or size.

- Project staffing. Project staffing has been identified as a critical project success factor (Shenhar and Dvir, 1996). It describes the average number of people scheduled to work on a project each day, thus capturing the concentration of labour resources on the project. All else being equal, scheduling more people to concurrently work on a project, that is, increasing overlapping, could decrease project duration (Farris et al., 2006).

- Priority. Priority relates to both top management support and project urgency (Pinto and Slevin, 1987, 1989). It indicates the importance (urgency) assigned to a project by top management. Project priority can be rated on a scale from 1 to 9, with 1 representing the lowest level of priority and 9 representing the highest level of priority. All else being equal, a higher urgency project would be expected to achieve shorter project duration than a lower urgency project, because higher urgency projects would receive more attention and experience shorter turnaround times in resource requests and other administrative tasks (Farris et al., 2006).

- Level of monitoring. This value, given on a scale of 0–10 with 1 representing the lowest level of monitoring and 9 representing the highest level of monitoring, represents the process of control, monitoring, and follow up procedures required for performing the project. This input also represents the degree of project complexity, the higher the complexity, the higher the level of monitoring (Vitner et al., 2006).

We use the following example to illustrate how to select from an array of 12 projects those better adapted to the organization's objectives. The data for this case study are shown in Table 9.2

Table 9.2 Data for the DEA application

Project number	Input variables (W)				Output variable (T)	
	Effort (W_1)	Project staffing (W_2)	Priority (W_3)	Level of monitoring (W_4)	Duration (T_1)	Quality (T_2)
1	456	0.06	7	6	1,616	5
2	589	0.09	9	9	1,934	8
3	405	0.04	5	8	1,850	9
4	552	0.06	8	5	945	7
5	348	0.05	6	7	864	6
6	420	0.03	9	6	1,735	7
7	374	0.04	7	8	875	4
8	485	0.06	4	5	1,458	8
9	520	0.04	6	4	1,326	9
10	480	0.05	8	6	1,258	6
11	390	0.04	9	8	1,035	7
12	515	0.06	7	5	990	8

In the general DEA analysis, efficiency can be defined as:

$$\frac{\text{Value of project's output}}{\text{Value of project's input}} \tag{9.1}$$

Thus, for project 1 we have:

$$\frac{1,616T_1 + 5T_2}{456W_1 + 0.06W_2 + 7W_3 + 6W_4}$$

where T_r is the price or value of one unit of output r, and W_s is the cost of one unit of input s. The DEA approach uses the following ideas to determine whether a project is efficient (Winston, 2003):

1. No project can be more than 100 per cent efficient. Thus, the efficiency of each project must be less than or equal to 1. Thus, for project 1

$$\frac{1,616T_1 + 5T_2}{456W_1 + 0.06W_2 + 7W_3 + 6W_4} \leq 1$$

Since linear programming cannot handle fractions we need to transform the formulation. Multiplying both sides of this inequality by $\left(456W_1 + 0.06W_2 + 7W_3 + 6W_4\right)$ yields:

$$\left(\frac{1,616T_1 + 5T_2}{456W_1 + 0.06W_2 + 7W_3 + 6W_4}\right) * \left(456W_1 + 0.06W_2 + 7W_3 + 6W_4\right) \leq \left(456W_1 + 0.06W_2 + 7W_3 + 6W_4\right)$$

$$1,616T_1 + 5T_2 \leq 4566W_1 + 0.06W_2 + 7W_3 + 6W_4$$

$$456W_1 + 0.06W_2 + 7W_3 + 6W_4 - 1,616T_1 - 5T_2 \geq 0$$

2. If the efficiency of project *i* equals 1, then it is efficient; if the efficiency is less than 1, then it is inefficient.

3. To simplify computations, output prices may be scaled so that the cost of project *i*'s inputs equals 1. Thus, e.g. for project 1 we add the constraint:

$$456W_1 + 0.06W_2 + 7W_3 + 6W_4 = 1$$

4. Each input cost and output price must be strictly positive. If, e.g., $T_i = 0$, then DEA model could not detect an inefficiency involving output *i*; if $W_j = 0$, then DEA model could not detect an inefficiency involving input *j*.

Points (1)-(4) lead to the following linear programming problem to measure the efficiency of project 1:

Max $1,616T_1 + 5T_2$ (9.2)

Subject to $-1,616T_1 - 5T_2 + 456W_1 + 0.06W_2 + 7W_3 + 6W_4 >= 0$ (9.3)

$$-1,934T_1 - 8T_2 + 589W_1 + 0.09W_2 + 9W_3 + 9W_4 >= 0 \quad (9.4)$$

$$-1,850T_1 - 9T_2 + 405W_1 + 0.04W_2 + 5W_3 + 8W_4 >= 0 \quad (9.5)$$

$$-945T_1 - 7T_2 + 552W_1 + 0.06W_2 + 8W_3 + 5W_4 >= 0 \quad (9.6)$$

$$-864T_1 - 6T_2 + 348W_1 + 0.05W_2 + 6W_3 + 7W_4 >= 0 \quad (9.7)$$

$$-1,735T_1 - 7T_2 + 420W_1 + 0.03W_2 + 9W_3 + 6W_4 >= 0 \quad (9.8)$$

$$-875T_1 - 4T_2 + 374W_1 + 0.04W_2 + 7W_3 + 8W_4 >= 0 \quad (9.9)$$

$$-1,458T_1 - 8T_2 + 485W_1 + 0.06W_2 + 4W_3 + 5W_4 >= 0 \quad (9.10)$$

$$-1,326T_1 - 9T_2 + 520W_1 + 0.04W_2 + 6W_3 + 4W_4 >= 0 \quad (9.11)$$

$$-1,258T_1 - 6T_2 + 480W_1 + 0.05W_2 + 8W_3 + 6W_4 >= 0 \quad (9.12)$$

$$-1,035T_1 - 7T_2 + 390W_1 + 0.04W_2 + 9W_3 + 8W_4 >= 0 \quad (9.13)$$

$$-990T_1 - 8T_2 + 515W_1 + 0.06W_2 + 7W_3 + 5W_4 >= 0 \quad (9.14)$$

$$456W_1 + 0.06W_2 + 7W_3 + 6W_4 = 1 \quad (9.15)$$

$$T_1, T_2, W_1, W_2, W_3, W_4 >= 0.0001 \quad (9.16)$$

Equation (9.2) maximizes the efficiency of project 1; constraints (9.3)–(9.14) ensure that no project is more than 100 per cent efficient; constraint (9.15) implies that the total cost of project 1's inputs equal 1. Constraint (9.16) ensures that each input cost and output price is strictly positive. Operating in the same way for the rest of the projects the results shown in Table 9.3 are obtained. Four projects (project 3, 6, 8 and 9) form part of the efficient frontier (i.e., are 100 per cent efficient) whilst the other six (project 1, 12, 2, 11, 5, 10, 4 and 7) are rated as non-efficient.

Table 9.3 Results for the DEA application

Project number	Objective	Output price		Input cost			
		T_1	T_2	W_1	W_2	W_3	W_4
3	1.0000000	0.000541	0.000000	0.000620	0.000000	0.022045	0.079822
6	1.0000000	0.000576	0.000000	0.001723	9.212605	0.000000	0.000000
8	1.0000000	0.000596	0.016389	0.000000	0.000000	0.250000	0.000000
9	1.0000000	0.000000	0.111111	0.000000	24.07407	0.005291	0.001323
1	0.9535369	0.000590	0.000000	0.000677	0.000000	0.024064	0.087135
12	0.8568417	0.000000	0.107105	0.001518	0.000000	0.000000	0.043643
2	0.8153680	0.000422	0.000000	0.000484	0.000000	0.017194	0.062258
11	0.8076923	0.000000	0.115385	0.002564	0.000000	0.000000	0.000000
5	0.7758621	0.000000	0.129310	0.002874	0.000000	0.000000	0.000000
10	0.7244965	0.000444	0.027714	0.000813	0.000000	0.012678	0.084685
4	0.7098655	0.000000	0.101409	0.001437	0.000000	0.000000	0.041322
7	0.5121766	0.000585	0.000000	0.002674	0.000000	0.000000	0.000000

References

Abdul-Raman, H., Yahya, I.A., Berawi, M.A., and Wah, L.W. 2008. Conceptual delay mitigation model using a project learning approach in practice. *Construction Management and Economics*, 26(1), 15–27.

AbouRizk, S. 2010. Role of simulation in construction engineering and management. *Journal of Construction Engineering and Management*, 136(10), 1140–53.

Ackoff, R.L. 1970. *A Concept of Corporate Planning*. New York: Wiley.

Ahmad, I. and Minkarah, I. 1990. *Decision analysis and expert system technology: A construction industry perspective*. Proc., Int. Sym. On Building Economics and Construction Management, CIB, Sydney, Australia, 363–372.

Aibinu, A.A. and Jagboro, G.O. 2002. The effects of construction delays on project delivery in Nigerian construction industry. *International Journal of Project Management*, 20, 593–99.

Aibinu, A.A. and Odeyinka, H.A. 2005. Construction delays and their causative factors in Nigeria. *Journal of Construction Engineering and Management*, 132, 667–77.

Alaghbari, W., Kadir, M.R.A., Salim, A., and Ernawati. A. 2007. The significant factors causing delay of building construction projects in Malaysia. *Engineering, Construction and Architectural Management*, 14(2), 192–206.

Al-Gahtani, K.S. 2009. Float allocation using the total risk approach. *Journal of Construction Engineering and Management*, 135, 88–95.

Al-Subhi Al-Harbi, K. 2001. Application of the AHP in project management. *International Journal of Project Management*, 19, 19–27.

Amiri, M. and Golozari, F. 2011. Application of fuzzy multi-attribute decision making in determining the critical path by using time, cost, risk and quality criteria. *International Journal of Advanced Manufacturing Technology,* 54(1–4), 393–401.

Ang, A.H. and Tang, W.H. 1975. *Probability Concepts in Engineering and Design.* New York: John Wiley & Sons.

Association for Project Management (APM). 2006. *Body of Knowledge,* 5th ed. High Wycombe: Project Management Institute.

Azaron, A. and Tavakkoli-Moghaddam, R. 2006. A multi-objective resource allocation problem in dynamic PERT networks. *Applied Mathematics and Computation,* 181(1), 163–74.

Barraza, G.A., Back, W.E., and Mata, F. 2000. Probabilistic monitoring of project performance using S-curves. *Journal of Construction Engineering and Management,* 126(2), 142–48.

——2004. Probabilistic forecasting of project performance using stochastic S curves. *Journal of Construction Engineering and Management,* 130(1), 25–32.

Bein, W.W., Kamburowski, J., and Stallmann, M.F.M. 1992. Optimal reduction of two-terminal directed acyclic graphs. *SLAM Journal of Computing,* 21, 1112–29.

Bell, D.V., Keeney, R., and Raiffa, H. 1978. *Conflicting Objectives in Decisions.* New York: International Institute for Applied Systems Analysis.

Bellas, C.J. and Samli, A.C. 1973. Improving new product planning with GERT simulation. *California Management Review,* 15(4), 14–21.

Bergantinos, G. and Sanchez, E. 2002a. How to distribute costs associated with a delayed project. *Annals of Operations Research,* 109, 159–74.

Bergantinos, G. and Sanchez, E. 2002b. NTU PERT Games. *Operations Research Letters,* 30, 130–40.

Berny. J. and Howes, R. 1982. Project management control using real-time budgeting and forecasting models. *Construction Papers,* 2(1), 19–40.

Blyth, K. and Kaka, A. 2006. A novel multiple linear regression model for forecasting S-curves. *Engineering, Construction, and Architectural Management*, 13(1), 82–95.

Brans, J.P. 1982. *L'ingénierie de la décision: élaboration d›instruments d'aide à la décision. Le méthode PROMETHEE.* Colloque d'aide à la decision. Quebec, 183–213.

Brans, J.P. and Vincke, P.H. 1985. A preference ranking organization method: The PROMETHEE method for multiple-criteria decision-making. *Management Science*, 31(6), 647–56.

Branzei, R., Ferrari, G., Fragnelli, V., and Tijs, S. 2002. Fuzzy temporal characteristics of operations for project management on the network models basis. *Annals of Operational Research*, 109, 359–74.

British Standard (BS 6079-1). 2002. *Guide to Project Management*. London: British Standards Institutions.

Bromilow, F.J. 1974. Measurement and scheduling of construction time and cost performance in the building industry. *The Chartered Builder*, 10(9), 189–96.

Butcher, W.S. 1967. Dynamic programming for project cost-time curves. *Journal of the Construction Division, Proceedings of the ASCE*, 93, 59–73.

Cagno, E., Caron, F., and Perego, A. 2001. Multi-criteria assessment of the probability of winning in the competitive bidding process. *International Journal of Project Management*, 19(6), 313–24.

Castelaz, P., Angus, J., and Mahoney, J. 1987. Appliction of neural networks to expert systems and command and control systems. *Proc., IEEE Western Conference on Expert Systems*, 118–125.

Castro, J., Gómez, D. and Tejada, J. 2012. A project game for PERT networks. *Operations Research Letters*, 35, 791–98.

Chan, A.P.C. 1999. Modeling building durations in Hong Kong. *Construction Management and Economics*, 17(2), 189–96.

Chanas, S. and Zielinski, P. 2003. On the hardness of evaluating criticality of activities in a planar network with duration intervals. *Operations Research Letters*, 31, 53–59.

Chanas, S., Dubois, D., and Zielinski, P. 2002. On the sure criticality of tasks in activity networks with imprecise durations. *IEEE Transactions on Systems, Man and Cybernetics, Part B*, 32, 393–407.

Chao, L.C. and Chien, C.F. 2009. Estimating project S-curves using polynomial function and neural networks. *Journal of Construction Engineering and Management*, 135(3), 169–77.

Chao, L.C. and Skibniewski, J.M. 1994. Estimating construction productivity: Neural-network-based approach. *Journal of Computing and Civil Engineering*, 8(2), 234–51.

Charnes, A. and Cooper, W.W. 1962. A network interpretation and a directed subdual algorithm for critical path scheduling. *Journal of Industrial Engineering*, 13(4), 213–19.

Chen, H.L., Chen, C.I., Liu, C.H., and Wei, N.C. 2013. Estimating a project's profitability: A longitudinal approach. *International Journal of Project Management*, 31, 400–10.

Chen, S.F. 2007. Analysis of critical paths in a project network with fuzzy activity times. *European Journal of Operations Research*, 183, 442–59.

Chen, S.P. and Hsueh, Y.J. 2008. A simple approach to fuzzy critical path analysis in project networks. *Applied Mathematical. Modeling*, 32, 1289–97.

Cheng, E.W.L. and Li, H. 2004. Contractor selection using the analytical network process. *Construction Management and Economics*, 22(10), 1021–32.

Cheng, M.Y. and Roy, A.F.V. 2011. Evolutionary fuzzy decision model for cash flow prediction using time-dependent support machines. *International Journal of Project Management*, 29(1), 56–65.

Cheng, Y.M., Yu, C.H., and Wang, H.T. 2011. Short-Interval Dynamic Forecasting for actual S-curve in the construction phase. *Journal of Construction Engineering and Management*, 137, 933–41.

Cicmil, S. and Hodgson, D. 2006. New possibilities for project management theory: A critical engagement. *Project Management Journal*, 37(3), 111–122.

Clark, C.E. 1961. The greatest of a finite set of random variables. *Operations Research*, 9, 145–162.

Crowston, W.B. 1971. Models for project management. *Sloan Management Review*, 12(3), 25–42.

Crowston, W.B. and Thompson, G.L. 1967. Decision CPM: a method for simultaneous planning, scheduling and control of projects. *Operations Research*, 15, 407–26.

——1970. Decision CPM: network reduction and solution. *Operations Research*, 21, 435–45.

Curiel, I. 1997. *Co-operative Game Theory and Applications: Co-operative Games Arising from Combinatorial Optimization Problems*. Boston, MA: Kluwer Academic.

Davis, E.W. 1966. Resource allocation in project network models-A survey. *Journal of Industrial Engineering*, 17, 177–88.

Dawson, C.W. and Dawson, R.J. 1995. *Towards more flexible management of software systems development using metamodels. Software Engineering Journal*, 10(3), 79–88.

De la Garza, J.M., Prateapusanond, A., and Ambani, N. 2007. Preallocation of total float in the application of a critical path method based construction contract. *Journal of Construction Engineering and Management*, 133, 836–45.

De la Garza, J.M., Vorster, M.C., and Parving, C.M. 1991. Total float traded as commodity. *Journal of Construction Engineering and Management*, 716–27.

De, P., Dunne, E.J., Ghosh, J.B., and Wells, C.E. 1995. The discrete time-cost tradeoff problem revisited. *European Journal of Operations Research*, 81, 225–38.

——1997. Complexity of the discrete time-cost tradeoff problem for project networks. *Operations Research*, 45, 302–6.

Deckro, R.F., Henert, J.E., Verdini, W.A., Grimsrud, P.H., and Venkateswar, S. 1995. Nonlinear time/cost tradeoff models in project management. *Computers Industrial Engineering*, 28(2), 219–29.

Deng, J.L. 1982. Control problem of grey system. *Systems and Control Letter*, 1(5), 288–94.

——1989. Introduction to grey system theory. *Journal of Grey System*, 1, 1–24.

Drezner, S.M. and Pristker, A.A.B. 1965. Use of generalized networks in scheduling. In: Depot Scheduling and Control Conference. Rand Corporation, Santa Monica, California, 1–3 December 1964.

Drucker, P. 1974. *Management: Tasks, Responsibilities, Practices*. New York: Harper & Row.

Dubois, D., Fargier, H., and Galvagnon, V. 2003. On the latest starting times and floats in activity networks with ill-known durations. *European Journal of Operations Research*, 147, 266–80.

Duckstein, L. and Opricovic, S. (1980). Multiobjective optimization in river basin development. *Water Resources Research*, 16(1), 14–20.

Dutta, S. and Shekhar, S. 1988. Bond rating: A non-conservative application of neural networks. *IEEE International Conference on Neural Networks*, New York, vol. II, 443–450.

Eisner, H.A. 1962. A generalized network approach to the planning and scheduling of a research project. *Operations Research*, 10(1), 115–25.

Elmaghraby, S.E. 1964. An algebra for the analysis of generalized activity networks. *Management Science*, 10(3), 494–514.

——1977. *Activity Networks: Project Planning and Control by Networks Models*. New York: Wiley.

——1993. Resource allocation via dynamic programming in activity networks. *European Journal of Operations Research*, 64, 199–215.

——1995. Activity Nets: A guided tour through some recent developments. *European Journal of Operations Research*, 82, 383–408.

El-Rayes, K. and Kandil, A. 2005. Time-cost-quality trade-off analysis for highway construction. *Journal of Construction Engineering and Management*, 131(4), 477–86.

Estevez-Fernandez, A. 2012. A game theoretical approach to sharing penalties and rewards in projects. *European Journal of Operations research*, 216, 647–57.

Fong, P.S.W. and Choi, S.K.Y. 2000. Final contractor selection using the analytical hierarchy process. *Construction Management and Economics*, 18(5), 547–57.

Ford, L.K. and Fulkerson, D.K. 1962. *Flows in Networks*. Princeton: University Press.

Fulkerson, D.R. 1961. A network flow computation for project cost curves. *Management Science*, 7, 167–78.

Galbraith, J.K. 1985. *The New Industrial State*. Boston: Houghton Mifflin.

Gallant, S. 1988. Connectionist expert systems. *Communications*, 31(2), 152–69.

Gessford, G.N. 1966. An investigation of the utility of critical path time and cost analysis as an aid to budgeting and administrative control by construction firms. PhD thesis. University of California.

Golenko-Ginzburg, D. 1972. *Statistical Methods in Network Planning and Control*. Moscow: Nauka (in German).

——1988. Controlled alternative activity networks in project management. *European Journal of Operations Research*, 37, 336–46.

——1993. A two-level decision-making model for controlling stochastic projects. *International Journal of Production Economics*, 32, 117–27.

Golenko-Ginzburg, D. and Blokh, D.A. 1997. *A generalized activity network model. Journal of the Operations Research Society*, 48, 148–63.

Golenko-Ginzburg, D., Gonik, A., and Kesler, S. 1996. Hierarchical decision-making model for planning and controlling stochastic projects. *International Journal of Production Economics*, 46–47, 39–54.

Golenko-Ginzburg, D., Kesler, S.S., and Livshift, S.E. 1997. *Statistical Modeling in Project Management*. Leningrad: Leningrad University Press (in Russian).

Gong, D. 1997. Optimization of float use in risk-based network scheduling. *International Journal of Project Management*, 15(3), 187–92.

Grubbs, F.F. 1962. Attempts to validate certain PERT Statistics, or: Picking on "PERT". *Operations Research*, 10, 912–15.

Hannan, E.L. 1978. The application of Goal Programming techniques to the CPM problem. *Socio Economic Planning Sciences*, 12, 267–270.

Hartley, H.D. and Wotham, A.W. 1966. A statistical theory for "PERT" critical path analysis. *Management Science*, 12, 469–81.

Hasting, M.A. and Mello, J.M. 1979. *Decision Networks*. New York: Wiley.

Hatush, Z. and Skitmore, M. 1997. Criteria for contractor selection. *Construction Management and Economics*, 15(1), 19–38.

Haykin, S. 1999. *Neural Networks: A Comprehensive Foundation*. New Jersey: Prenctice-Hall.

Hertz, D.B. 1979. Risk analysis in capital investment. *Harvard Business Review*, 57(5), 169–81.

Hespos, R.F. and Strassman, P.A. 1965. Stochastic decision trees for the analysis of investment decisions. *Management Science*, B11, 244–59.

Hillier, F.S. and Lieberman, G.J. 2001. *Introduction to Operations Research*. Seventh ed., Singapore: McGraw-Hill.

Hinderlang, T.J. and Muth, J.F. 1979. A dynamic programming algorithm for decision-CPM networks. *Operations Research*, 27, 225–41.

Householder, J.L. and Rutland, H.E. 1990. Who owns float? *Journal of Construction Engineering and Management*, 116(1), 130–33.

Hwang, C.L. and Yoon, K. 1981. *Multiple Attribute Decision Making: Methods and Applications*. New York: Springer-Verlag.

Hwee, N.G. and Tiong, R.L. 2002. Model of cash flow forecasting and risk analysis for contracting firms. *International Journal of Project Management*, 20(5), 351–63.

Ireland, V. 1983. The role of managerial actions in the cost, time and quality performance of high rise commercial building projects. PhD thesis. University of Sydney, Australia.

Kaka, A.P. 1999. The development of a benchmark model that uses historical data for monitoring the progress of current construction projects. *Engineering, Construction and Architectural Management*, 6(3), 256–66.

Kaka, A.P. and Price, A.D.F. 1993. Modeling standard cost commitment curves for contractors' cash flow forecasting. *Construction Management and Economics, ASCE*, 11, 271–83.

Kamarthi, S.V., Sanvido, V.E., and Kumara, R.T. 1992. Neuroform-Neural network system for vertical formwork selection. *Journal of Computing in Civil Engineering*, 6(2), 178–99.

Kandathil, G.M. 2003. Prediction of spacecraft project duration: Adaptation of Markoff Chain analysis. *Journal of Spacecraft Technology*, 13(1), 1–10.

Kaufmann, A. 1975. *Introduction to the Theory of Fuzzy Subsets. Vol. 1: Fundamentals Theoretical Elements*. New York: Academic Press.

Keeney, R.L. and Raiffa, H. 1976. *Decisions with Multiple Objectives: Preferences and Value Tradeoffs*. New York: Wiley.

——1993. *Decisions with Multiple Objectives: Preferences and Value Tradeoffs*. Cambridge and New York: Cambridge University Press.

Kelley, J.E. and Walker, M.R. 1959a. Critical path planning and scheduling. In: Eastern Joint Computer Conference, 1–3 December 1959. Boston.

Kelley, J.E. and Walker, M.R. 1959b. *Critical Path Planning and Scheduling-an Introduction*. Ampler, Pennsylvania: Mauchly Associates.

Kelly, J.E. 1961. Critical path planning and scheduling. Mathematical Basis. *Operations Research*, 9, 296–320.

Kenley, R. and Wilson, O.D. 1986. A construction project cash flow model. An ideographic approach. *Construction Management and Economics, ASCE,* 4, 213–32.

Kidd, J.B. 1990. Project management software-are we being over-performed? *International Journal of Project Management,* 8(2), 109–15.

——1991. Do today's projects need powerful network planning tools? *International Journal of Production Research,* 29(10), 1969–78.

Kim, B.C. 2007. Forecasting project progress and early warnings of project overruns with probabilistic methods. PhD thesis. University of Texas.

Ko, C.H. and Cheng, M.Y. 2007. Dynamic prediction of project success using artificial intelligence. *Journal of Construction Engineering and Management,* 133(4), 316–24.

Kolisch, R. 1999. Resource allocation capabilities of commercial project management software packages. *Interfaces,* 29(4), 19–31.

Kutcha, D. 2001. Use of fuzzy numbers in project risk (criticality) assessment. *International Journal of Project Management,* 19, 305–10.

Lambropoulos, S. 2007. The use of time and cost utility for construction contract award under European Union legislation. *Building and Environment,* 42(1), 452–63.

Lee, S.M., Moeller, G.L., and Digman, L.D. 1981. *Network Analysis for Management Decisions.* Boston: Kluwer-Nijhoff.

Lerner, A.Y. 1990. Artificial blood circulation: stabilization, physiological control and optimization. *Artificial Organs,* 14(2), 110–17.

Levine, H.A. 1986. *Project Management using Microcomputers.* Berkeley, CA: Osbourne, McGraw-Hill.

Lewis, C.D. 1982. *Industrial and Business Forecasting Methods: A Practical Guide to Exponential Smoothing and Curve Fitting.* London: Butterworth Scientific.

Liberatore, M.J. and Pollack-Johnson, B. 2006. Extending project time-cost analysis by removing precedence relationships and task streaming. *International Journal of Project Management*, 24(6), 529–35.

Lin, M.C., Tserng, H.P., Ho, S.P., and Young, D.L. 2012. A novel dynamic progress forecasting approach for construction projects. *Expert Systems with Applications*, 39, 2247–55.

Lindo Systems, 2002. Lingo version Lindow32. Chicago.

MacCrimmon, K.R. and Ryavec, C.A. 1962. An analytical study of the PERT assumptions. *Operations Research*, 12, 16–37.

——1964. *An analytical study of the PERT assumptions*. Rand Memorandum RM-3408-PR.

Madhi, L., Riley, M., Fereig, S., and Alex, A. 2002. A multi-criteria approach to contractor selection. *Engineering Construction and Architectural Management*, 9(1), 29–37.

Malcolm, D.G. 1963. Reliability maturity index (RMI) An extension of PERT into reliability management. *Journal of Industrial Engineering*, 14, 3–12.

Malcolm, D.G., Roseboom, J.H., Clark, C.E., and Fazar, W. 1959. Application of a technique for research and development program evaluation. *Operations Research*, 7, 646–69.

Mao, M. and Chirwa, E.C. 2006. Application of grey model GM (1,1) to vehicle fatality risk estimation. *Technological Forecasting and Social Change*, 73, 588–605.

Maravas, A. and Pantouvakis, J.P. 2012. Project cash flow analysis in the presence of uncertainty in activity duration and cost. *Journal of Project Management*, 30(3), 374–84.

Mavrotas, G., Caloghirou, Y., and Koune, J. 2005. A model on cash flow forecasting and early warning for multi-project programs: application to the operational program for the information society in Greece. *International Journal of Project Management*, 23(2), 121–23.

Mawby, D. and Stupples, D. 2002. Systems thinking for managing projects. In. *IEMC-2002: IEEE International Engineering Management Conference*, vols, I and II, 344–49. Piscataway, New Jersey.

McGartland, M.R. and Hendrickson, C.T. 1985. Expert systems for construction project monitoring. *Journal of Construction Engineering and Management*, 111(3), 293–307.

Microsoft (2007), Computer software.

Miskawi, Z. 1989. An S-curve equation for project control. *Construction Management and Economics, ASCE*, 7, 115–24.

Moder, J.J. and Philips, C.R. 1964. *Project Management with CPM and PERT*. New York: Reinhold.

Moder, J.J., Philips, C.R., and Davis, E.W. 1983. *Project Management with CPM, PERT, and Precedence Diagramming*. 3rd ed. New York: Van Nostrand Reinhold Company.

Moeller, J.J. 1972. *VERT*, Technical papers: Twenty-third Institute Conference and Convention. Anaheim, California, 31 May–3 June 1972. American Institute of Industrial Engineers.Moeller, G.L. and Digman, L.A. 1981. Operations Planning with VERT. *Operations Research*, 29(4), 676–97.

Mons, D.L., Cheng, C.H., and Lu, H.C. 1995. Application of fuzzy distributions on project management. *Fuzzy Sets and Systems*, 73, 227–34.

Moore, L.J. and Clayton, E.R. 1976. *GERT Modeling and Simulation: Fundamentals and Applications*. New York: Petrocelli-Charter.

Moore, L.J. and Taylor, B.W. 1977. Multiteam, multiproject research and development planning with GERT. *Management Science*, 24(4), 401–10.

Moore, L.J., Taylor, B.W., Clayton, E.R., and Lee, S.M. 1978. Analysis of a multicriteria project crashing model. *AIIE Transaction*, 10(2), 164–69.

Moselhi, O., Hegazy, T., and Fazio, P. 1991. Neural networks as tools in construction. *Journal of Construction Engineering and Management*, 117(4), 606–625.

Murray, J.E. 1963. Considerations of PERT assumptions. *IEEE Transactions on Engineering Management*, 10, 94–99.

Myerson, R.B. 1991. *Game Theory: Analysis of Conflict*. Cambridge, MA: Harvard University Press.

Odeh, A.M. and Battaineh, T. 2002. Causes of construction delay: traditional contracts. *International Journal of Project Management*, 20, 67–76.

Office of the Secretary of Defence and the National Aeronautics and Space Administration, 1962. DOD/NASA Guide to PERT/COST Systems Design, June.

Opricovic, S. and Tzeng, G.H. 2004. Compromise solution by MCDM methods: A comparative analysis of VIKOR and TOPSIS. *European Journal of Operations Research*, 156(2), 445–55.

Panagiotakopoulos, D. 1977. A CPM time-cost computational algorithm for arbitrary activity cost functions. *INFOR*, 15, 183–95.

Pao, Y.H. 1989. *Adaptive Pattern Recognition and Neural Networks*. Reading, Mass: Addison-Wesley Publishing Co.

Pohekar, S.D. and Ramachandran, M. 2004. Application of multi-criteria decision making to sustainable energy planning-A Review. *Renewable and Sustainable Energy Reviews*, 8, 365–381.

Pollack-Johnson, B. 1995. Hybrid structures and improving forecasting and scheduling in project management. *Journal of Operations Management*, 12, 101–17.

Ponce de León, G. 1984. Schedule submittals: to approve or not to approve. *Strategem*, 2(1), 1–12.

Pritsker, A.A.B. 1966. *GERT: Graphical Evaluation and Review Technique.* Memorandum RM-4973-NASA, the RAND Corporation, Santa Monica, California.

——1979. *Modeling and Analysis using Q-GERT Networks*. 2nd ed. New York: John Wiley/Halsted Press.

Pritsker, A.A.B. and Happ, W. 1966. GERT: Graphical evaluation and review technique. Part 1. Fundamentals. *Journal of Industrial Engineering*, 17, 267–74.

Pritsker, A.A.B. and Whitehouse, G.E. 1966. GERT: graphical evaluation and review technique. Part II. Probabilistic and industrial engineering applications. *Journal of Industrial Engineering*, 17(6), 293–300.

Project Management Institute (PMI). 2004. *A Guide to Project Management Body of Knowledge*, 3rd ed. Pennsylvania: Project Management Institute, Inc.

Rajagopalan, S. 1994. Capacity expansion with alternative technology choices. *European Journal of Operations Research*, 77, 392–403.

Razz, T. and Marshall, B. 1996. Effects of resource constraints on float calculations in project networks. *International Journal of Project Management*, 14(4), 241–48.

Robinson, D.R. 1975. A dynamic programming solution to cost-time tradeoff for CPM. *Management Science*, 22, 158–66.

Rommelfanger, H.J. 1994. Network analysis and information flow in fuzzy environment. *Fuzzy Sets and Systems*, 67, 119–28.

Roy, B. 1964. *Les problèmes d'ordonnancement*. Paris: Dunod.

Saaty, T.L. 2000. *Fundamentals of Decision Making and Priority Theory with AHP*. Pittsburgh: RWS Publications.

Samli, A.C. and Bellas, C. 1971. The use of GERT in the planning and control of marketing research. *Journal of Marketing Research*, 8, 335–39.

San Cristóbal, J.R. 2009. Time, Cost, and Quality in a road building project. *Journal of Construction Engineering and Management*, 135(11), 1271–74.

Shamblin, J.E. and Stevens G.T. 1974. *Operations Research: A Fundamental Approach*. Bogota: McGraw-Hill.

Shankar, N.R., Sireesha, V., Rao, K., and Vani, N. 2010. Fuzzy critical path method based on metric distance ranking of fuzzy numbers. *International Journal of Mathematical Analysis*, 4(20), 995–1006.

Shapley, L.S. 1953. A value for n-person Games. *Annals of Mathematical Studies*, 28, 307–17.

Simon, M.A. 1977. *The New Science of the Management Decision*. New York: Prentice-Hall.

Skitmore, M. 1998. A method for forecasting owner monthly construction project expenditure flow. *Journal of Forecasting*, 14, 17–34.

Slyeptsov, A.L. and Tsyhchuk, T.A. 2003. Fuzzy temporal characteristics of operations for project management on the network model basis. *European Journal of Operations Research*, 147, 253–65.

Spooner, J.E. 1974. Probabilistic estimating. *Journal of the Construction Division*, 100, 65–77.

Stacey, R. 2001. *Complex Responsive Processes in Organisations: Learning and Knowledge Creation*. London: Routledge.

Stewart, R. and Mohamed, S. 2002. IT/IS project selection using multi-criteria utility theory. *Logistics Information Management*, 15(4), 254–70.

Stumpf, G.R. 2000. Schedule delay analysis. *Cost Engineering*, 42(7), 32–43.

Taha, H.A. 2003. *Operations Research: An Introduction*. Seventh ed., New Jersey: Prentice-Hall.

Tavares, L.V. 2002. A review of the contribution of operational research to project management. *European Journal of Operations Research*, 136, 1–18.

Taylor, B.W. and Moore, L.J. 1980. R&D project planning with Q-GERT network modelling and simulation. *Management Science*, 26(1), 44–59.

Tijs, S.H. and Driessen, T.S.H. 1986. Game theory and cost allocation problems. *Management Science*, 32(8), 1015–28.

Topcu, Y.L. 2004. A decision model proposal for construction contractor selection in Turkey. *Building and Environment*, 39(4), 469–81.

Tuker, S.N. 1988. A single alternative formula for Department of Health and Social Security S-curves. *Construction Management and Economics, ASCE*, 6, 13–23.

Voropajev, V.I., Ljubkin, S.M., and Golenko-Ginzburg, D.A. 1997. A model approach in reducing uncertainty and risk in project management. *Professional Magazine of PM Association Finland*, 3(1), 40–43.

Voropajev, V.I., Ljubkin, S.M., Titarenko, B.P., and Golenko-Ginzburg, D. 2000. Structural classification of network models. *International Journal of Project Management*, 18, 361–68.

Vrat, P. and Kriengkrairut, C. 1986. A goal programming model for project crashing with piecewise linear time-cost trade-off. *Engineering Costs and Production Economics*, 10, 161–72.

Wassermann, P.D. 1989. *Neural Computing: Theory and Practice*. New York: Van Nostrand-Reinhold.

Whitehouse, G.E. 1973. *Systems Analysis and Design using Network Techniques*. New Jersey: Prentice-Hall, Englewood Cliffs.

Whitehouse, G.E. and Pritsker, A.A.B. 1969. GERT, Part III: Generating functions, conditional distributions, counters, renewal times and correlations. *AIIE Transaction*, 1(1), 45–56.

Winston, W.L. 2003. *Operations Research: Applications & Algorithms*. 4th ed. Thomson Business Press.

Wood, M. 2002. Mind the gap? A processual reconsideration of organizational knowledge. *Organization*, 9(1), 151–71.

Wu, L., Liu, S., and Wang, Y. 2012. Grey Lotka-Volterra model and its applications. *Technological Forecasting and Social Change*, 79, 1720–30.

Yu, P.L. 1973. A class of solutions for group decision problems. *Management Science*, 19(8), 936–46.

Zadeh, L.A. 1978. Fuzzy sets as a basis for a theory of possibility. *Fuzzy Sets and Systems*, 1, 3–28.

Zamori, F A., Braglia, M., and Frosolini, M. 2007. A fuzzy multi-criteria approach for critical path definition. *International Journal of Project Management*, 27, 278–91.

——2009. A fuzzy multi-criteria approach for critical path definition. *International Journal of Project Management*, 27(3), 278–91.

Zeleny, M. 1982. *Multiple Criteria Decision Making*. New York: McGraw-Hill.

Zielinski, P. 2005. On computing the latest starting times and floats of activities in a network with imprecise durations. *Fuzzy Sets and Systems*, 150, 53–76.

Zimmermann, H.J. 1984. *Fuzzy Sets and Decision Analysis (TIMS/Studies in the Management Sciences)*. Amsterdam: North-Holland, Elsevier.

——2001. *Fuzzy Set Theory and its Applications*. Boston: Kluwer Nijhoff.

Index